Weaponized Whiteness

Studies in Critical Social Sciences Book Series

Haymarket Books is proud to be working with Brill Academic Publishers (www.brill.nl) to republish the *Studies in Critical Social Sciences* book series in paperback editions. This peer-reviewed book series offers insights into our current reality by exploring the content and consequences of power relationships under capitalism, and by considering the spaces of opposition and resistance to these changes that have been defining our new age. Our full catalog of *SCSS* volumes can be viewed at https://www.haymarketbooks.org/series_collections/4-studies-in-critical-social-sciences.

Series Editor
David Fasenfest (SOAS University of London)

Editorial Board
Eduardo Bonilla-Silva (Duke University)
Chris Chase-Dunn (University of California–Riverside)
William Carroll (University of Victoria)
Raewyn Connell (University of Sydney)
Kimberlé W. Crenshaw (University of California–LA and Columbia University)
Heidi Gottfried (Wayne State University)
Karin Gottschall (University of Bremen)
Alfredo Saad Filho (King's College London)
Chizuko Ueno (University of Tokyo)
Sylvia Walby (Lancaster University)
Raju Das (York University)

WEAPONIZED WHITENESS

The Constructions and Deconstructions
of White Identity Politics

FRAN SHOR

Haymarket Books
Chicago, IL

First published in 2019 by Brill Academic Publishers, The Netherlands.
© 2019 Koninklijke Brill NV, Leiden, The Netherlands

Published in paperback in 2020 by
Haymarket Books
P.O. Box 180165
Chicago, IL 60618
773-583-7884
www.haymarketbooks.org

ISBN: 978-1-64259-364-8

Distributed to the trade in the US through Consortium Book Sales and Distribution (www.cbsd.com) and internationally through Ingram Publisher Services International (www.ingramcontent.com).

This book was published with the generous support of Lannan Foundation and Wallace Action Fund.

Special discounts are available for bulk purchases by organizations and institutions. Please call 773-583-7884 or email info@haymarketbooks.org for more information.

Cover design by Jamie Kerry and Ragina Johnson.

Printed in United States.

10 9 8 7 6 5 4 3 2 1

Library of Congress Cataloging-in-Publication Data is available.

Contents

Acknowledgements   VII
Introduction   1

PART 1
Terrors in the Constructions of White Identity Politics

1   U.S. "Savage" Wars and White Terror   9

2   The Past of Present Terrors   22

3   White Identity Politics and the Terrors of Trumpism   32

PART 2
Dilemmas in the Deconstructions of White Identity Politics

4   Unveiling Whiteness: White Student Activists in the Civil Rights Movement   47

5   Exorcising the Ghosts of the Past: From Civil Rights Murders to Confederate Monuments   68

6   The Deconstruction of Whiteness in a "Post-racial" America   81

7   Challenging Weaponized Whiteness: Black Lives Matter   90

Conclusion   99
Epilogue   107
Afterword   119
    Frank Joyce

Bibliography   133
Name Index   151
Subject Index   155

Acknowledgements

The research and writing for this collection of essays has occupied a decade or more of scholarly engagement with a variety of subject matter related to whiteness, white supremacy, and white identity politics. On the other hand, political concerns related to racial justice, as will be especially evident in Chapter 4, have occupied most of my life. It is a daunting and impracticable task, therefore, to acknowledge all of those academics and activists who, over the years, have made significant contributions to the thinking that informs these essays. During my transition from a full-time Professor in the History Department of Wayne State University to a retired Emeritus Professor, I have enjoyed the benefits of collegial interactions that have informally influenced the perspectives and analysis contained herein. Moreover, the privilege of encountering other academics at conferences and professional meetings has also obviously had its impact on my thinking. To acknowledge all those colleagues, both near and far, who provided inspiration and/or feedback to the various essays is, unfortunately, beyond my powers of remembrance.

In deference to those who may be inadvertently unrecognized in these acknowledgements, I am abstaining from producing a large and rambling list of colleagues and comrades who may have played even a minor role in shaping my observations on the various topics covered in this collection. On the other hand, I do wish to acknowledge those academic colleagues who have given specific encouragement and help for this project over the last few years, whether directly or indirectly. First and foremost, I must thank David Fasenfest for securing a contract and for moving this project to publication with additional technical assistance. Those other colleagues and comrades who have rendered differing levels of support and engagement include: Tom Abowd, Ron Aronson, Roxanne Dunbar-Ortiz, Michael Ezra, Jerry Harris, Gloria House, Dolores Janiewski, Bob Jensen, John Marciano, and, last but not least, David Roediger. Dave's guidance, through his groundbreaking and prolific work on the history of white supremacy and personal contact, has been invaluable.

For many years, I have assumed, perhaps arrogantly, the title and role of "public intellectual." My understanding of that role is that one uses intellectual skills honed as a scholar to create writings more accessible to a broader public outside of the academy. Being grounded in local and national organizations and writing for a wide variety of print and online political journals has afforded some legitimacy to the lofty ideal of public intellectual. Again, there are too many individuals to enumerate for my appreciation. However, I do want to offer a "shout-out" to the editors of two of those journals to which I've contributed for their assistance: Dan LaBotz and Lois Weiner of *New Politics* and Jeffrey St. Clair of *CounterPunch*.

Also, there are numerous organizations to which I've been affiliated that have had a meaningful impact on my life and writings. The longest connection to any organization has been my involvement as a Board Member and Advisory Board Member to the Michigan Coalition for Human Rights (MCHR). Throughout the years I have organized many programs and spoken to and on behalf of MCHR. Among my comrades in MCHR who have become part of the important antiracist and human rights work conducted over the years are the following: Dorothy Aldridge, Abayomi Azikiwe, Brenda Bryant, Jose Cuello, Karl Gregory, Frank Hammer, Gloria House, Barb and Bob Ingalls, Frank Joyce, Cary McGehee, Fred Pearson, Kim Redigan, Ed Rowe, Marge Sears, Rudy Simons, Heaster Wheeler, and Bill Wylie-Kellerman. Other organizational affiliations, although more limited in time and scope and, therefore, without any individual attribution, are: Historians for Peace and Democracy and local affiliates of BlackLivesMatter, Gray Panthers, Indivisible, Move-On, Occupy, and Peace Action. Also, my involvement with the Huntington Woods Peace Group and Social Justice Committee of the Birmingham Temple has provided significant opportunities to put my knowledge and values to work. Again, there are so many individuals with whom I've worked on myriad peace and justice projects in the aforementioned organizations that I am reluctant to attempt citing each and every one. On the other hand, there are a few individuals from these organizations that have had a more direct and significant connection to this project. They are Rich Feldman, Gloria House, Frank Joyce, and Kim Redigan. In particular, my exchanges with Frank Joyce at convivial breakfast meetings and through email have expanded and deepened my understanding of all of the pernicious effects of white supremacy and how to combat those effects.

Finally, family and friends, too numerous to mention, have sustained me, if not directly contributing to this project. Among those family members are my progeny, Molly, Miriam, and Finn, and my inestimable wife and fellow traveler (except for all those interminable meetings), Barbara Logan. It is to the youngest members of my immediate family, granddaughters Ruby and Iris, to whom I dedicate this book. May the love surrounding them from family and friends radiate into a national and global beloved community. And may they inhabit a sustainable world where justice and equity truly reign.

Introduction

In the aftermath of Donald Trump's 2016 ascent to the presidency of the United States, an ascent aided by the corporate media, voter suppression, Russian involvement, the flaws of Hillary Clinton, and the arcane and slaveholding-rooted Electoral College, journalistic accounts of racially motivated white voters became a common reference point for explaining his electoral victory. Because the preponderance of white voters, including 52% of white women, voted for a well-known misogynist, racist, xenophobe, many in the liberal media bemoaned a "white identity politics" that motivated Trump supporters. Very few pundits traced this back beyond Richard Nixon's "Southern Strategy" and his implicit racial appeal for law and order. One of the more recent versions of this truncated historical perspective even argued that Trump has completed a Republican Party transformation that has "embedded white ethno-nationalism in its DNA" (Patterson 2018).[1]

It is the contention of this collection of essays that white identity politics, as an expression and instrument of white supremacy, are deeply embedded in the history of the United States. Indeed, the foundational document, the Constitution, reflects the framers' white supremacist positions. On the other hand, although there are certain white supremacist threads that run through U.S. history, in no sense is it the contention of the essays contained herein that white identity politics is an unchanging and ahistorical trope. Indeed, legal and activist challenges have eroded much of the reign of white supremacy without, however, eliminating certain institutional and ideological support for white identity politics. These essays examine the ways in which specific historical conditions informed and continue to inform white identity politics, both in its implicit and explicit form, the latter being an expression of the weaponized whiteness that has become the hallmark of Trumpism and much of the Republican Party (Knowles and Tropp 2018). Beyond the critique of whiteness and a reconstituted white supremacy, the book will provide the reader with an understanding of and, hopefully, a commitment to ending the terrors of white identity politics.

Because I believe that confronting that legacy is essential to enacting transformational change in the United States, these essays not only reconstruct the critical contexts of white identity politics but also offer a way forward by highlighting the role of white and black activists in challenging those white racial

---

[1] Tim Wise, the anti-racist author and activist, has denounced the Republican Party as a "white identity cult" (Wise 2018).

constructions. In addition, I share Kai Wright's reflections after visiting the Equal Justice Institute's moving Brooklyn Museum exhibit on the history of lynching and white terrorism. Writing in *The Nation*, Wright concluded the essay noting that "there is no road forward for progressive politics without confronting white identity politics ... (including) owning the legacy of white terrorism ... white citizens who want to dredge their communities of the hateful morass in which Trump wallows will nonetheless have to bravely, publicly claim their history, knowing that the truth is the only thing that will set them free" (Wright 2017).

While I am skeptical of the civic literacy of my fellow citizens, especially in an era marked by "civic illiteracy" (Giroux 2018: 90, 197), I am too committed as an historian and racial justice activist to deny the very real need to reveal the truths of our past and present realities. It is the task of the historian to track down difficult truths, wherever they may lead. In writing history of the kind contained herein, I take seriously the admonition of Black Lives Matter organizer, DeRay McKesson, that "we must never cede the reality of what transpired to partial truths, even if what we gain is the more palatable story – indeed, especially when that is the case" (McKesson 2018: 166). Therefore, without dredging up the racist muck of the past and those moments, both in the past and present, when racial justice activists contested white identity politics, we cannot expect to find that elusive truth and its potentially liberating aspects.

Before I provide an overview of the structure of this collection of essays, I want to specify the relationship between white supremacy and white identity politics. As a guiding definition for the chapters that follow, white supremacy entails "a sociopolitical system of domination based on racial categories that benefits those defined and perceived as white" (DiAngelo 2018: 30). Obviously, definitions and perceptions change over time as a consequence of shifting material conditions and the contesting of definitions and perceptions by self-conscious agents of change. Nonetheless, as an instrument of that sociopolitical system of domination, white identity politics establishes a value system that advantages whites to the detriment of racialized others, creating, in the process, a "value gap that is in our national DNA" (Glaude Jr. 2016: 30–31).

Historically, while the enactment of white supremacy over time has created control mechanisms that have oppressed and disadvantaged racialized others designated as non-white, the operation of a socially constructed racial binary of black and white has been the most egregious and consistently violent.[2] According to Keenga-Yamahtta Taylor, "White supremacy has historically existed

---

2 For an examination beyond the binary of black and white, see, for example, Wu 2002.

to marginalize Black influence in social, political, and economic spheres while also obscuring differences in experience in the social, political, and economic spheres among white people. Like slavery, this was necessary to maximize productivity and profitability while dulling the otherwise sharp antagonisms between the richest and poorest white men" (Taylor 2016: 210). On the other hand, white supremacy is not limited to the historical oppression of African Americans, but also informs how people of color, in general, have become racialized others and victimized as such (Takaki 2008). As noted recently by Natasha Leonard, Trump's "immigration policy is a matter of white supremacist social engineering aimed at excluding and decimating poor, predominantly nonwhite immigrants" (Leonard 2018).

White identity politics, thus, has been a contingent corollary of white supremacy even as white supremacy underwent historical and social transformations as a consequence of legal challenges (Brown v. Board of Education) and movement contestations, especially in the modern civil rights and black power incarnations. Therefore, white identity politics remains a material expression of the structural racism still extant in the United States. Although not exclusively targeting African Americans, nonetheless, structural racism manifests its most potent and pathological expressions in "the policies, programs, and practices of public and private institutions that result in greater rates of poverty, dispossession, criminalization, illness and ultimately mortality of African Americans" (Taylor 2016: 8).[3]

White identity politics also reflect the constructions of whiteness as a racial category with roots in the American colonial experience. As an outgrowth of the establishment of a regime of social control that attempted to incorporate all whites into a relatively privileged space vis-à-vis Native peoples and people of African descent, whiteness represents a long, albeit contested, institutional and ideological legacy. As argued by David Theo Goldberg, "whiteness ... stands socially for status and superiority, politically for power and control, economically for privilege and property, culturally for self-assertion and arrogance, but also and dialectically for anxiety and a crisis of confidence" (Goldberg 2002: 196). Indeed, whiteness has a long history of being "weaponized," especially in the American political landscape in order to terrorize and, otherwise, dominate racialized others (Roediger 2010). On the other hand, "racism and racial animus are not fixed characteristics of an already defined group of people, but a situational dimension of our common political life that is repeatedly mobilized" (Singh 2017: 176).

---

3 For an excellent extended historical and sociological overview of structural racism in the United States, see Feagin 2014.

Examining the mobilization of that political life in the long history of the United States through the present predicament is the focus of Part 1, "Terrors in the Constructions of White Identity Politics." Chapter 1, "U.S. 'Savage' Wars and White Terror," reviews how the expansion of the United States across the continent and, then, overseas through wars of aggression was rationalized as "civilizing missions" against "savage" populations. Such savage wars enacted forms of "racial nationalism" (Singh 2017: 33) that spread white terror from the western frontiers of the U.S. in the nineteenth century through wars in the Philippines, Vietnam, Afghanistan, and Iraq during the twentieth and twenty-first century. Highlighting both the institutional and ideological expressions of savage war locates the intimate connection between racial nationalism and white identity politics.

Chapter 2, "The Past of Present Terrors," follows the thread of the Indian Wars and Indian Removal up through the present punitive policies against "racialized others" at the militarized southwestern border. The related historical role of repressive policing and vigilante actions against African Americans further elaborates how violence, performed at the local and national levels from the nineteenth through the twenty-first centuries, was and remains an instrument of weaponized whiteness and white identity politics. As expressed by Nikhil Pal Singh in his essential study, *Race and America's Long War*, "what we are experiencing today is like a series of afterimages" (Singh 2017: 122).[4] It is these afterimages that provide the past resonances in the present.

Chapter 3, "White Identity Politics and the Terrors of Trumpism," considers not just the reprehensible racist politics and policies of the Trump Administration, but also situates Trumpism in a socio-economic, socio-cultural, and socio-psychological context that has emerged, in particular, over the last several decades. Hence, explaining the electoral victory and political rule of Trump within this context also locates the factors that animate white identity politics. How the pull of reconstructing an imagined past also is explored for their implications in binding certain sectors of the white population to the Trump agenda.

Part 2, "Dilemmas in the Deconstructions of White Identity Politics," underscores the fact that white supremacy has undergone numerous challenges. Starting with the modern civil rights movement, those challenges, especially from anti-racist whites, wrestled with certain contradictions and dilemmas. Chapter 4, "Unveiling Whiteness: White Student Activists in the Civil Rights

---

[4] A parallel formulation of the continuing influence of the past on the present are the reflections of Richard Rothstein (2017) on the persistence of housing segregation – "the public policies of yesterday still shape the racial landscape of today" (178).

Movement," explores how and why white students during the 1960s had to confront their own whiteness as part of their commitment to civil rights and the black freedom struggle. Linking some connections from my own background to those of my student activist cohorts, the chapter delves deeply into the ways that we white participants in the civil rights movement reflected and reacted against our white privileges in contesting institutionalized racism.

Chapter 5, "Exorcising the Ghosts of the Past: From Civil Rights Murders to Confederate Monuments," examines two contested arenas within which, in particular, Southern justice and history have been challenged and transformed. The first arena considers the murders of 1960s civil rights leaders in Mississippi by briefly looking at the life of Medgar Evers, the head of the Mississippi NAACP during the civil rights era, and the man who assassinated him, Byron De La Beckwith. The trials and re-trials of Beckwith help to reveal the degree to which well-meaning whites, like prosecuting attorneys and political officials, sought closure to the past terrors of white supremacy even as they took refuge in the ghostly illusions of colorblind "post-racialism." The second arena is the recent battle over Confederate Monuments throughout the South. Even though the erection of these monuments is part and parcel of the rule of the old order of white supremacy in the South, the contemporary debate over and deconstruction of these monuments has led to a confrontation with the ghosts of the past.

Chapter 6, "The Deconstructions of Whiteness in Obama's 'Post-Racial' America," delineates the constructions and deconstructions across the political spectrum during the Obama presidency. From a reactionary right-wing posture of paranoid whiteness to the liberal embrace of multi-cultural colorblindness to the more radical challenges of anti-racist whites, whiteness and post-racialism are probed for their contradictions and ongoing dilemmas.

Chapter 7, "Challenging Weaponized Whiteness: Black Lives Matter," analyzes the emergence of the black lives matter movement and its explicit contestation of racial injustices and implicit challenges to white identity politics. I believe this is an appropriately compelling conclusion to this section since I share Joel Olson's perspective on how "African American freedom struggles have advanced democracy, possibly more than any other kind of movement in the United States, because they explicitly challenge the connections between whiteness and citizenship" (Olson 2004: xxiii). The insistence that "black lives matter" offers a way out of those institutional and ideological prisons that have victimized not only African Americans but also all those racialized others who have borne the brunt of a weaponized whiteness.

The "Conclusion" discusses how to challenge and change the "white racial frame" that implicitly sustains white identity politics and what Robin DiAngelo identifies as "white solidarity" (DiAngelo 2018: 57). In highlighting how white identity politics interacts with national identity, immigration, the gun culture, and the promises of an inclusive pluralist democracy, major tropes explored in the prior chapters will be reviewed, especially with an eye towards the difficulties in transcending race.

The "Epilogue" will focus on how the class system, in particular, creates conditions that exacerbate racial divisions and tensions. The first part will look at how corporate capital has deindustrialized Detroit's auto industry and, in the process, caused untold damage to the employment opportunities and living standards of the African-American community in Metro Detroit. The second part of this "Epilogue" will consider how the social psychological dynamics of white identity politics in the most recent past recapitulates some of the lasting traumas of white supremacy. Re-presenting Lynn Nottage's award-winning play, *Sweat*, about the intersectional injuries to workers as a result of contemporary economic dislocations and factory closings, provides a reminder that the suffering caused by white identity politics not only harms its victims, but also exacts a physical, mental, and political-economic toll on those workers who turn their class injuries into racial resentments and weaponized whiteness.[5] Ultimately, Nottage's play affords a template for better understanding how weaponized whiteness cannot be separated from the class and gender dimensions that define the hurt and harm inflicted on racialized others.

---

5   See, for example, Metzl 2019.

PART 1

Terrors in the Constructions of White Identity Politics

∴

CHAPTER 1

U.S. "Savage" Wars and White Terror

The long arc of racial injustice in the United States bends towards whiteness, an historical fiction whose construction led to the domination of racialized others. Even before the establishment of the United States, white terror defined the physical and socio-cultural boundaries between white European settlers, the indigenous population of North America, and Africans brought to the continent. From the earliest European settlements on the North American continent to the U.S. "War on Terror," the malleable construction of the frontier provided both a physical and ideological border from which an assault was waged against "savages" in the name of "civilization" (Nugent 2009: 304). Indeed, as argued by Richard Slotkin, "the story of American progress … took the form of a fable of race war, pitting the symbolic opposites of savagery and civilization, primitivism and progress, paganism and Christianity against each other…. The doctrine of 'savage war' depended upon the belief that certain races are inherently disposed to cruel and atrocious violence" (Slotkin 1985: 53). The irony, of course, was that in the expansion of the United States and the development of an American Empire, both formal and informal, engaging in savage wars became inherent in its so-called civilizing mission (Atwood 2010; Nugent 2009).

While there were numerous motivating forces and ideological rationales for conducting savage wars for over four centuries, from economic and geopolitical imperatives to gendered expressions, white terror was part and parcel of wars that "exterminated 'savages' who stood in the path of Anglo-American expansion" (Drinnon 1997: xi).[1] Whether those "savages" occupied territory on the continental United States or in Mexico, the Philippines, Vietnam, Afghanistan, or Iraq, American military forces unleashed white terror against racialized others. In highlighting the policies and practices that informed these savage wars, this chapter will make clear the continuities in the construction of white identity politics, even in the face of changed conditions. As Janne Lahte contends in her recent study of the U.S. fifty year war against the Apache nation, the "United States was born, manufactured, and maintained through conquest and war" (Lahte 2017: 20). It will be the focus of this chapter to emphasize

---

1 For a classic text on the economic motivations for American empire, see Williams 1982. On the connections between war capitalism and race war, see Singh 2017: 74–97. For an example of how "martial manhood" informed American expansion, see Greenberg 2005.

the ways in which savage war and white terror have been integral components in the historical trajectory of the United States.

It is not surprising that the author of the Declaration of Independence, having cited fomenting "insurrection" by "merciless Indian savages" as one of the grievances against King George III, would, himself, become the advocate for merciless policies towards Native Americans. Although Thomas Jefferson hoped to convert Native Americans into yeomen farmers, he undertook courses of action that led to the dispossession of immense parcels of Indian Territory. Whenever there was any resistance by Indigenous peoples to what Jefferson considered benevolent policies of a "Great White Father," he reacted with what would become the guiding rationale for white terror. In instructing his Secretary of War in 1807 on the preparations for military engagements against any recalcitrant or resisting Native Americans, Jefferson spelled out "the danger they are bringing on themselves … and that if ever we are constrained to lift the hatchet against any tribe, we will never lay it down until that tribe is exterminated, or driven beyond the Mississippi" (quoted in Drinnon 1997: 96).[2] While pursuing what Jefferson called an "empire of liberty" and what John Quincy Adams, in the aftermath of the Louisiana Purchase, labeled the "whiteness of innocence," that innocence was belied by the spread of white terror.

The very exemplar of white terror was Andrew Jackson who made no pretenses about the "whiteness of innocence."[3] Indeed, as Roxanne Dunbar-Ortiz argues, "Jackson was the Dark Knight in the formation of the United States as a colonialist, imperialist democracy" (Dunbar-Ortiz 2014: 108). Jackson led both mercenaries and U.S. soldiers against various Indian nations from genocidal war against the Muskogee nation in Tennessee in 1814 to Seminole "savage wars" in Florida in 1817–1818 (Drinnon 1997: 104–111; Dunbar-Ortiz 2014: 98–99; Rosen 2015). (In the latter war, Jackson's white terror campaign against the Seminole intruded into the territorial claims of Spain.) Jackson continued his predations against native peoples during his Presidency with policies that would lead to Indian Removal. Indeed, the Indian Removal Act of 1830 "mandated federal troops to push Native Americans beyond the Mississippi and extinguish their titles to their land" (Grandin 2019, *The End of the Myth*: 58). As a

---

2 For a brilliant study of the interaction with native peoples throughout the history of the United States, see Dunbar-Ortiz 2014. The campaigns waged by the U.S. to dispossess indigenous peoples of their land and to expand the nation as a "white possession" are discussed in Moreton-Robinson 2015.

3 On the connections between whiteness and innocence, the African-American philosopher George Yancy notes: "As long as whiteness constitutes an ensemble of power relations that places whites in positions of advantage and power … vis-à-vis nonwhites, whiteness will never be innocent." See Yancy 2004: 6.

consequence of such brutal expulsion thousands of Cherokees, in particular, were to perish in the wake of Jacksonian white terror, a terror that "was directed equally toward racial enemies within and without" (Singh 2017: 34).

But, what of those white citizens not under Jackson's command in the savage wars or those not on the frontier wresting the land from the indigenous inhabitants? Did they endorse the white terror behind the dispossession of Indian territories? Writing in the 1830s about how many whites rationalized this dispossession and hid behind the ideological veils of "progress" and "civilization," the French political observer, Alexis de Tocqueville noted: "The world belongs to us (white Americans), they tell themselves every day: the Indian race is destined for final destruction which one cannot prevent and which is not desirable to delay. Heaven has not made them to become civilized; it is necessary that they die.... In time I will have their lands and will be innocent of their death" (Tocqueville 1971: 206.). Tocqueville's indictment of what would become a fundamental element in the construction of white political identity in the nineteenth century further reveals how white terror could be made invisible to those benefitting from its imperial plunder.[4]

As the United States was expanding in the 1830s, gobbling up, in the process, Mexican territories, Native Americans across the continent faced exterminationist attacks by white settlers, enabled by rich industrial and real estate barons. In 1834, California Native Americans numbered around 150,000. (By the end of the nineteenth century the number would be less than 20,000.) Seeking the land occupied by those indigenous inhabitants, Leland Stanford and other wealthy white transplants financially underwrote what were euphemistically called "Indian-hunting expeditions" that were, in fact, murderous assaults on California Native Americans. When Stanford became Governor of California in 1861, he appropriated state finances to expedite further extermination, all, of course, in the name of white civilization and the march of progress (Duster 2017).

On the other hand, there were serious debates in the nineteenth century about U.S. expansion and the so-called march of civilization, especially around the issues of annexation during the Mexican War (Slotkin 1985: 173–190). Probably the most critical and prophetic of those in Congress challenging not only possible war with Mexico but also the endless wars on Native Americans, was the ex-President, John Quincy Adams. Fearful that annexation of Texas would further reinforce "the nation's habituation to racist wars," Adams admonished

---

[4] On the contradictions of Tocqueville's perspectives on U.S. national identity and his advocacy of white hegemony, see Behdad 2005: 48–75.

his congressional colleagues that "racism and war would be the only thing that gave the republic meaning" (Grandin 2019, *The End of the Myth*: 85). In his Congressional address in 1836, Adams confronted the Speaker of the House, James Knox Polk with these damning queries: "Do not you, an Anglo-Saxon, slaveholding exterminator of Indians, from the bottom of your soul, hate the Mexican-Spaniard-Indian, emancipator of slaves and abolisher of slavery? Have you not Indians enough to expel from the land of their fathers' sepulchres, and to exterminate" (quoted in Grandin 2019, *The End of the Myth*: 86)?

Although another slave apologist, Senator John Calhoun of South Carolina, favored annexing Texas, he feared absorbing Mexico with its "mixed blood" population. For Calhoun, the Union should be preserved for the "Caucasian race" (Love 2004: 21–22). Abolitionists, such as Frederick Douglass, who opposed both the Mexican War and a slave republic that excluded those of African descent from citizenship, condemned the war, as "disgraceful, cruel and iniquitous … Mexico seems a doomed victim to Anglo-Saxon cupidity and love of domination" (quoted in Zinn 1995: 155). Other abolitionists, especially in New England, criticized the war, as well as those, like a young Abe Lincoln in Illinois, who opposed the expansion of slavery. Yet, there were white abolitionists who opposing slavery, nonetheless, heralded a racialized "manifest destiny." The abolitionist Theodore Parker "declared that expansion was inevitable as a consequence of racial gifts and that it would bring with it a regime of Anglo-Saxon dominance" (Slotkin 1993: 46).[5]

This racialized version of Anglo-Saxon identity not only informed the policies and practices of aggressive expansionism, but also provided racial markers for new immigrants, especially those arriving from Ireland in the 1840s. According to Matthew Frye Jacobson, "'Anglo-Saxon' performed two distinct, exclusionary functions within the reigning ideology of American nationalism: it separated racially 'pure' Americans from 'mongrelized' and 'degenerate' Mexicans on one front; and it divided virtuous self-governing Anglo-Saxon citizens from the pathetic Celtic newcomers on another" (Jacobson 1999: 206). Yet, the main ideological thrust of this racialized fetishism of Anglo-Saxonism is thoroughly revealed in Josiah Strong's 1886 paean, *Our Country* and his embrace of imperialist Anglo-Saxonizing of the world (Jacobson 1999: 207). "Is there any room for reasonable doubt," Strong wrote, "that this race … is destined to

---

5   On the racial meanings of manifest destiny, see Horsman 1981, especially where he maintains that by "the 1850's it was generally believed that a superior American race was destined to shape the destiny of much of the world. It is also believed that in their outward thrust Americans were encountering a variety of inferior races incapable of sharing America's republican system and doomed to permanent subordination or extinction" (6).

dispossess many weaker races, assimilate others, and mold the remainder, until ... it has Anglo-Saxonized mankind?" (quoted in Jacobson 1999: 207).

It was in the context of expanding that regime of Anglo-Saxon dominance to the Philippines that U.S. savage war enacted new imperial geopolitical aims, along with the retention of the ideological tropes of white identity politics. One of the leading proponents of the imperial "civilizing mission" in the Philippines was Theodore Roosevelt. To Roosevelt, those who opposed the war in the Philippines were "Indian-lovers" and "traitors to their race." For Roosevelt, the war was a struggle between "civilization and barbarism.... Whether the barbarian be the Red Indian on the frontier of the United States, the Afghan on the border of British India, or the Turkoman who confronts the Siberian Cossack, the result is the same ... without force, fair dealing usually amounts to nothing" (quoted in Slotkin 1993: 52 and 106).

The United States did not just apply force in the Philippines, it let loose forms of white terror that recalled the Indian Wars and presaged the wars on Southeast Asia, Afghanistan, and Iraq. The massacres that were part of the white terror against native peoples at Sand Creek (1864), the Washita (1869), White Mountain (1870) and Wounded Knee (1890) were rehearsals for the violence visited upon Filipinos. "If 'Indian' was the racial epithet for Filipinos preferred by the high command, the second most popular – and the one preferred by the rank and file – was 'nigger'" (Slotkin 1993: 114). According to Walter Nugent, "Senior American officers who were veterans of the Indian Wars easily equated the Filipinos with the 'savages' of the Plains, deserving extermination. Common soldiers, many of them lightly trained volunteers, were unlimited in their patriotism and their racism. One wrote, 'I am in my glory when I can sight my gun on some dark skin and pull the trigger'" (Nugent 2009: 270). The atrocities that followed from this white terror were so disturbing that they actually led to court-martials of commanding officers. However, the General who demanded that Samar be made a "howling wilderness" faced a court-martial that resulted in nothing more than his forced retirement.

Nevertheless, the use of torture, such as the "water cure" (later to become used in Iraq as water-boarding), the murder of prisoners and civilians, rape and even the killing of anyone on the island of Samar above the age of eleven were all part of this notorious enactment of savage war. As reported at the time in the Philadelphia *Ledger*: "Our men ... have killed to exterminate men, women, children, prisoners and captives, insurgents and suspected people ... (the) prevailing idea that the Filipino, as such, was little better than a dog, a noisome reptile in some instances, whose best disposition was the rubbish heap.... It is not civilized warfare, but we are not dealing with civilized people. The only thing they know and fear is force, violence, and brutality, and we give it to them" (quoted in Slotkin 1993: 113). Another reporter recorded later the words of an American officer in the Philippines: "We exterminated the American Indians, and I guess most of us are proud of it, or, at least, believe the end justifies the means; and we must have no scruples about exterminating this other race standing in the way of progress and enlightenment" (quoted in Drinnon 1997: 314).

Although over a half-century later, the U.S. imperial intervention in Vietnam replicated the kinds of atrocities committed against other racialized Asians, including the murder and mutilation of innocent civilians as in the Philippines and during the centuries long Indian wars. As Frances Fitzgerald pointed out connecting that long history to what transpired in Vietnam: "The Americans were once again embarked upon a heroic ... conquest of an inferior race. To the American settlers the defeat of the Indians had seemed not just a nationalist victory, but an achievement made in the name of humanity – the triumph of light over darkness, of good over evil, and of civilization over brutish nature. Quite unconsciously, the American officers and officials used a similar language against the (Vietnamese) National Liberation Front" (Fitzgerald 1972: 491–492).

In Vietnam, a primary ground tactic promoted by those American officers and officials was a "search and destroy" tactic. As several studies of the ground war in Vietnam have graphically confirmed, this tactic produced a prodigious amount of carnage (Appy 1993; Turse 2017). Certain high-profile atrocities, such as My Lai, achieved prominent media coverage (nearly a year after the incident, however). Nonetheless, My Lai was seen by a majority of the American public either as an aberration or the result of a few bad apples, like Lt. William Calley, the officer leading the My Lai massacre. In fact, while Calley was found guilty by a military court of the massacre of hundreds of men, women, and children, his punishment was relatively minor. In his discussion of the massacre and the response to My Lai and the conviction of Lt. Calley, Tom Englehardt cites polls that indicated both overwhelming support for Calley and indifference to the atrocity (Englehardt 1995: 215–227).

The kind of savage war waged by the U.S. military in Southeast Asia meted out terror against an uncivilized brown enemy. Although the suffering inflicted on the Vietnamese, Cambodians, and Laotians could be rationalized, opposition grew as that suffering was broadcast on the nightly news and as more and more U.S. soldiers returned home in body bags. As the war dragged on, it was clear the "killings of civilians ... were widespread and routine." Nick Turse attributes these atrocities "to the U.S. command policies" noting, however, "face-to-face atrocities were responsible for just a fraction of the millions of civilian casualties in South Vietnam. Matter-of-fact mass killings that dwarfed the slaughter at My Lai normally involved heavier fire power and command policies that allowed it to be unleashed with impunity" (Turse 2017: 22).

That heavier firepower was evident in the massive amount of bombs dropped on Southeast Asia. Four times the tonnage of bombs were dropped on Vietnam, Cambodia, and Laos than that were used by the U.S. in all theaters of operation during World War II. Not only were thousands of villages in Vietnam destroyed, but also civilian deaths, numbering close to 3 million, resulted in a large part from such indiscriminate bombing. Integral to the bombing strategy was the use of terror weapons that violated international laws, such as napalm and anti-personnel fragmentation bombs. As a consequence of the establishment of free-fire zones anything and everything could be attacked, including hospitals, leading to the deliberate murder of most civilians (Gibson 2000; Turse 2017). As a consequence of such massive civilian deaths and the exposure of the horrors of the Vietnam War through a variety of mainstream and alternative media, protests against the war expanded (Appy 2015; Small 2002).

Because such indiscriminate bombing became the source of much of the criticism of the prosecution of the war in Southeast Asia, later wars tried to deflect any criticism of bombing by touting so-called precision and clean weapons. In the first Gulf War, under President George H.W. Bush, the Pentagon, learning from the lack of control of visual images in Vietnam, tightly managed nightly news broadcasts with videos of so-called precision bombing. While the American public rallied behind the troops, the rest of the world saw the vicious unleashing of techno-war. This high-tech slaughter was most evident in the massacre of retreating Iraqis from Kuwait in what became known as the "Highway of Death." Although the Pentagon controlled to a great extent the televised images, this massacre did find some fleeting moments in television reporting. CNN, at least for its U.S. audience, framed the devastation as just retribution for Iraqi torturers and thieves. Yet, it was clear to other reporters that this fleeing convoy of conscripts and civilians had been repeatedly bombarded by U.S. warplanes using cluster bombs and anti-personnel weapons. Even British military officials decried this slaughter, bridling at how U.S. pilots had boasted about their participation in what they called "The Turkey Shoot" (Kellner 1992: 404–408).

When the United States initiated the war in Afghanistan in 2002, the claim was again made that there would be precision bombing without any deliberate "collateral damage" to civilians. However, from the very beginning and continuing throughout the now seventeenth year of U.S. military engagement in Afghanistan, constant reports of bombings of wedding parties and family gatherings have proliferated. One such example happened in a village north of Kandahar that was strafed by AC-130 gunships, resulting in the death of at least ninety-three civilians. The blunt response by one Pentagon official was that "the people were dead because we wanted them dead." Trying to avoid any further probing of the incident, then Secretary of Defense, Donald Rumsfeld, said, "I cannot deal with that particular village." In a June 28, 2002 *Los Angeles Times* story about the civilian deaths, one Afghan who had lost his wife angrily lamented: "I put a curse on the Americans who did this. I pray they will have the tragedy in their lives that I have had in mine." Given such indiscriminate killing, it should not be surprising that U.S. policy in Afghanistan has only succeeded in re-legitimizing a guerilla insurgency, led by a renewed Taliban, creating further tragedies for the Afghan people (Rashid 2008).

Hence, what was christened as a "War on Terror" has in many respects become a terror war waged by the United States for geo-political reasons and underlined by the persistence of a white supremacist agenda. If not yet fully recognized as such by the American people, especially given the white blind spot that often operates to dilute the brutal realities of U.S. savage wars, others in strategically significant parts of the world readily understand how the presence of the U.S. military, in whatever guise, embodies the pursuit of imperial projects underscored by racism. According to the Indian activist and writer, Arundhati Roy, "It's become clear that the War against Terror is not really about terror, and the War of Iraq not only about oil. It's about a superpower's self-destructive impulse toward supremacy, stranglehold, global hegemony" (Roy 2004: 34).[6]

In the second Gulf War, with the actual invasion of Iraq under President George W. Bush, the U.S. military, facing an intransigent Sunni civilian population, resorted to the use of cluster bombs and to free-fire zones in the early aerial assaults throughout Iraq from Hilla to Fallujah. In Fallujah, Sunni residents, whether combatants or civilians, described by a U.S. Marine as "strange, sullen, wild-eyed" with a "rough analogy to American Indians" were "burned alive with the white phosphorus that U.S. forces used in Vietnam" (Singh 2017: 16). As a consequence of the bombing of cities, there were heavy civilian casualties. Occasionally, criticism of the type of ordnance used in Iraq found its way into the mainstream U.S. press, especially when left-over cluster bomblets looking like yellow food packages blew up in children's hands or depleted uranium weapons were inadvertently dropped on British soldiers. However, questions in the corporate media about the immorality of "shock and awe" bombing strategy were often buried deeper than any of the cluster bomblets. (Donnelly and Schlesinger 2003).

---

6 On the U.S. wars on and of terror in the aftermath of 9/11, see Dower 2017, esp. 87–125.

The racism that led the U.S. military to see every "gook" as Viet Cong in Vietnam also reappeared in Iraq. According to one British commander in Iraq, American troops often saw Iraqis as "untermenschen" – the Nazi expression for sub-humans. Although embedded U.S. reporters rarely provided an insight into this racist mentality, Mark Franchetti of the *London Times* quoted one U.S. soldier as asserting that "Iraqis are sick people and we are the chemotherapy" (Franchetti 2003). And with chemotherapy if the sick person dies it was only to help cure that person. This reminds one of the infamous pronouncement by a U.S. military office on the destruction of a Vietnamese village during the war that ravaged that country: "We had to destroy the village in order to save it."

The view of the Iraqis as "sick people," framed in obvious racist terms, is very evident in the 2014 popular film, *American Sniper*, directed by Clint Eastwood and based on the autobiography of Chris Kyle, a Navy SEAL sniper "who boasted of having killed over 250 people during his four deployments as a sniper in Iraq" (Miller 2013). While deliberately downplaying the geo-political context and the victimization of the Iraqi people at the hands of the U.S. military, the film attempts to cast Kyle as a reluctant hero who, nonetheless, following the advice of one commanding officer in the film puts "the fear of God into the savages." Kyle embraces his role as crusader for a civilizing mission that is legitimized in the film against the backdrop of the viciousness of two enemy figures, Mustapha, a Syrian sniper, and the "Butcher," an Iraqi torturer. Indeed, one sees the brutal "Butcher" torturing a father and child, creating a cinematic context for Kyle's killings to be seen as righteous. Thus, the film turns the war into another struggle between civilization and savagery, recapitulating in the process many of the tropes of the cinematic Western (Soberon 2017).

The metaphor used in the film of Kyle as a "sheep-dog," protecting the world against wolves, like the Iraqi bad-guys, obliterates the role of the U.S. in the torture at Abu Ghraib and countless incidents of U.S. military terror. The film even depicts Kyle equivocating when a boy tries to pick up an RPG launcher. Mumbling to himself for the kid to drop it, Kyle manifests much relief when the boy lets go of the weapon and runs away. However, both the real Kyle and other U.S. soldiers exhibited an entirely different attitude toward Iraqi children, recalling the orders given in the Philippines to fire on anyone over ten. According to a news story that appeared in the April 8, 2003 *Sydney Morning Herald*, Army Private Nick Boggs rationalized killing a 10 year-old Iraqi child. "I did what I had to do. I don't have a big problem with it but anyone who shoots a little kid has to feel something.... I think they thought we wouldn't shoot kids. But we showed them we don't care. We are going to do what we have to do to stay alive and keep ourselves safe."

While both the cinematic Kyle and the real Kyle were devoted to the "mission" and saving one's own, the real Kyle was actually little more than a bloodthirsty killer who embraced his role as an instrument of white terror. He writes in his autobiography: "We're here and we want to fuck with you ... You see us? We're the people kicking your ass. Fear us because we will kill you, motherfucker. I wish I could kill all of you fucking savages. None of you deserve to live. I only wished I had killed more ... I never once fought for the Iraqis. They're all a bunch of raghead savages and shit on my boot. I could give a flying fuck about them" (quoted in Langman and Lundskow 2016: 170). No "innocence of whiteness" in these racist rantings! Kyle did, however, demonstrate concern for his fellow U.S. soldiers even after his four tours of duty, helping with Iraqi war veterans with PTSD (including the one who later murdered Kyle on a gun-range). However, this kind of nationalistic and cultural chauvinism made it impossible for Kyle and many of his fellow Americans to comprehend the kind of savage war perpetrated on the Iraqis.

While much of the killing in Iraq was buried under a patriotic gaze deployed in the portrait of Chris Kyle in the film, *American Sniper*, the release of documents and films of the Iraq War by WikiLeaks in 2010 brought into the light of day the kinds of military operations that wreaked havoc on Iraq. The release by WikiLeaks of close to 400,000 reports, authored by those U.S. and U.K. soldiers engaged in military operations in Iraq from 2004 to 2009, provided compelling testimony to the viciousness of the war and occupation. Certainly, such glimpses reinforced the sense that the massive killing of civilians was not incidental, but part and parcel of a campaign to sow death and destruction. Therefore, it is understandable why the Pentagon wanted to suppress WikiLeaks and why the Trump Administration requested extradition for Julian Assange, the founder of WikiLeaks, for his role is disseminating the documentation of the U.S. war crimes in Iraq.

It is indisputable that WikiLeaks added essential elements to that public record. Among these are the greater involvement of the U.S. military and its Iraqi allies in torture. For those U.S. soldiers, like Josh Steiber, who witnessed such violations of human rights and helped, at some point, with the release of documents and videos, WikiLeaks and the U.S. public owe them, unlike Chris Kyle, a debt of gratitude. Steiber, in particular, spoke out around the country about the process of desensitizing that he underwent in his operational activities in Iraq. However, soldiers, like Steiber and Chelsea Manning, who served several years of imprisonment for the alleged leaking of material and most recently (as of April 2019) has been imprisoned for her refusal to testify before a grand jury investigating WikiLeaks, demonstrate that they can transcend the murderous programming which the military and civilian authorities promulgate in the pursuit of war.

On the other hand, as important and courageous as these ground and grunt level perspectives are, they still exist within the matrix of U.S. imperialism. In other words, while they may record the victimization of the other, they tell us little about what Iraqis observed and felt about the war and occupation. In order, therefore, to get beyond the limited vision found even in the WikiLeaks documents, we should enhance those reports with an authentic Iraqi perspective from this same period. Fortunately, there exist at least two collections of such reports, entitled *Baghdad Burning,* written by a twenty-something educated Iraqi woman who blogged from 2004 to 2007 under the name of "Riverbend." The few entries below may help to break through the insularity found in the WikiLeaks documents and expand our own vision of what the U.S. imperial intervention and white terror in Iraq have wrought.

One of the more remarkable findings by WikiLeaks is that of unaccounted civilian deaths in Iraq numbering in the tens of thousands. While trying to discern the actual numbers of people killed in the war is still in dispute, it seems that the earlier 2006 study in the respected medical journal *The Lancet* has been relegated to historical amnesia. However, one can cite the following October 18, 2006, entry by "Riverbend" on why the figure of 600,000 dead, projected as the maximum by *The Lancet,* was not unimaginable given the lethal environment of the war. According to the blog, Riverbend writes that "we literally do not know a single Iraqi family that has not seen the violent death of a first or second degree relative these last three years. Abductions, sectarian violence, revenge killings, assassinations, car-bombs, suicide bombs, American military strikes, Iraqi military raids, death squads, armed robberies, executions, detentions, secret prisons, torturing, mysterious weapons – with so many different ways to die is the number so far-fetched?"

From the perspective of "Riverbend" the violence against Iraqi civilians, and, particularly, incidents of rape, were not just relegated to the sectarian war unleashed by the U.S. invasion and occupation. Rape, as recounted in this July 11, 2006 entry, was endemic to the U.S. prosecution of the war:

> The poor girl Abeer was neither the first to be raped by American troops, nor will she be the last. The only reasons this rape was brought to light and publicized is that her whole immediate family was killed with her ... We've been hearing whisperings about rapes in American controlled prisons and during sieges of towns like Haditha and Samarra for the last three years. The naiveté of Americans who can't believe their "heroes" are

committing such atrocities is ridiculous. Who ever heard of an occupying army committing rape???

"Riverbend's" angry and ironic final question underscores the blinkered vision most U.S. citizens still have about the wars in Iraq and Afghanistan. Even with the massive amount of documentary materials now available through WikiLeaks, the silence on issues like rape and the massacres in cities like Fallujah, a city in which Chris Kyle was stationed and did many of his sniper killings, is deafening. The constant bombardment of militaristic propaganda purveyed by the Pentagon and embedded in the corporate media and mass-mediated culture tries to instill the kind of hyper patriotic illusions of "clean" wars and "heroic" warriors. Instead of recognizing that war atrocities are part of daily operations, something that WikiLeaks does help to reveal, U.S. citizens, for the most part, remain blind to the horrors visited upon others in our name.

It is imperative, therefore, that we heed the voices of people like "Riverbend" and keep them in our consciousness, even as we have gained the additional essential information disseminated by WikiLeaks. For this reason alone, the following comments of "Riverbend" have particular relevance to the thrust of this chapter concerning savage war and white terror. In contesting the Pentagon's insistence that all of its heinous weapons, from cluster bombs to phosphorous and depleted uranium, are merely conventional arms, she reveals the lies embedded in the American fog of war. As noted by "Riverbend" in her November 17, 2005 entry: "This war has redefined 'conventional.' It has taken atrocity to another level. Everything we learned before has become obsolete. 'Conventional' has become synonymous with horrifying. Conventional weapons are those that eat away the skin in a white blaze; conventional interrogation methods are like those practiced in Abu Ghraib and other prisons ... Quite simply ... conventional terror" (Riverbend 2005).

The white blaze referred to by "Riverbend" is most certainly white phosphorous which was used throughout Iraq in contravention of international law banning such weapons. However, the white blaze could also metaphorically be the white terror unleashed by the U.S. execution of savage wars from those against the Indians on the U.S. content to Iraqis in their native land. Writing in the midst of the Vietnam War and a domestic war against advocates of black liberation, James Baldwin prophetically asserted:

> As long as white Americans take refuge in their whiteness – for so long as they are unable to walk out of this monstrous of traps – they will allow

millions of people to be slaughtered in their name, and will be manipulated into and surrender themselves to what they will think of – and justify – as a racial war. They will never, as long as their whiteness puts so sinister a distance between themselves and their own experience and the experience of others, feel themselves sufficiently human, *sufficiently worthwhile*, to become responsible for themselves, their leaders, their country, their children, or their fate. (Baldwin 1971)

CHAPTER 2

The Past of Present Terrors

While the snarling rabid minions of the mobilized alt-right seek to cloak themselves in the mantle of "free speech," their provocative marches are, instead, the most extreme recrudescence of a white nationalist distemper. Indeed, the spike in incidents since 2017 promulgated by angry whites affiliated with the alt-right on people of color has left scores dead or injured (Hankes and Amend 2018). Emboldened by the white supremacist Trump Administration and the constant racist tweeting of its ersatz Fuehrer, other "aggrieved" whites look to the White House to express and rationalize their racial resentments.

Of course, those racial resentments are deeply rooted in the political culture of the United States, especially as expressions of state and vigilante violence against people of color. When white Europeans invaded the American continent in the fifteenth and sixteenth centuries, they either sought to plunder the wealth of the indigenous population or to establish colonies as an extension of the war capitalism practiced by their competing nation states, turning these wars prosecuted by the Crown and American colonists into "race wars" (Grenier 2005: 12). To satisfy the need for labor, European settlers imported enslaved Africans in the seventeenth century, enacting, in the process, a harsh regime of exploitation throughout the colonies (Horne 2018). Once these North American colonies achieved their independence through the formation of the United States in the late eighteenth century, those states continued to engage in war and expansion against the Native Americans and to increase the enslavement of people of African descent.

Indeed, the foundational document of these United States, the Constitution, was a perfect reflection of a slave republic, built on empire, expansion, and exclusion. According to Barbara Jean Fields, "racial ideology supplied the means of explaining slavery to people whose terrain was a republic founded on radical doctrines of liberty and natural rights" (Fields 1990: 114). The Second Amendment to that Constitution inscribed militias as a vehicle of state violence against both the Indigenous and enslaved populations (Dunbar-Ortiz 2018). Hence, hiding beneath the ideological veil of liberty and security was an iron fist of state violence, especially against people of color, whether red, black, or brown (Singh 2017: 35–73).

In the early republic racial ideology and state violence were also often incorporated into patriarchal constructions of a "civilizing mission" towards Native

Americans. Both Thomas Jefferson and Andrew Jackson, in particular, relied on the symbol of the "Great White Father." Jackson's slave-owning background informed his sense of this civilizing mission "in whose name he removed Indians. But that slave model of paternalism, appropriate enough to Indian removal, contained force and violence at its core" (Rogin 1976: 169). When Jackson signed the actual Indian Removal Act of 1830, it began a decade long forced evacuation of these Indigenous peoples from their homelands to so-called Indian Territory west of the Mississippi. Prior to his presidency, Jackson had a long history, especially in Tennessee, of terrorizing Native Americans. In the military operation against the Muskogee, "Jackson's mercenaries killed hundreds of Muskogee civilians, pursuing without mercy even homeless and starved refugees seeking shelter and safety" (Dunbar-Ortiz 2014: 99).

During the 1830s tens of thousands of Native Americans were brutally uprooted and marched, often in the dead of winter, across the Mississippi. When even the U.S. Supreme Court ruled in 1832 against such forced relocation, President Jackson defied the court. The violent removal of these Indian nations continued under Jackson's successor, Martin Van Buren, concluding in 1838 with the Cherokee being put into detention camps before being forced out of Georgia and Alabama in a winter march, later to be known as the "Trail of Tears." Over 8000 of those Cherokee, including women and children, died under these horrific conditions. One of the U.S. Army soldiers who later recounted his involvement in this violent uprooting of Cherokee noted: "I fought through the Civil War and have seen men shot to pieces and slaughtered by thousands, but the Cherokee removal was the cruelest work I ever knew" (quoted in Dunbar-Ortiz 2014: 113).

Throughout the 1830s, "the homelands of the Choctaw, the Chickasaw, the Creek, the Seminole, and the Cherokee had, through the military power and legal authority of the United States of America, been converted into a vast reserve for the cultivation of whiteness" (Johnson 2013: 31). That whiteness reflected both white supremacy and the massive growth of cotton on the slave labor camps in these former homelands of these aforementioned Native peoples. The brutal regime that drove enslaved Africans under constant torture to harvest the dominant export commodity of the United States during this time was cotton. In turn, cotton was at the core of an expanding world market that garnered economic rewards for the white enslavers throughout the pre-Civil War period (Baptist 2014). Hence, cultivating whiteness in this historical epoch entailed levels of cruelty and violence against both enslaved and indigenous populations. In the case of the enslaved, a system of violence and cruelty through abduction and torture enacted an accumulation by possession. In the case of Native Americans, a system of violence and cruelty through displacement and extermination enacted an accumulation by dispossession.

The contemporary forced separation of asylum seeking and immigrant parents and children at the southwest border, while not as cruel or as violent as the 1838 Cherokee removal, has, nonetheless, unleashed a different "trail of tears." Many of those desperate families have fled from violence in countries like El Salvador, Guatemala, and Honduras, countries where U.S. imperial interventions in the late twentieth and early twenty-first centuries exacerbated harsh conditions confronting the poor (Grandin 2007). According to a 2015 Doctors Without Borders study of these Central Americans seeking asylum, at least 40% had lost a family member to the endemic gang violence plaguing their countries. Desperate families with young children from these Central American countries are continuing the hazardous trek to the U.S. Southern border.

While overall immigration since 2000 has declined, the repressive response by U.S. authorities at that border has increased, especially in the aftermath of 9/11 and the expansion of a regime of detentions and deportations. President Barack Obama's Administration oversaw a massive ramping up of deportations (Golash-Boza 2016). It is estimated that during his time as president a record 2.7 million foreign nationals were deported (Chardy 2016). One historical irony of his policy is that in legitimizing the coup against the democratically elected President of Honduras, violence spread in that country and led to even more desperate refugees seeking asylum in the United States. In addition, in the summer of 2014 with a surge in families and unaccompanied minors crossing the border, the Obama Administration used detention centers as a stopgap until the courts intervened to demand their release while cases for asylum were under review.

During the Republican primary campaign, Donald Trump repeatedly and maliciously referred to Mexican "rapists" and "criminals" pouring over the border, necessitating an even harsher regimen, including the building of a wall to prevent further immigration of these brown people from the south. Channeling his hero, Andrew Jackson, Trump longed for reconstituting a white republic by criminalizing those seeking refuge in the United States. Once inside the White House, the Trump administration began separating families at the border. Starting in 2017 with then-secretary of Homeland Secretary John Kelly announcing these separations as a "deterrence" through now ex-Homeland Secretary, Kirstjen Nielsen, defending taking children away from their parents "in the interest of the child," thousands of children have been essentially kidnapped by a "zero-tolerance" policy. Viewing the parents as "smugglers" of their own children, Attorney General Jeff Sessions vowed in May 2018 to continue family separation, using biblical passages the following month to justify the Administration's actions.[1]

The hue and cry raised by international human rights agencies denouncing such forced separations, along with reports from the ACLU and immigration attorneys, of hundreds of claims of abuse by the Border Patrol of these children, galvanized an already outraged public that such cruelty against immigrant families must desist. Although Trump was forced to promulgate an executive order on June 20, 2018 to keep immigrant families together, the process of reuniting and protecting these families remains an open question. Immigrants are still being sent to detention centers where thousands are already languishing in such understaffed and overcrowded facilities. As noted by Henry Giroux, "the caging of young immigrant children who were forcibly separated from their parents at the southern border for months at a time ... resonates with deeply disturbing events of a dark past in which violent separation of families was the hallmark feature of fascist cruelty, barbarism, and brutality" (Giroux 2018). Thousands of these young immigrant children still remain under various forms of custody on the U.S. Southern border.

On the other hand, one does not have to invoke fascism as a historical precedent for recognizing the white supremacist roots of such cruelty to refugee families and migrants at the U.S. Southern border. Indeed, the long history of the Border Patrol, beginning in 1924, is replete with incidents of racist violence by Border agents, some of whom were members of the Ku Klux Klan. These agents regularly physically abused migrants along the border, at times relying on rape and murder. During the 1970s the *New York Times* ran a series of articles that reported on Border Patrol agents kidnapping children and keeping them imprisoned in "ice box" cells. As a recent brief overview of the Border Patrol makes clear: "The viciousness we are witnessing today at the border, directed at children and adults, has a long history, a fact that should in no way mitigate the extraordinary cruelty of Donald Trump. But it does suggest that if the U.S. is to climb out of the moral abyss it has fallen into, it has to think well beyond Trump's malice. It needs a historical reckoning with the true cause of the border crisis: the long, brutal history of border enforcement itself" (Grandin 2019).

While those who have occupied the frontlines of border enforcement have, at times, exhibited and continue to exhibit sadistic and racist tendencies towards people of color, especially those arriving at the border from Central American countries, the more generalized policy of border management is

---

1 As noted by Behdad (2005: 166): "the predicament of the border is generalized to the point where the state's politics of exclusion becomes a matter of public opinion and racism against nonwhite immigrants becomes a legitimate form of nationalism."

historically connected to state control and disciplinary power. Such control and disciplinary power is a vehicle "to authorize … perpetual surveillance and control of the immigrant population and to transform the average citizen into a vigilante who internalizes disciplinary power" (Behdad 2005: 161). The history of vigilante activity as an extension of white identity politics is "the modern face of the military tradition of frontier homicide" (Estes 2019: 194).[2] It also represents a more thoroughgoing version of the use of "private violence for public ends" (Slotkin 1993: 99).

Nowhere has that use of both state and private violence been more evident that in the disciplinary power meted out to African Americans, whether under slavery, Jim Crow, and on up to the present. While this recent vicious policy on the southwest border recalls the use of military violence against Native Americans and reflects the punitive policies of the present, African Americans in even greater numbers have faced both state and vigilante violence over the centuries. State controls of repression were enacted both as war measures and domestic policing. That policing, especially in order to uphold slavery, incorporated whites into disciplinary and repressive regimes with a license to kill blacks. As noted in one study of slave patrols during the eighteenth and early nineteenth century in the Southern states, "the new American innovation in law enforcement … was the creation of racially focused law enforcement groups" (Hadden 2001: 4).

Especially with white supremacy as the dominant ideological order through the nineteenth and twentieth centuries, African Americans suffered at the hands of white vigilantes and law enforcement officials (Hadden 2001: 203–220). In a dozen southern states between 1877 and 1950 there were over 4,000 lynchings. One historian's reflection on the role of lynching described them as "theatrical spectacles of white supremacy, as whites claimed their economic, cultural, and social dominance over blacks through ritualized forms of mob violence carried out in official public spaces" (Romano 2014: 17). Furthermore, according to racial justice activist, Bryan Stevenson, "lynching created an environment where racial subordination and segregation could be maintained for decades with limited resistance. Most critically, lynching reinforced a legacy of racial inequality that has never been adequately addressed in America" (Stevenson 2017: 14). These public spectacles of lynching and racial violence, especially during and after World War I, also were intended to prevent black migration from the South while keeping African Americans under a repressive political and economic regime (Anderson 2016: 39–44).[3]

---

2 For an examination of the multiple meanings of the "frontier" throughout the history of the United States right up to and including Trump's wall, see Grandin 2019, *The End of the Myth*.
3 Lynching, of course, was not limited to African Americans. Especially in the West and Southwest, white mobs and vigilantes deployed lynching against Native Americans, Mexicans, and

In the Southern states, in particular, right through the 1960s, police and white vigilantes were part of terrorist networks that punished any black person who violated the rules of white supremacy. Moreover, that terrorist network implicated all of the agencies of the state, particularly those in the South, where "at least through the late 1960s, white men could murder blacks and their allies without fearing any meaningful retribution ... (since) the state ... shared some responsibility for racial violence of the era. And the unwillingness of juries to convict shows that many whites understood that upholding the racial status quo necessitated turning a blind eye to murder" (Romano 2014: 43–44.) Thus, the practice of white supremacy and white identity politics doomed many African Americans in the South to a reign of terror and a forfeiting of any hope for racial justice.

White supremacy did not disappear with the overcoming of segregation and second-class citizenship. If it no longer relied on white sheets to promulgate its terror, it could always find blue uniforms to hide behind whenever travesties were committed against the African-American community. Of course, the police had been implicated in terror networks, like the KKK, especially in the South. On the other hand, as Richard Rothstein's study of *de jure* housing segregation across the nation makes clear, federal and state authorities at all levels of law enforcement enabled discriminatory practices against African Americans, in particular, while institutionalizing legal advantages for whites. Moreover, according to Rothstein, "During much of the twentieth century, police tolerance and promotion of cross burnings, vandalism, arson, and other violent acts to maintain residential segregation was systematic and nationwide" (Rothstein 2017: 143).

With cries for "law and order" and the pointed use of drug and criminal justice policies, the African-American community faced renewed state violence and police brutality in the late twentieth century. As the "war on poverty" of the 1960s morphed into a "war on crime," African Americans became the target of punitive policing as a consequence of racist presumptions about the "pathologies" of the black community. With the insurgencies of those black communities from Newark in 1964 to Detroit in 1967, innocent African Americans fell victim to the mayhem of malevolent police and military repression. Policing in Detroit and Chicago took an ominous turn with the creation of "special" police units that waged a "reign of terror" against black men in

---

Chinese. For an overview of lynching and racist violence against Mexicans and Mexican Americans on the Southwest border in the late nineteenth and early twentieth century, see Grandin 2019, *The End of the Myth*: 156–167. A lynching party attacked the small Chinese population in Los Angeles in 1871, murdering, in the process, at least nineteen of the one hundred seventy two Chinese living there. See Wu 2002: 61.

particular. The STRESS ("Stop the Robberies, Enjoy Safe Streets") squad in Detroit in the first years of its existence in the early 1970s murdered a young African-American male a month (Hinton 2016: 99, 109–110, 191–202; Goergakas and Surkin 1998: 167–173). In Chicago the counterinsurgency techniques and torture practiced in Vietnam found their way into a police unit that subjected over one hundred African-American criminal suspects over a twenty year period to those brutal methods deployed first in Vietnam and then later used by some of the very same police in the "enhanced interrogation" at Guantanamo (Singh 2017: 68–69).

Especially in the aftermath of the Black Power insurgencies of the 1960s, aggressive militarized policing and punitive policies towards African Americans resulted in the "exponential growth of imprisonment" of black men (Hinton 2016: 178; Taylor 2016: 66–67). This physical and legal harassment of African Americans not only led to higher rates of incarceration, but also continued a legacy of white supremacy when it came to the criminal justice system. As noted by Keeanga-Yamatha Taylor, although, "there have been many changes in Black life, politics, and culture, ...the threat and reality of police surveillance, scrutiny, violence, and even murder has remained remarkably consistent. The daily harm caused by the mere presence of police in Black communities has been a consistent feature of Black urban history, and, increasingly, Black suburban history. Police brutality has been a consistent badge of inferiority and second-class citizenship" (Taylor 2016: 107–108).

Among the most recent incidents of police violence against unarmed young blacks is the tragic, but instructive, incident of the murder of Michael Brown in 2014. The six bullets fired by Ferguson police officer Darren Wilson did more than terminate Michael Brown's life with extreme prejudice. Brown's death and its repercussions once more demonstrate the persistence of racial injustice and the contradictions inherent in how local, state, and national authorities pursue their blinkered sense of justice. At the local level the outrageous and arrogant behavior of the overwhelmingly white Ferguson police force and political establishment towards African Americans is not just an egregious example of the continuing rule of white supremacy in the suburbs of St. Louis. It is reflective of institutional and ideological patterns that inform cities and suburbs across the United States, especially when it comes to meting out "justice" to Black and Brown youth. Whether through the operation of racial profiling in the criminal justice system or extrajudicial killings of people of color by police or white vigilantes, punitive measures disproportionately target minority communities (McKesson 2018: 52–67).

As clinical professor of law and director of the Civil Rights and Police Accountability Project at the Edwin F. Mandel Legal Aid Clinic, Craig Futterman notes: "For all too many people out there, when people think of the words 'criminal,' 'drug dealer' or 'gangbanger,' images of Black and Brown folks come to mind and that's equal with respect to police." Hence, implicit bias, operating on a racialized white subconscious that relies on the long history of racial stereotypes, targets, in particular, young people of color. Indeed, as Futterman's research shows concerning police perceptions of young Black and Brown men, they see those young men as a "potential criminal or a potential danger, and that also makes that police officer far more likely to feel threatened and far more likely to shoot" (quoted in Muhammad 2012).

While the exact sequence of events that led to the killing of Michael Brown is still in dispute, what is indisputable, based on the independent autopsy report by Dr. Michael Baden, former chief medical examiner of New York City, is that Brown was a defenseless victim of police violence. Instead of immediately arresting Darren Wilson, the Ferguson police department put him on paid leave. During the whole period of the investigation of the murder of Michael Brown, these same police and political forces were selectively releasing information about Brown intended to cast aspersions on his innocence, as if any such information could justify his extrajudicial murder.

According to Brigitt Keller, executive director of the National Police Accountability Project, "excessive force by police ... is getting worse." She identifies possible causes as the militarization of the police, ongoing police impunity, and an exaggerated sense of what police confront, no doubt reinforced by the spread of Homeland Security horror stories. Certainly, when it comes to African Americans the police and homegrown white terrorists are more a threat than foreign terrorists of color (Lindorff 2014). Yet, there remains a deep racial divide when it comes to assessing the inequities of police violence. A Pew Research poll taken in the aftermath of Michael Brown's murder reported that 80% of blacks thought Michael Brown's death raised "important issues about race that need to be addressed" against only 37% of whites who agreed with that sentiment.

This divide is nothing new when it comes to how justice has been meted out to people of color, those in the lower classes, and anyone deemed "dangerous" to the law and order of the land. It was just over fifty years ago that white supremacist vigilantes aided by local police murdered civil rights workers, Chaney, Goodman, and Schwerner. For many whites in Mississippi these civil rights workers had it coming to them since they were disturbing the "peace" of a racially sanctioned order. "The racial murders of the 1950s and 1960s," declares one of the best histories of the murders of those decades and the trials that followed, "operated as a tool of racial terrorism, driven by a desire to stifle black protest and uphold white supremacy" (Romano 2014: 19).

Now fifty years later those in Ferguson seeking justice confront local and state police forces that curtail their civil rights and threaten them with violence. When unarmed demonstrators marched to the command center in Ferguson on the evening of August 17th they were met with tear gas and armored vehicles. Seeking to charge the demonstrators with provoking the violence, the police authorities made unsubstantiated claims about the use of Molotov cocktails and small arms fire. Not unlike what happened fifty years ago in the Gulf of Tonkin when the Johnson Administration lied about North Vietnamese attacks in order to justify its own escalating aggression, the authorities fabricated incidents to rationalize their own violence.

Although state and federal authorities deployed a variety of changing strategies and tactics to calm the situation in Ferguson, they either dithered at the expense of justice or demonstrated their own hypocrisy when it came to sanctioning extrajudicial killings. While President Obama droned on about our "shared humanity," his real drones assassinated victims throughout the Middle East. "According to one study, as of 2015, U.S. attempts to kill forty-one individuals resulted in more than one thousand deaths" (Singh 2017: 32). In defending such extra-legal assassination, even in the face of so many innocent victims, Attorney General Eric Holder analogized the situation as one similar to a policeman stopping a suspect's flight by relying on deadly force. Before his government position in the Obama Administration, Holder helped establish, as U.S. attorney for the District of Columbia, an early version of the notorious "stop-and-frisk" policy (Singh 2017: 71). In his private practice, Holder also defended Chiquita against charges that their funneling money through a subsidiary to right-wing paramilitary groups in Colombia had led to the murder of labor and political opponents of banana estate authoritarianism.

On the other hand, with the ascension of Donald Trump to the presidency, his administration has developed a range of extra-judicial terror engagements, both domestically and internationally. Trump used an executive order to overturn Obama's meager efforts to reign in the CIA's role in the drone assassination program. By granting more authority to the CIA for targeting individuals and countries in which they resided, Yemen and Somalia, for example, have recorded a three-fold increase in drone killings. In addition, the CIA established new operations in Niger in order to strike targets in Africa (Kaufman 2018). The level of state violence against people of color in the United States has increased. Indeed, the lethal white terror manifests a direct correlation with the political fortunes of Donald Trump. From the outrageous racist claims about Mexicans to the Gestapo-like tactics of ICE to the kidnapping of brown children and their detention or deportation of their parents, Trump relies on racial fears and resentments of whites to advance and institutionalize such white aggression and violence towards people of color. "Trump's scapegoating rhetoric of demonization and bigotry not only dehumanizes racialized others, it also prepares the ground for encouraging hate groups and an intensification of hate crimes" (Giroux 2018, "Neoliberal Fascism").

Certainly, the very real decline of living standards and the attendant rise in morbidity statistics among some white workers, especially those in rural areas, has created an environment where racism and xenophobia can be mobilized (Metzl 2019). "Perceived threats to national security and/or unemployment" are breeding grounds for "anti-immigrant attitudes" (Lamont 2000: 92). When those kinds of domestic conditions are combined with a toxic brew of white nationalism and imperialism, the resort to racism becomes inevitable. Hence, "the degraded popular image of Arabs and Islam and official policies towards visitors and immigrants from Arab countries are all too indicative of a rising tide of racism in the US that may do untold future damage both internally and internationally" (Harvey 2005: 197).[4] Once more, U.S. military interventions in Arab and Islamic countries and restrictive immigration patterns reflect and promote racial animosities both at home and abroad.

In the next few decades people of color will become a majority of the American working class. Attacks by Trump and the Republican Party on people of color represent desperate attempts to mobilize whites and divide the working class for their own political benefits. Unfortunately, for the fortunes of the working class as a whole, the appeals to white racial resentments go beyond the fringe extremist elements of the alt-right. They go to the core of a persistent white identity politics – a core that needs to be confronted and removed if there is any hope for transformative change in the United States. Furthermore, "as long as capitalism exists, material and ideological pressures push white workers to be racist and all workers to hold each other in general suspicion. But there are moments of struggle when the mutual interests of workers are laid bare, and when the suspicion is finally turned in the other direction – at the plutocrats who live well while the rest of us suffer" (Taylor 2016: 215–216).

---

4   This negative image of Arabs and Islam has a long history in the West. As noted by Sardar and Davies: "The basic representation of Muslims as militant, barbaric fanatics, corrupt, effete sensualists, people who have lived contrary to natural law, developed early in Western scholarship and has been resistant to change" (2002: 52).

CHAPTER 3

White Identity Politics and the Terrors of Trumpism

To understand how white identity politics forms one of the central elements of Trumpism,[1] one must put both the man and the phenomenon in a larger critical historical context. The rise and rule of Donald Trump embodies much that is disturbingly new from his almost daily narcissistic rants on Twitter to his overt racist, misogynist, and xenophobic public pronouncements. Especially menacing is Trump's "racist vocabulary ... that ... registers a move from the coded language of benign neglect to policies marked by malignant cruelty" (Giroux 2018, "Neoliberal Fascism"). This racist vocabulary, as noted by Ta-Nehisi Coates, reflects "white supremacy in all its truculent and sanctimonious power." Coates delineates the precise content of Trump's white supremacy from his outspoken advocacy of the "death penalty for the eventually exonerated Central Park Five to the slandering of Barack Obama under the ideological cover of 'birtherism' to denunciations of Mexicans as 'rapists'" (Coates 2017).

On the other hand, there are broader and deeper historic roots to many of the positions articulated by Trump during his presidential campaign and adopted during his presidency. In particular, Trumpism as a historically determined political expression must, therefore, be examined for its underlying social and cultural connections. Thus, as argued by Naomi Klein, "Trump is not a rupture at all, but rather a culmination – the logical end point – of a great many dangerous stories our culture has been telling for a very long time. That greed is good. That the market rules. That money is what matters in life. That white men are better than the rest. That the natural world is there for us to pillage. That the vulnerable deserve their fate and the one percent deserve their golden towers. That anything public or commonly held is sinister and not worth protecting. That we are surrounded by danger and should only look after our own" (Klein 2017: 257–258).

It is these "dangerous stories," anchored in material conditions and ideological orientations that constitute the phenomenon known as Trumpism. In order to illuminate further the contexts out of which Trumpism emerged I want to highlight several overlapping domains from the socio-economic to the socio-cultural to the socio-psychological. Then, I will consider how these

---

[1] The chapter is a revised and expanded version of my article "'A Troll at the Bridge': Trump, Trumpism, and White Identity Politics," *New Politics* March 3, 2018. http://newpol.org/content/-troll-bridge-trump-trumpism-and-white-identity-politics.

domains inform Trumpism as an electoral and governmental project, especially, but not exclusively, as a representation of white identity politics.[2] Finally, I will assess the forms of resistance that have challenged Trumpism and what the future of democracy might be given the persistence of white supremacy and the "resilience of racism's historical legacies and current appeal" (Singh 2017: x and 152–177).

One cannot separate Trumpism from the reign of the neoliberal order that has marked capitalism in the United States and around the world since the 1970s. This rendering of neoliberalism follows the insights of Thomas Piketty on the growth of inequality inherent in contemporary global capital (Piketty 2014) and David Harvey on how capital, through a variety of fixes, has continued to accumulate through dispossession (Harvey 2005: 137–182). Citing the "unholy alliance between state powers and the predatory aspects of finance capitalism," Harvey identifies this variant of neoliberalism as "vulture capitalism" (Harvey 2005: 136). Paul Kennedy's take on neoliberal economics, which he calls "vampire capitalism," is reflected in the following analysis: "During the last 40 years or so a disruptive and largely predatory model of capitalism has become established ... whereby a minority of low or non-paying capitalists ... have been able to commandeer a large portion of the wealth generated from economic growth while failing to either reinvest this in ways that creates jobs and raise the incomes of everyone else or to remunerate their employees in proportion to the latter's contribution to creating new values" (Kennedy 2017: 29.)

Of course, the neoliberal project has global dimensions that rely on transnational capital to intimidate workers and national governments to adhere to their demands from lowering wages to eliminating trade and environmental protections. On the other hand, neoliberalism on the global level also had a direct impact on U.S. domestic politics. As argued by Robert Kuttner, "the economic turbulence of the 1970s opened space for elites to weaken democratic counterweights to capital, substantially using globalization as their instrument. The resulting policies were perverse for efficiency as well as equality" (Kuttner 2018: xiv). Those policies, while not exclusively embedded in the Republican political agenda, nonetheless, expanded under President Reagan and have now "accelerated" under President Trump. They consist of "deregulating restrictions on corporate power, cutting taxes for the rich, expanding the military, privatizing public education, suppressing civil liberties, waging a war

---

2 According to Arlie Hochschild, "Trump was the identity politics candidate for white men" (2016: 230).

against dissent, treating Black communities as war zones, and dismantling all public goods" (Giroux 2018: 9).[3]

Another mechanism in the "dismantling all public goods" is the way in which vulture capitalism has imposed forced bankruptcy on cities, such as Detroit, and countries, such as Puerto Rico. By seizing public assets, vulture capitalism rewards those financial institutions that hide behind the ideological cloak of "market fundamentalism." In turn, this hollowing out of public treasuries by private enterprises further exacerbates the income inequality that is a trademark of contemporary capital. Such inequality has a profound impact beyond just the socio-economic domain. Indeed, economic inequality informs the degree to which social, cultural, and psychological bonds are disrupted and, even, destroyed. According to Sasha Abramsky, "the more unequal our society becomes, the more common understandings ... cease to function. At a certain point the bonds of empathy collapse, to be replaced by suspicion and fear" (Abramsky 2017: 202).

Before exploring more in depth the suspicion and fear that demarcate the socio-psychological domain, I want to underscore how the socio-economic order of neoliberalism bleeds into the socio-cultural domain. In its "obsession with commodities, productivity, and disposability" neoliberalism engenders "consumerist logics that travel far beyond shopping centers and the workplace and find their way into personal relationships ... Human values of kindness, love, compassion, and the need for communion with others are eventually reduced to mere afterthoughts in the wake of our market driven culture" (Obineme 2018). As an expression of the branding phenomenon in our market driven culture, Trumpism glories in a pathological narcissism that marks both the man and his business operations. Eschewing even a scintilla of compassion, Trump revels in a ruthless "deal-making" model that recalls the popularity of "reality" television series like "Survivor." As indicated by one critic of "Survivor," a hallmark of the television program was its message about the devaluation of "trust, compassion and mercy." That same critical interpreter of the cultural moment represented by "Survivor" explained "if you are not tougher and less scrupulous than all the others, you will be done in by them, with or without remorse" (Bauman 2003: 88–89).

As part of that narcissistic and callous media culture, television, in particular, has lent itself also to the trivialization and corruption of discourse, a trivialization and corruption censured by media critics like Neil Postman and Thomas Frank. Not surprisingly, having built his "reputation on insults, humiliations, and a discourse of provocation and hate," on "The Apprentice," Trump

---

3 On the racial implications of neoliberalism, see Hohle 2015.

translated his cultural capital achieved through television into political capital during the Republican primaries and beyond (Giroux 2018: 151–152). Yet, ironically, Trump's representation in "The Apprentice" as a savvy billionaire businessman with "impeccable business instincts and unparalleled wealth" (Keefe 2019: 35) was on one level the same kind of con job by the producers of the program as any and every business venture of the Trump organization. Trump's rise in popularity through "The Apprentice" was as much a reflection of the dumbing down of intelligence by the purveyors of such TV programming as it was a prelude to the pomp that surrounded Trump's announcement of his run for the presidency from the gold-colored escalator in the atrium of Trump Tower (Keefe 2019: 40).

With the addition of the short-handed messaging in social media and the continuing assault on intelligence by certain TV programming like "The Apprentice," the media environment proved conducive, in particular, to a media personality like Trump. Television and social media have become breeding grounds for what Henry Giroux calls "civic illiteracy" which "mistakes opinion for informed arguments, (and) erases collective memory." He further notes that the election of Trump "is a case study in how politics has been emptied of any viable meaning and civic illiteracy has been normalized ... His victory makes clear that ignorance rather than reason, emotion rather than informed judgment, and the threat of violence rather than critical exchange appear to have more currency in the age of civic collapse" (Giroux 2018: 197 and 90).

In particular, the manipulation of social media, by various agencies and agents, from Russian to Macedonian to the alt-right in the United States, created a semiotic environment that favored Trump while creating havoc, especially on Facebook, during the 2016 presidential campaign. After being investigated by Robert Mueller and the Senate Intelligence Committee, Facebook took stock of the level of Russian interference in the 2016 presidential election. In October 2017, Facebook identified tens of thousands of posts by Russian agents that may have been read by nearly a hundred and twenty-six million Americans (Osnos 2018: 43). Facebook and other social media have clearly exacerbated the degree of "civic illiteracy" spread by unwitting consumers of deeply flawed social media sources.

On the other hand, "civic illiteracy" extends beyond the media environment to what constitutes a fundamental erosion of a democratic ethos in our political culture, an erosion that Cornel West contends is part of the "imperialist meltdown" infecting both the Republican and Democratic Party establishments. According to West, while Trump is a "sign of our spiritual bankruptcy – all spectacle and no substance, all narcissism and no empathy, all appetite and greed and no wisdom and maturity, his triumph flows from the implosion of a

Republican party establishment beholden to big money, big military and big scapegoating of vulnerable peoples of color, LGBTQ peoples, immigrants, Muslims, and women.... It also flows from a Democratic party establishment beholden to big money, big military, and the clever deployment of peoples of color, LGBTQ peoples, immigrants, Muslims, and women to hide and conceal the lies and crimes of neoliberal policies here and abroad; and from a corporate media establishment that aided and abetted Trump owing to high profits and revenues" (West 2018).

However, to the degree that the Republican Party and Trump have weaponized whiteness, the terrors of Trumpism threaten whatever remains of the vestiges of a political democracy in the United States. Indeed, as numerous recent studies have made clear, the U.S. political environment represents more of an oligarchy than a democracy (Formisamo 2017; Page and Gillens 2017). Those oligarchic tendencies preceded Trump and Trumpism, especially in the political mechanisms mobilized by a wealthy elite for the perpetuation of their economic interests. In the process, the political corruption by what Jane Mayer calls "dark money" manipulated legislation that accrued to the benefit of the corporate and wealthy elite at the expense of the vast majority of the population (Mayer 2017). Although using populist rhetoric about the predations of the economic globalist elite during the presidential campaign, Trump and his Administration have blatantly exacerbated these oligarchic tendencies in their bald-faced and shameless exploitation of governmental resources for their personal economic benefit.

Another critical component of Trumpism that heightens the contradictions in American political culture is the tradition of anti-intellectualism. Reinforced by civic illiteracy, newer forms of anti-intellectualism have risen to the level of a "post-truth" realty that manifests antagonism even to empirical facts. While anti-intellectualism has been part of American culture for some time, as historian Richard Hofstadter discussed in his classic study from the 1950s, *Anti-intellectualism in American Life*, more recent analyses of its persistence, especially among religious fundamentalists, bears out the connections between Trumpism and a new and more destructive wave of anti-intellectualism (Jacoby 2009). "Under Trump," asserts Henry Giroux, "language and memory are disabled as words are emptied of substantive content and the space of shared reality crucial to any democracy is eviscerated.... State-sanctioned attacks on the truth, facts and scientific reason in Trump's America are camouflaged as one would expect when led the by the first reality TV president" (Giroux 2018, "Neoliberal Fascism").

Education, especially at public schools from the elementary to the university level, has seen rising resentments about the "costs" that often have racial and class implications. Stoking those resentments about public education are part of what Jonathan Metzl calls "conservative backlash politics." His analysis of the decimation of Kansas public schools by its Republican governor identifies the class and racial injuries reinforced by a political agenda that mirrors Trump's education secretary, Betsy De Vos.[4] Of course, there is a significant class cultural component to this antagonism to college education and the role, in particular, of elite professionals. While the costs for many working class families for higher education has become prohibitive, the confidence in the value of such education has diminished. As Joan Williams (2017) and Arlie Hochschild (2016) remind us in their examinations of the white working class, the culture wars, fueled by right-wing media and politicians, take aim not at the financial elite but at supposed arrogant professionals who disparage and talk down to white workers.

As the hidden injuries and humiliations built into the class cultural system have taken their toll on significant segments of the white working class, the increase of fear, anger, and resentment, all part of the socio-psychological domain, has opened up the political space for demagogues like Trump. "Primed to fear a long list of despised 'others' by endless exposure to sensational cable television news reports, to social media, and to talk radio, a critical mass of voters in such an anxious age will throw their lot in with demagogic figures who pander to their anxieties" (Abramsky 2017: 15). Such demagogic figures also appeal to those seeking authoritarian leaders, like Trump, who, in the pursuit of a vindictive agenda of targeted "enemies," undermine legal and political norms that provide some semblance of democratic control (Achen and Bartels 2016: 316).

This socio-psychological domain is especially awash with racial resentments that have been nurtured by politicians and pundits since the so-called age of racial backlash under Nixon and revamped in the so-called post-racial age of Obama. Especially during the presidency of Barack Obama, long festering racial resentments gained new immediacy as racist rhetoric targeting the Obamas became the staple of political discourse among the right wing (King and Smith 2011; Sugrue 2010; and Tesler 2016), providing, in the process, a fertile ground for mobilization of those racial resentments by Trump. As argued by Henry Giroux: "In an age of armed ignorance, racism is back both as a spectacle and as a driving force of American politics and has once again come to life as a result of a racist populist discourse that leaves nothing hidden in its blitzkrieg of rhetorical hate, bigotry, and invective" (Giroux 2018: 142–143).

---

4   Metzl 2019: 191–267.

Of course, the long trajectory of racism, nativism, and xenophobia in American politics almost guarantees demagogic appeals, especially during times of economic and social dislocation. Indeed, tracing those persistent currents back into the nineteenth century, as historians like David Roediger, Alexander Saxton, and Ronald Takaki, among others, have done, invariably raises questions about historically-constructed racial identities. While seemingly invisible for much of its history, given its normalized hegemonic rule, white racial identity has become more visible as it has assumed a more "aggrieved" posture. According to Mike King: "Aggrieved whiteness is a white identity politics aimed at maintaining white socio-political hegemony through challenging efforts to combat actual material racial inequality, while supporting heavily racialized investments in policing, prisons, and the military, and positing a narrative of anti-white racial oppression loosely rooted in an assortment of racialized threats" (King 2017).[5]

White identity politics is, thus, a historical and social construct that is oppressive when premised, either consciously or unconsciously, on race-based hierarchies of power mediated, in turn, by class, gender, sexuality, geographic, and national identity privileges. The privileges of white identity politics with its attendant "possessive investment in whiteness" (Lipsitz 2006) are evident throughout American history, albeit often submerged in so-called "race neutral" social programs (Katznelson 2005). On the other hand, as noted by Ruth Frankenberg, "whiteness as a site of privilege is not absolute but rather crosscut by a range of other axes of relative advantage or subordination; these do not erase or render irrelevant race privilege but rather inflect or modify it" (Frankenberg 1993: 76). Unlike the representations of white supremacist hate groups, like the KKK and neo-Nazis, "white identity politics is packaged much more decorously and clearly part of mainstream opinion" (Jardina 2017). On the other hand, while Trump's appeal to white identity politics clearly contained white supremacist tropes, not all of those who voted for Trump did so out of a sharing of that white supremacy.

Certainly, in attempting to account for Trump's electoral appeals to a certain segment of the white working class, one is confronted with a number of contradictions. When one considers the loss of manufacturing jobs, especially in small manufacturing towns of the Rustbelt, it is not surprising that in their desperation, significant numbers of white workers voted for Trump in the 2016

---

5 Aggrieved whiteness, reinforced by gender and class privilege, was on full display during Brett Kavanaugh's alternatively weepy and blustery performance before the Senate Judiciary Committee in response to the allegations of Dr. Christine Blasey Ford concerning her experience of being assaulted by him in high school.

presidential election (Davis 2017; Perusek 2017). From the perspective of one analyst: "A generation of working-class stagnation and political decline (deunionization, deindustrialization, social service cuts, shifting the tax burden of the rich and onto the better paid segments of the working class) has symbiotically coincided with a nativist white politics of cacerality and class hatred for the racialized poor who have been hit the hardest by these political-economic shifts" (King 2017). Furthermore, "disenchanted by ... a political and economic culture of exploitative greed and gridlock," these white working class, Rustbelt voters were responsive to Trump's denunciations of unfair trade deals, like NAFTA and the TPP, and corporate and Washington corruption (Gest 2016: 191). Although racial resentment was a major factor in Trump's electoral victory, for many white workers their "quest for recognition in the context of their downward mobility" was also significant (Lamont et al. 2017).

On the other hand, the vast majority of Trump voters, coming from suburban and rural locations, were either upper middle class, self-employed, or nonunionized white workers. Furthermore, according to the Pew Research Center, Trump's advantage among those whites without a college degree was almost forty percentage points, the largest margin since the 1980 exit polls. While Trump's faux populism resonated with some of these voters, others, having bought into the constant Republican attacks on public sector workers, consisting of large numbers of women and people of color, constituted the white majority of men and women who gave Trump his electoral, but not popular vote, victory. The white majority was aided by a weaponized whiteness that had purged large numbers of African Americans and Latinos through the use of elaborate voting restrictions like repressive voter ID laws and the closing down of polling places. In Wisconsin, alone, a state that Trump won by around 23,000 votes, an estimated 200,000 voters were eliminated from the election rolls. Added to the purges and disenfranchisement of ex-felons of color, fewer blacks and more whites comprised the 2016 electorate (Fraga et al. 2017; Berman 2017).

The white nationalist mythology embedded in Trump's campaign promises, especially under the slogan of "Make America Great Again" (MAGA), may have mobilized whites seeking psychological compensation for the loss of economic and political status at the local, national, and international level. Indeed, as argued in a recent study of Trump voters, "evidence points overwhelmingly to perceived status threat among high-status groups (i.e., whites, Christians, and men) as the key motivation underlying Trump support. White Americans declining dominance in the United States ... and American insecurity about whether the United States is still the dominant global economic superpower combined to prompt a classic defensive reaction among members of dominant groups" (Mutz 2018). The interface of this sense of American insecurity with calls by Trump to "Make America Great Again" appealed to a racialized nostalgia, tinged with restorative fantasies (Hochschild 2016: 49). Yet, when one considers how these appeals to "white nationalism and supremacy" at times redounded to the detriment of some of those white supporters of Trump, especially in the area of health care, one can see how potent and potentially self-destructive such myths are (Metzl 2019: 187–188).

When one considers Trump's perspective on foreign affairs, it is hard not to agree with labor and racial justice activist, Bill Fletcher, that it represents "the politics of racial and imperial revenge" (quoted in Cheung-Miaw and Elbaum 2019). Putting "America First," with resonances from the proto-fascist American movements of the 1930s, nonetheless, coincides with ongoing anxieties about the declining global status of the United States (made worse by Trump's "America First" rhetoric and policies), unending foreign wars with disproportionate losses suffered by the working class, and increasing injection of people of color into mainstream American culture. Thus, "this MAGA tale has the advantage of tactical flexibility in that it can be used to justify retrenchments and withdrawals as well as the massive use of military force, while fostering national/racial chauvinism and hostility towards other countries" (Cheung-Miaw and Elbaum 2019). The xenophobic and racist nationalism articulated by Trump cannot avoid pronouncements and policies that generate arrogance and aggression towards people of color around the world and in the United States. Given the decline of American power, the question remains: "Can the land of liberty and privilege, even amidst its decline, learn to be a land that treats everyone everywhere as equals" (Wallerstein 2003: 215).

Obviously, Trump's "America First" approach runs up against the geopolitical concerns of the bi-partisan foreign policy elite. When Trump goes "off the rails," so to speak, and announces withdrawals from Syria and Afghanistan, Washington and Pentagon hegemonists begin to howl and find ways to impede such precipitous, albeit legitimate, action on Trump's part. Even more cringeworthy from the elites' perspective was Trump's re-tweeting of a right-wing racist trope about white farmers being set upon by blacks in South Africa. Still, the convergence of Trump's agenda with the geopolitical U.S. hegemonists finds common ground in establishing a counterforce in Africa to parry Chinese moves, to isolate China in Asia, and, indeed, to prevent China from emerging as a "global threat" to the United States (Cheung-Miaw and Elbaum 2019). While Trump's provocative moves to foster a coup in Venezuela reflects the coveting of Venezuela's massive oil reserves, the bi-partisan desire to destroy any socialist model in the hemisphere (as compromised as Venezuela is as such a model because of embargoes, sanctions and falling oil prices), and a domestic political agenda with appeals to reactionary Cuban and Venezuelan immigrant constituencies, in particular, in Florida, it also exhibits a strong dose of "white supremacy," especially when those in Venezuela being supported by the U.S. are overwhelmingly white and historically antagonistic to the advances of poorer and darker Venezuelans (Palast 2019).

On the other hand, Trump's refusal to see the crisis in Central America as one linked to prior U.S. policies allows him to utilize racist and xenophobic tropes in his dismissal of any asylum claims from Central Americans fleeing violence in their countries. One can see how Trump's constant references to "building a wall" could resonate with these anxious and resentful white voters, tapping into historical and contemporary expressions of white supremacist xenophobia (Coaston 2018). Embedded in the reference to the wall is a white supremacist appeal to stopping so-called illegal immigration, especially of Latinos attempting to escape from dire economic circumstances, often created by global capitalism and U.S. trade policies, and/or massive violence in their native lands. The sense of "aggrieved whiteness" that informs many whites who mistakenly believe that jobs are being stolen away by Latino immigrants does feed the demands for border "security." In addition, Trump's Islamophobia, shared by many in the right-wing Republican base, has been particularly evident in all of the attempted bans on refugees coming from predominantly Islamic countries.

It is not surprising, therefore, that among the first executive orders promulgated by Trump was entitled "Executive Order Protecting the Nation from Foreign Terrorist Entry into the United States." The effort to tie refugees to terrorism has continued throughout the Trump presidency even in the face of the facts concerning those seeking refuge in the U.S. "Over more than four decades, not a single American has been killed on U.S. soil by someone who entered the country as a refugee" (Isaacs 2019). Employing such racist ideology against refugees has fueled Trump's deliberate and radical reduction of admission of refugees, resulting in 22,491 refugees admitted in 2018, a number even lower than the first few years after 9/11 (Isaacs 2019).

Throughout his first year in office, Trump has used the aptly named "bully pulpit," greatly expanded through the deployment of Twitter, to mobilize racial and class resentments of his shrinking base. In particular, Trump's public denunciations of protesting NFL players, led by ex-Forty-Niner's quarterback, Colin Kaepernick, target a league of well-paid mostly African-American players (estimated to be at seventy percent). Trump rarely misses an opportunity to launch either racially-coded or explicit racial verbal assaults on people of color, whether those in the Black Lives Matter movement or dark-skinned immigrants, in the case of the latter, in particular, forwarding outrageous white supremacist conspiracy theories. One of the more recent egregious racist remarks in his meeting with members of Congress was Trump's reference to Haiti and certain African countries as "shitholes" (Jean-Pierre 2018).

Trump also has relied on anti-Native racism through his constant tweeting put-downs of Senator Elizabeth Warren as "Pocahontas" or in his patronizing and racist asides during a presidential session with Navajo code talkers. Beyond his tweets and disrespectful comments are the practices of the Trump organization and policies of the Trump presidency. In the attempt to block the expansion of American Indian casinos in New York, Trump's casino company underwrote ads that portrayed American Indians as vicious law-breakers even as the Trump organization was violating campaign finance laws. Once installed as U.S. President Trump turned the Department of Indian Affairs into an operation for resource extraction, denying in the process "Native self-determination and sovereignty" (Four Arrows 2019).

When one considers the composition of Trump's Cabinet, consisting of billionaires, militarists, and know-nothings, there is little that separates Trump's politics and policies from the dominant tendencies in the Republican Party. Indeed, as pointed out by Naomi Klein, the Cabinet and Trumpism as a "political and economic project" is representative of deeply rooted Republican positions: "the deconstruction of the regulatory state; a full-bore attack on the welfare state and social services (rationalized in part through bellicose fear mongering and attacks on women for exercising their rights); the unleashing of domestic fossil fuel frenzy (which requires the sweeping aside of climate science and the gagging of large parts of the governmental bureaucracy); and a civilizational war against immigrants and 'radical Islamic terrorism' (with expanding domestic and foreign theaters)" (Klein 2017: 5–6). The convergence of Trumpism and the reactionary Republican agenda, thus, promulgated policies and legislation that further inscribed white identity politics into the oligarchic national regime.[6]

On the other hand, the instability of this white nationalist and reactionary Republican agenda had difficulty maintaining itself, as evidenced by the so-called "Blue Wave" in the Congressional elections of 2018. Both in the short term and long term, as argued by Mike Davis: "Trumpism, whatever its temporary successes cannot unify millennials economic distress with that of older white workers because it counterposes geriatric white privilege as the touchstone of all its policies ... The real opportunity for transformational political change belongs to the Sanderistas but only to the extent that they remain rebels against the neoliberal Democratic establishment and support the resistance in the

---

6 According to Singh, the Republican agenda of this "racially homogeneous far-Right political party" that predated Trump consists of "social conservatism, a near fanatical commitment to upward wealth distribution, climate change denial, the rejection of socially useful public spending, hostility to taxation in support of transfer payments to the poorer and most vulnerable, racially coded appeals to law and order, and anti-immigrant animus" (2017: 153–154).

streets" (Davis 2017). The resistance in the streets has been impressive from Trump's opening day in office when millions around the country, led by a revitalized women's movement, marched in massive numbers in Washington, DC, and cities around the country. Following these demonstrations, many then poured into airports protesting Trump's travel bans and onto the frozen fields around Standing Rock.[7] Emerging from all of these mobilizations were the outlines of multi-racial alliances, building on other movements like BlackLivesMatter, that have challenged Trump, if not yet Trumpism.

Nonetheless, there remains the problem of white identity politics, in either its explicit or implicit form. Whatever becomes of President Trump as a consequence of crimes uncovered by various investigative bodies, the fact remains that he, and, more precisely, Trumpism have conjured up some of the worst representations of white supremacy and white nationalism. It seems that the genie of white identity politics has been let out of the bottle of white supremacy even though the bottle may seem outdated and near empty. Nonetheless, as noted by Joel Olson, "Today there is still the white problem – its expectations, its power, its solidarity, its imagination. Even after the civil rights movement, whiteness stands at the path to a more democratic society like a troll at the bridge. The political task ... is to chase the troll away, not to ignore or invite it to the multicultural table" (Olsen 2004: 37). Unless or until white identity politics is confronted head-on, little can be expected from a resistance that shies away from the troll at the bridge and the lingering terrors of Trumpism.

Beyond confronting and overcoming white identity politics and those terrors, there is a broader agenda of which Cornel West reminds us: "Race matters in the 21st century are part of a moral and spiritual war over resources, power, souls, and sensibilities. There can be no analysis of race matters without earth matters, class matters, gender matters and sexuality matters and, especially, empire matters. We must have solidarity on all these fronts. As we fight back, we remember the great visionary and exemplary figures and movements of the past. These precious memories focus our attention on things that really matter – not spectacle, image, money, and status but integrity, honesty, dignity, and generosity" (West 2018). While the terrors of Trumpism may fade, there is still much work to be done to enable and enact a transformative agenda that not only addresses the residual impact of white identity politics but also the constellation of political challenges, as noted by Cornel West, that impedes the achievement of justice and dignity for all.

---

7 Noting the extreme repression meted out by state authorities against Standing Rock demonstrators, Indian activist and scholar, Nick Estes contends, "what happened at Standing Rock was the most recent iteration of an Indian war that never ends" (Estes 2019: 10).

PART 2

Dilemmas in the Deconstructions of White Identity Politics

∴

CHAPTER 4

Unveiling Whiteness: White Student Activists in the Civil Rights Movement

When four black students from North Carolina Agricultural and Technical College sat down at a "whites-only" lunch counter in Greensboro, North Carolina on February 1, 1960, they precipitated more than a momentary challenge to the segregated facilities at this particular Woolworth store. Although this was not the first civil rights protest led by students, the Greensboro sit-in galvanized the imagination of black and white students throughout the country. Cleveland Sellers, then a sixteen-year-old African-American student in Denmark, South Carolina, later wrote that the Greensboro sit-in "hit me like a shot of adrenalin" (Sellars 1973: 18). That shot resonated throughout the South where thousands of mostly black students initiated what one study of the civil rights movement called a "decade of disruption" (Morris 1984: 195–228).

In the furious few months that followed the 1960 Greensboro sit-in, black students in the South, particularly at movement centers such as Nashville, Atlanta, and Washington, DC, and white students on northern campuses from Boston to Berkeley became the shock troops of the civil rights movement. In the process they formed critical student-based national organizations beginning with the founding of the Student Non-Violent Coordinating Committee (SNCC) in April of 1960 and offshoots such as the Northern Student Movement (1961) and Friends of SNCC (1962) (Carson 1982; Hogan 2007; Stoper 1989; Zinn 1964). The civil rights protests and networks informed the early activities of Students for a Democratic Society (SDS), founded in 1960 (Gitlin 1989; Miller 1994; Polletta 2002; Sale 1974), and the Southern Student Organizing Committee (SSOC), founded in 1964 (Michel 2004). By contesting segregation at the local, state, and federal level, student activists underscored their commitment to the expressions of moral politics and participatory democracy that helped to define the protests of the 1960s (Farber 1994; Farrell 1997; Morgan 1991).

However, beyond those expressions of moral politics and participatory democracy, white students who involved themselves in the black freedom struggle had to contend with the contradictions of their own white privileges, especially, although not exclusively, in the South where white students were targeted as "nigger lovers" and race traitors. Indeed, confronting segregation and racial oppression led many white student civil rights activists to begin to question the very meaning of "whiteness" for them and the society as a whole. By identifying that whiteness as a social construct that perpetuated "race privilege," the very "naming" or unveiling of whiteness created the space to challenge the often "unnamed" role of racial dominance (Frankenberg 1993: 6).

As an undergraduate student at the University of Pittsburgh from 1963–1967, I became involved with the Friends of SNCC and SDS on campus. However, instead of "going South," my civil rights activism, at first very episodic and driven by events in the South, was an introduction into contesting the persistence of racial oppression on the national level and in a northern city. As Wesley Hogan has asserted in her study of SNCC, "In peculiar ways, this northern front of the civil rights movement would also challenge the national culture of white supremacy. Though many northern whites were committed to racial equality, they had almost no experience with making it happen. The racial divide was in everyone, they would discover" (Hogan 2007: 96). That discovery of the internal racial divide was a slow and difficult process during the years of my civil rights activism. In many respects, my understanding of that period would require a psychological and historical distance achieved through a much later connection to studying the civil rights movement from a scholarly (albeit still activist) perspective.

What I propose to undertake in this chapter is a bifurcation of an autobiographical overview of my activism measured against the rendering of the historical context and developments influencing mostly northern white student activism in the civil rights movement from 1963–1967. To some extent reflecting on what I lived through in my own personal world, as compared to the impersonal and global forces at work during this period, should provide some insight into not only how the "personal is political" but also how the racial divide was constructed and deconstructed internally and externally for those white students who went South and those who, as I did, stayed in the North. In order to facilitate that interrogation of that racial divide, I want to apply the well-known metaphor of the "veil" deployed by W.E.B. DuBois throughout his classic, *The Souls of Black Folk* (DuBois 1961: 16–17 and *passim*). While for DuBois, the veil was intimately connected with the double-consciousness imposed on African Americans wrestling with their African and American heritage, I want to shift the racial lens from blackness to whiteness and explore the double consciousness on the personal and political planes.

Whiteness has a structural location of privilege or advantage in a social order based on racial hierarchy and oppression. It also inhabits a subjectivity that is generally taken for granted under normal circumstances but becomes problematic and open to challenge under crises situations, such as those in the 1960s. In turn, these privileges and subjectivities are mediated further by class, gender, sexuality, and place (Bush 2004; Feagin 2009; Frankenberg 1993; Hartigan 1999; Lipsitz 1998; Martinot 2010; Roediger 1994). Of course, the utility of employing whiteness as a descriptive and analytical trope occupies a contested interpretive terrain (ILWCH Forum 2001). As Howard Winant points out, "Our new found attention to whiteness must be understood as a product of both the accomplishments and the containment of the postwar movements of racially defined minorities, especially the black movement. It should be seen, too, in light of the partial, contradictory, and inadequate racial reform policies enacted during the 1960s" (Winant 2001: 97). As a movement that destabilized racial categories and acted as a catalyst to the unveiling of whiteness, the civil rights movement of the 1960s also raised the question of how citizenship, or American national identity, was racially constituted (Glenn 2002; Olson 2004).

Certainly, the post-World War II period provided the historical background that heightened the contradictions between racialized citizenship and an inclusive democracy. With the defeat of fascism questions about racial oppression in the United States and throughout the third world were highlighted, especially through anti-colonial struggles among people of color. Moreover, the contradictions of the Cold War raised on-going concerns about the legitimacy of U.S. claims as the leading defender of democracy. As Mary Dudziak reminds us in her study of the intersection of the Cold War and civil rights, that intersection "is in part the story of a struggle over the narrative of race and democracy" (Dudziak 2000: 250). Finally, the narrative of race and democracy was made even more insistent in the South as it was incorporated into the national economy and life of the United States, giving rise to a self-conscious black freedom movement.

While the civil rights phase of this black freedom movement offered opportunities for white students to aid in the defeat of racial segregation, those same students operated against an historical backdrop of privileged citizenship (Thompson 2001: 41–111). The New Deal and post-World War II legislation promoted a form of white affirmative action (Katznelson 2005) that has been labeled "the possessive investment in whiteness" (Lipsitz 1998). In attempting to dispossess that possessive investment in whiteness, white students joined the black freedom struggle often cognizant of some of the ways in which their privileges were impediments to becoming active citizens in an authentic democracy. In late 1963 Ralph Allen, a white student imprisoned in Americus, Georgia as a consequence of his work with SNCC, responded to a letter from a local young black student inquiring about why he would leave his safe white haven (which the student called "heaven") to join the civil rights movement. Allen's response acknowledged his own subjective journey from "the conceited, loud self-centered All-American free white and twenty-one college boy." However, he notes that "something happened to make me human, something I don't yet understand" (quoted in Zinn 2002: 184).

Reflecting later on these white students who became "human" though their commitment to civil rights and racial justice, Mark Warren argues that these activists may "start off being against racism out of a moral impulse, (but) that they end up being for racial justice in pursuit of a moral and political vision. They come to understand white people's interest in racial justice as a central part of achieving a better society for all" (Warren 2010: 21). Striving for such a just society provided white student activists with a movement environment that "filled a missing link between feelings of alienation and historical opportunity – a link that was not only practically effective but morally compelling" (Flacks 1988: 135).

Part of the moral compulsion for white student involvement in civil rights was that sense of alienation and guilt rooted in the privileges of middle class suburban life, a life fostered by white affirmative action programs such as the FHA and GI Bill. In Alice Walker's novel, *Meridian,* about black and white students in the civil rights movement, one of the main characters, Lynne Rabinowitz, is a northern white suburban-raised student. Lynne insists that she was "saved" by the civil rights movement from being "as dumb as my mother was. Even if I practiced not knowing what the world is like, even if I lived in Scarsdale or some other weird place, and never had to eat welfare food in my life, I'd still know. By nature I'm not cut out to be a member of the oppressors. I don't like them; they make me feel guilty all the time" (Walker 1976: 181). Commenting on the non-fictional Jewish women who went "South" to participate in the black freedom struggle, Debra Schultz asserts: "Going South gave northern Jewish women an opportunity to create existential meaning in their lives through moral action" (Schultz 2001: 24).

Moral action was, indeed, a compelling factor for those Southern white students attracted to the civil rights movement and especially SNCC. In fact, the first white student volunteers with SNCC were almost overwhelmingly from Christian social gospel networks. A number of SNCC student activists from the South, including Sam Shirah, Bob Zellner, Mary King, and Jane Stembridge, had fathers who were either Methodist or Baptist ministers. In commenting on the social gospel preached by her Methodist Minister father, Mary King wrote: "The gospel was to him the radically transforming news that each individual is precious in God's sight, and therefore personal salvation was all but meaningless to my father if it was devoid of concern for fundamental justice for others" (King 1987: 54).

Making that message for social justice integral to their civil rights activism, white Southerners often confronted racist barriers even as they committed themselves to anti-racist activism. One study of anti-racist white Southern activists in the civil rights movement suggests that they had to "redefine their identity as white Southerners without white supremacy" (Chappell 1994: xxii). Such a redefinition or deconstruction of whiteness and white supremacy often led to confrontations with the white power structure and racist authorities. When Bob Zellner attempted to act on his religious beliefs related to racial justice by joining with black students from Alabama State to worship together at black churches in Montgomery, Alabama, he and the other four white students from his college, the all-white Methodist school, Huntingdon College, were asked to withdraw from their college (Zellner 2008: 48–72).

Other white Southern students, especially women, became involved with SNCC out of their pre-existing reformist Christian networks (Curry et al. 2000). Constance Curry, reared in vacation Bible schools and church camps, parlayed her role as the Southern Human Relations Project Director for the National Student Association in 1960 into becoming an early advisor to SNCC. Jane Stembridge, "full of Christian existentialism," became SNCC's first office secretary. Sue Thrasher and Joan Browning were in Nashville in 1961, becoming part of James Lawson's workshops while transitioning into SNCC activism. In Austin, Texas, Dorothy Dawson Burlage and Sandra "Casey" Cason brought their anti-racist activism as members of interracial religious organizations, such as the YWCA and Christian Faith and Life Community, into early efforts with SNCC (Rossinow 1998).

On the other hand, like the fictional Lynne Rabinowitz, other northern white middle class women were attracted to SNCC's work in the South, bringing with them their pre-existing connections to either left or pacifist networks. One northern female student coming from a secular Jewish and left background who headed south was Dorothy Miller. After graduating from Queens College she secured a job in June of 1961 with the Southern Regional Council in Atlanta and then moved over to SNCC to aid the Atlanta black student leader and *Student Voice* editor, Julian Bond. For Miller, who, during this time, would marry southern white student activist, Bob Zellner, the experiences in the South and in SNCC were her "first exposure to Black culture and ... to ministers and religious people" (quoted in Schultz 2001: 6). Another northern student, Penny Patch, went to southwest Georgia in 1962 from her freshman year at Swarthmore, becoming in the process the first white woman to participate in a SNCC project in the Deep South. Patch's commitment to helping blacks overcome the devastating restrictions of racial oppression was, nonetheless, complicated by her naive approach to the explosive dynamics of a white woman working alongside black men (Curry et al. 2000: 133–170; Olson 2001: 242). On the other hand, both female and male white students brought a range of cultural assumptions and political orientations that were challenged by the racial conditions they encountered in the South.

Certainly, feelings of alienation, guilt, and the desire to create existential meaning through moral action were critical motivations in my turn towards civil rights and initial confrontation with the veil of whiteness. As a Jew growing up in suburban Pittsburgh, I was only barely aware of the invisible privileges that surrounded me. However, my Jewish identity definitely made me feel marginal to the dominant WASP community in which I lived. Moreover, I had a vague sense of connection to marginalized others, especially African Americans, primarily as a consequence of black music and my identification with the sensuality of that music. Listening to the only black station in the Pittsburgh area, WAMO, I thrilled to songs like "Work with Me, Annie" by Hank Ballard and the Midnighters (which was later given a more tepid and less sexual white cover in "Dance with Me, Henry" by Georgia Gibbs). Thus, the lure of black popular culture began to penetrate, to some extent, the veil of whiteness. As one interpreter of white middle class youth during this period contends: "Black culture, through music, was the dialectical accompaniment, the alter ego, to white middle-class teenage life. Like the early civil rights movement that penetrated the consciousness of white America with dramas, rock and roll was a racial subtext in postwar America" (Breines 1992: 152).[1]

On a related level, as provocatively presented in the following passage from Eldridge Cleaver's *Soul on Ice,* young whites were re-discovering the pleasures of the body even as they began to challenge the body politic. "The white youth of today have begun to react to the fact that the 'American Way of Life' is a fossil of history.... They couldn't care less about the old stiffassed honkies who don't like their new dances: Frug, Monkey, Jerk, Swim, Watusi. All they know is that it feels good to swing to way-out body-rhythms instead of dragassing across the dance floor like zombies to the dead beat of mind-smothered Mickey Mouse music" (Cleaver 1968: 81). Freeing my body from strictures of cold war and conformist culture led to the embrace of black popular culture even as Mickey Mouse still pervaded the educational and semiotic environment I inhabited.

There were, however, challenges to this veil of whiteness that emerged with the merger of the media and civil rights activism that marked the period from 1955–1965. James Baldwin's insight about white children growing up "with a grasp of reality so feeble that they can very accurately be described as deluded

---

[1] For other studies of the influence of black popular culture on the emergent youth culture, see Graebner 1990; Lipsitz 1990; Ward 1998.

about themselves and the world they live in" (Baldwin 1998: 431) certainly applied to the sheltered and shuttered life I lived and education I received. My earliest recognition of the odious and oppressive role of racism in American life came in December 1955. No, it was not in response to the arrest of Rose Parks for refusing to give up her seat on a bus in Montgomery, Alabama and the subsequent mobilization and bus boycott by the black community of that city. Unaware of those developments, I was, instead, attuned to the controversy surrounding the efforts by Southerners, from the governor of Georgia to the residents of New Orleans, to exclude the University of Pittsburgh's black fullback and linebacker, Bobby Grier, from playing in the Sugar Bowl game against Georgia Tech. Growing up in western Pennsylvania where football was integral to masculine rites-of-passage, I was outraged that racial discrimination could bar a talented athlete from performing on the gridiron. I was also a naïve ten-year-old, living in a predominantly white suburb of Pittsburgh and sheltered in so many ways within a racial order that provided certain advantages to whites while denying them to blacks.

It took a little while and the exposure to events in the South during the early 1960s to awaken fully my awareness about the appalling conditions under which African Americans had to operate. Especially the dramatic events in Birmingham during the spring of 1963, my graduating year from high school, drew my attention once more to the injustices of racial discrimination. When I was offered a track scholarship to Duke University, I asked the recruiter whether any blacks attended Duke. Not wanting to be part of such a whites-only college environment, I, instead, gladly accepted an athletic scholarship to the University of Pittsburgh. It was at Pitt that I gained a solid understanding of the historical roots and contemporary offshoots of racism while also becoming a civil rights activist.

My commitment to civil rights was also reinforced by the images being broadcast on television during the early 1960s as news programs began to feature stories from the civil rights struggle in the South. As noted by Sasha Torres, "race and racial conflict fed the new medium's enormous appetite for visual spectacle; …the mere fact of television's coverage served paradoxically to render racism visible in new ways, and to new audiences" (Torres 2003: 17). Watching those spectacles of confrontation between civil rights demonstrators and their vicious white tormentors, I began to formulate an "othering" of whiteness that separated me from those white Southerners resisting racial equality. Once the hoses and dogs were brought out against children in Birmingham in 1963 (Branch 1989: 756–781; McWhorter 2001: 370–374), I felt compelled to seek out ways to join the civil rights movement.

Starting college in the fall of 1963, I was immediately confronted by the rush of events from the bombing of the Birmingham Church with the resultant death of four little girls and the assassination of President Kennedy in Dallas in November. My angry reaction to the bombing and its tragic consequences was reinforced when my introductory psychology professor cancelled class because he was too upset about what had happened to conduct class. Immediately following the Kennedy assassination, the whole campus shut down. But my initial reaction was reflective of my strong sense that it was the South that was the site of racial and mindless violence. Nonetheless, I was still too bound up in my own world of sports and study in my freshman year to commit either to going South or throwing myself into political organizations dealing with civil rights.

On the other hand, the lure of the South for northern white student activists was a reflection of the increasing tempo of civil rights demonstrations in 1963, especially the Birmingham, Alabama and Cambridge, Maryland spring offensives, the latter featuring the leadership of a dynamic women, Gloria Richardson, with support from black students from surrounding Maryland college campuses and white students from the small liberal arts colleges in eastern Pennsylvania (Harley 2001: 174–196; Levy 2003), and the August March on Washington (Branch 1989: 846–887). Beyond the attendant assistance, from fundraising to clothes drives, student activists also sought to engage their desire for authentic social change. "We went South," according to one white student activist, "because we could see no way of making our own lives meaningful by working for change in our white world" (quoted in Fager 1967: 95). John Perdew, a middle class white student from Harvard, traveled to Georgia in 1963 with "only an abstract, intellectual concept of race relations" (quoted in Carson 1982: 72–73). After getting arrested in a civil rights march, going to jail, and getting arrested again after demonstrating upon his release, Perdew began to get some sense of the racial injustice encountered on a daily basis by southern blacks. As one study of northern middle class students suggests, "exposure to the southern judiciary and personal suffering stemming from the limitations of federal as opposed to state power ... served to teach lifelong lessons to those young people in American democratic reality" (Louis 1970: 110).

Another American democratic reality, Jim Crow political disfranchisement, drew northern white student activists to volunteer for civil rights campaigns in the South. One of those campaigns was the brainchild of Allard Lowenstein, a former president of the National Student Association and Cold War liberal, who became immersed in civil rights issues after the murder of Medgar Evers in June 1963. As a dean of student affairs at Stanford in 1962 and with contacts at Yale, Lowenstein convinced Bob Moses to sponsor a "Freedom Vote," a mock election intended to empower Mississippi blacks. With the aid of some sixty to one hundred white students from Stanford and Yale in the fall of 1963, black voters turned out by the tens of thousands in the face of constant harassment and violence (Branch 1999: 118–123 and 156–159; Dittmer 1994: 200–210; Foreman 1985: 354–358; King 1987: 229–231 and 239–241). While some of those white student volunteers suffered similar harassment and violence, others brought with them a kind of northern white paternalism that was to mark some of the early intervention of privileged whites with southern African Americans. One such egregious example of that paternalist privilege was evident in a Yale student's recruiting pitch: "Any white Northerner who's had the good fortune to achieve even an average education in the North is going to be, just by virtue of this fact, so much more talented than the Negro leadership in the movement is the South, that in one day, he can make a significant contribution" (quoted in Branch 1999: 156). Such attitudes raised doubts in the minds of many of the black student activists in SNCC concerning recruiting northern white volunteers for projects in the southern African-American communities.

Nonetheless, as a consequence of the lack of federal response to all of the violence and repression heaped upon those working for change in Mississippi, SNCC reluctantly agreed to bring hundreds of white students to Mississippi in the summer of 1964. This would become known as Freedom Summer. Much has been written about Freedom Summer of 1964 (Belfrage 1990; Holt 1965; McAdam 1988; Watson 2010). It was a probably both the high and low point of white student involvement with the civil rights movement in the South (although the following summer of 1965 would see another effort). At the end of 1964 Freedom Summer there were one thousand arrests, scores of bombings, beatings, and shooting incidents and the murder of six civil rights activists, the most dramatic being the killings of Michael Schwerner, a CORE organizer from New York, Andrew Goodman, a Freedom Summer student volunteer from Queens College, and James Chaney, a local black Mississippi youth who was working with Mickey Schwerner (Cagin and Dray 1988). While not diminishing the incredible drama of that summer, the Freedom Summers of 1964 and 1965 will be briefly reviewed for their impact on mobilizing northern white students to aid the civil rights agenda throughout the nation and on the increasing radicalization of those student activists in ways that challenged and confounded the privileges of whiteness (Rothschild 1982).

In order to recruit students for the 1964 Freedom Summer, SNCC relied on two mechanisms: (1) speaking engagements for SNCC leaders, such as Bob Moses, on college campuses; and (2) the expansion of activities of Friends of SNCC chapters. At an appearance on the Stanford campus in April of 1964, Moses addressed a rapt audience of some 400 students. Calling the "civil rights question ... the spearhead" for the examination of all the nation's ills, Moses engaged the potential recruits about the existential dilemmas they would face if they joined Freedom Summer. He continued this philosophical bent at a later training session in Oxford, Ohio for those students who had volunteered for Freedom Summer. "Don't come to Mississippi this summer to save the Mississippi Negro. Only come if you understand, really understand, that his freedom and yours are one" (quoted in Burner 1994: 155).

Earlier campus appearances by other SNCC leaders had nurtured the ground for an expansion of Friends of SNCC chapters from a handful in 1962 to over fifty in 1964. On the Madison campus of the University of Wisconsin, a campus visit by Diane Nash in the aftermath of the Freedom Rides and the involvement of other SNCC activists, such as Theresa Del Pozzo (Curry et al. 2000: 184–188) and Dion Diamond, established and expanded the functions of the Madison Friends of SNCC. Beyond the obvious fundraising and support efforts, the Madison group became a conduit for direct funding for projects in Mississippi during and after Freedom Summer. Those Madison students, such as Stuart Ewen, who went to Mississippi during the summer of 1964 came back later to campus as transformed activists. Ewen later recalled that the experience was "a political education that changed who I was ... I returned to Madison in the spring of 1965 as someone for whom politics and action had become central" (Ewen 1990: 180).

Part of that "political education" was, as mentioned earlier, the interaction with the repressive environment in the South through imprisonment, beatings, and harassment. One Harvard student found himself languishing in the Panola County Jail in Mississippi for more than the usual day sentence, "furious" at his irregular arrest. Nonetheless, he realized his predicament was an initiation into the oppressive world of Mississippi justice. In a letter to his family he opined that "abstract support for 'Civil Rights' – the newspapers and other outsiders call it Civil Rights and we call it Freedom – isn't worth much to people who are catching hell. You've got to catch some of the hell yourself" (quoted in Sutherland 1965: 133–136). Yet, in catching hell, some of those white students expressed the outrage and incredulity embodied in their privileged whiteness. One such white volunteer lamented that after being assaulted, his assailant was free to walk the streets, albeit after paying a surprising $25 fine. His final angry comment was: "I have no local protection. I have no Federal protection" (quoted in Sutherland 1965: 146). The kind of "righteous anger" reflected the moral outrage of white northern civil rights activists caught up in Southern justice (sic) that violated the "values of justice and equality with which these (students) have been brought up and in which they deeply believe" (Warren 2010: 27). Even when federal authorities from the F.B.I. or Department of Justice appeared, they often acted like antagonists rather than allies towards those who were challenging segregationist practices in the South. Such behavior from the federal government led to feelings of betrayal, especially among the white volunteers "whose political socialization had been fairly conventional. The government they had been led to believe to be powerful and essentially just was proving itself to be cowardly and amoral in its dealings with segregationists" (McAdam 1988: 130).

On the other hand, many of the white student volunteers who went South, despite their good intentions, brought with them attitudes and behaviors that created their own contradictions, especially with the black staff members of SNCC. A SNCC memo, under the heading of "Some Aspects of Black-White Problems as Seen by Field Staff," addressed some of these contradictions by observing that "missionary attitudes are really resented." The paper further argued "white people do come down without grappling with their own feelings about Negroes" (in Belfrage Papers). Commenting on this problem, another project report acknowledged "too many people are naive. I have met kids here who have hardly spoken to a Negro in the north and have no experience in civil rights work" (Cunnigham in Ewen Papers). Another particularly evident contradiction of privilege among the white student volunteers was the fact that they could return to rather comfortable environments if the going got tough. One white female student volunteer recognized that privilege: "As a white northerner I can get involved whenever I feel like it and run home whenever I get bored or frustrated or scared. I hate the attitude and position of Northern whites and despise myself when I think that way" (quoted in Sutherland 1965: 193).

Nevertheless, white northern students, especially because of their privileges, were the overwhelming recruitment pool for participating in Freedom Summer. While state universities, such as Wisconsin, Michigan, and UC Berkeley, provided a significant pool of student volunteers, Ivy League schools were even more prominently represented. Although colleges, such as Harvard and Yale, had been actively connected to the civil rights movement prior to the summer of 1964, there were even more concerted efforts to attract students from these schools for the various projects in Mississippi. One Yale applicant, for example, active with a Northern Student Movement tutorial program in New Haven, hoped to continue working with young black students in Mississippi not only for the impact it might have on the lives of those black youth, but also for the personal transformation offered by his own involvement (McAdam 1988: 42 and 47). According to James Forman, SNCC Executive Director, "we made a conscious attempt ... to recruit from some of the Ivy League schools ... you know, a lot of us knew ... what we were up against. So, that we were, in fact, trying to consciously recruit a counter power-elite" (quoted in McAdam 1988: 40).[2]

Forman, Moses, and other SNCC leaders knew that the media would follow the high-profile white students to the South, casting a national spotlight on Mississippi in a way that would further arouse the nation to support the civil rights agenda. Beyond the media glare, however, northern student supporters would become the shock troops pushing that agenda and keeping pressure on federal officials during the summer. When Schwerner, Goodman, and Chaney disappeared on June 21, 1964, Friends of SNCC chapters mobilized. In New York City hundreds of students participated in a picket line at the federal building in Manhattan. Friends of SNCC set up another picket line at the federal building in Boston. Even smaller towns where there were college campus supporters of SNCC, such as Urbana and Carbondale, Illinois, had demonstrations and vigils, even though the only federal facility for conducting the vigil in Carbondale was a post office (King 1987: 394 and 388).

Beyond the efforts to keep the focus on the dramatic events in Mississippi during the summer of 1964, there were more quiet transformations going on in the lives of Freedom Summer volunteers that would have profound consequences for student activism and the deconstruction of whiteness. One of those volunteers whose experience transformed him from a participant in the civil rights movement to a seminal student leader was Mario Savio (Cohen 2009). Savio had transferred from Queens College to Berkeley in the fall of 1963 and started interacting with Friends of SNCC and CORE activists. Joining a major demonstration by campus activists against discriminatory hiring practices by the Sheraton Palace hotel in San Francisco, he was one of the many arrested. He heard about Freedom Summer during his time in jail and decided to volunteer in order to be on the frontlines of the struggle against segregation and racial oppression.

When Savio returned to the Berkeley campus in the fall of 1964, he became the new president of the local Friends of SNCC chapter. As such, he, along with other civil rights campus activists, received notification from the university that they could no longer set up recruiting tables for literature distribution on university property. For Savio, with his strong Catholic background and moral commitment to civil rights, to accept the university's restrictions was to betray all of those endangered black Mississippians struggling for racial justice and freedom. Joining with civil rights veterans on campus and student organizations

---

2 One of the Freedom Summer recruits, Paul Cowan, later recalled "the Summer Project was as much an effort to work free from our own pasts as to help black people build a better future for themselves." See Cowan 1970: 37.

appalled by the curtailment of their free speech, Savio became the impassioned spokesperson for what would become a critical moment of student activism, the Berkeley Free Speech Movement (FSM) (Cohen and Zelnik 2002; Rosenfield 2012: 153–288). Without recounting all of the details of the FSM conflict, it is apparent that "for most of the leaders of the Berkeley revolt, the movement was seen as an extension of the civil rights struggle and the Summer Project in particular. The tactical, ideological, and personal imprint of Freedom Summer was everywhere evident in the events at Berkeley" (quoted in McAdam 1988: 162).

While the impact of Freedom Summer on white student activists and northern college campuses was instrumental in enlarging that activism in so many ways, SNCC suffered some fallout from the influx of northern white secular students and their unconscious undermining of developing indigenous black leadership. A few of the white Southerners in SNCC, nonetheless, understood the need to challenge the anti-black racism in the white community even before Freedom Summer began to raise concerns about in which communities white civil rights activists should work. Sam Shirah, a Southern white SNCC activist commented in early 1964: "Two years ago the frontier for the white student who wanted to be part of current history was to get on a Negro picket line against a segregated restaurant. That's still needed and all of us will be doing that, too. But the frontier today is elsewhere. It is for the white student to go into the white community and organize" (Michel 2004: 20). While SNCC provided a few organizing opportunities during Freedom Summer to work in Southern white communities, those organizing efforts weren't very successful.

Nonetheless, SNCC activists, both black and white, committed themselves to the establishment of the Mississippi Freedom Democratic Party (MFDP) as a political vehicle to challenge the racist and exclusionary politics of the regular Democratic Party. As an organizational vehicle for empowering marginalized blacks, the MFDP, according to one SNCC fieldworker, "was the best means of physically organizing the Negroes of Mississippi, of finding indigenous leadership, and building a political structure" (quoted in Belfrage 1990: 85). When the liberal establishment was marshaled to defeat the demands of the MFDP at the Atlantic City Democratic Convention in August 1964, Moses quipped: "The liberals getting upset at us was inevitable. We are raising fundamental questions about how the poor sharecropper can achieve the Good Life, questions that liberalism is incapable of answering" (quoted in Dittmer 1994: 318). In addition, there were questions about white supremacy that liberalism, for all its putative support for civil rights, could not forthrightly address and remedy.

In raising these fundamental questions, SNCC also found itself in an organizational and ideological crisis in 1964 that lasted into 1965 (Polletta 2002: 88–119). Certainly, as one historian has noted: "The pivotal events of August

1964 not only transformed the national context for the civil rights movement but also reshaped SNCC's political perspective, strategic approach, and evolving identity" (Ransby 2003: 331). SNCC's efforts to reshape its outlook and structure in the fall of 1964 reflected not only a break with liberalism, but a turn away from civil rights to black power. Sociologist Belinda Robnett contends that such a transition was a function of relational identity transformation within the organization brought on by a changing external political context (Robnett 2002: 266–285), a political context also influenced by the escalating Vietnam War in the aftermath of the Gulf of Tonkin war resolution. A white Freedom Summer volunteer who would go on to become an organizer for SDS underscored the impact of August 1964 on student activists: "For many of us the Gulf of Tonkin incident and the refusal to seat the MFDP were watershed events that convinced us that neither the Democratic Party nor liberals could be counted on for meaningful social change" (Pardun 2001: 70).

The dramatic events of 1964 reinforced my commitment to working with the civil rights movement and my own growing estrangement from liberalism. However, it was partly the attitude about being a privileged white northerner that prevented me from going South as well as my sense of finding a way to manifest my dedication to civil rights in the Pittsburgh area that moved me to get involved first with a chapter of Friends of SNCC at the University of Pittsburgh and then to work with whites and blacks together in the Hill District of Pittsburgh, the nearby ghetto to the university, in 1965–1967. As Friends of SNCC we mobilized in the aftermath of the events in Selma, Alabama in March of 1965 where on March 7th state police had brutally attacked a peaceful march, injuring scores and killing a young black man, Jimmy Lee Jackson. In response, demonstrations occurred on many northern campuses, including the University of Pittsburgh. In turn, two white supporters who traveled to Alabama for the follow-up protests, Boston minister, James Reeb and Detroit volunteer, Viola Liuzzo, were murdered (Branch 2006: 80–82 and 172–181; Romano 2014: 20, 52–53, 57–59, and 62–63). The murder of Rev. Reeb, in particular, unleashed even more campus activity from vigils to fundraising to recruiting additional volunteers for the Selma to Montgomery march. At Pitt, the university community organized a number of buses to attend the march. Again, I declined to go South, but vowed to find a way to make myself useful to the growing agitation in the Hill District in the fall of 1965.

Meantime, other white northern students had traveled South in the summer of 1965 to participate in the Southern Christian Leadership Conference version of Freedom Summer. Designated as Summer Community Organizing and Political Education, or SCOPE, this project attracted more students than the 1964 SNCC Freedom Summer, perhaps as a consequence of the national attention devoted to the events in Selma (Branch 2006: 196). Given these dramatic incidents, it is not surprising that the main motivation for many of the SCOPE volunteers was reflected in one student's perspective: "I feel that Civil Rights is the most pressing problem of our time and that working in Civil Rights is the most useful way I can spend my summer, both in terms of duty to humanity and deep personal value" (quoted in Rothschild 1982: 39).

Nevertheless, as one of the studies on these students' notes, "there was a substantial contingent of SCOPE workers who viewed SCLC as a second-best affiliation. To these people, SNCC represented the soul and the muscle of the movement by virtue of its more militant grassroots credentials when compared to SCLC" (Demerath, Maxwell, and Aiken 1971: 127). In fact, some of the SCOPE volunteers had worked in Mississippi in 1964, often as tutors at Freedom Schools throughout the state. One recent Smith graduate had worked in the Freedom School in Natchez during the summer of 1964. Another one of those SCOPE workers, Pete Blickman, had also worked in Natchez doing voter registration for the MFDP. As a recent graduate from the University of Wisconsin and an activist with Madison Friends of SNCC, Blickman represented the more militant and politically conscious summer volunteers. Other SCOPE volunteers, such as a Mills College senior, had been attracted to SNCC from programs highlighting SNCC's work at San Francisco State and a Bob Moses speech at the same venue.[3]

Although most SCOPE volunteers identified themselves as liberals, their liberalism reflected an increasing radicalization among student activists in the mid-1960s. Patti Alter, the Mills College senior, described herself as "a white liberal because I'm white and I'm from the North and I'm working with the Movement." Warren Drexel from San Jose State and Santa Clara Friends of SNCC recognized the need for white northerners to go South because it "brings the mass media down here when there are Northern white volunteers getting beat on the head." However, echoing Bob Moses's orientation admonition to the 1964 Freedom Summer volunteers, Drexel asserted: "I didn't come down here to help Negroes. I came down here with very selfish intentions to help myself because I live in this social structure and I would help to cure the sickness." The "shock of recognition" concerning the sickness of anti-black racism further reinforced a sense that liberalism was at best inadequate and at worst part of the problem. One student drew the following lesson from the summer: "I could no longer believe in the liberal myth in America" (Project South interviews with Warren Drexel and Patti Alter). As another

---

3 Interviews with cited SCOPE workers can be found in the Project South papers, SC 66, at the Department of Special Collections at Stanford University Library.

SCOPE volunteer acknowledged: "The contradiction between ideology and practice became acutely apparent – apparent to a degree I would not have been aware of if I had remained a 'northern-white liberal.' We're a sick people with a system fabricated on lies" (quoted in Demerath et al. 1972: 164 and 173.)[4] Among those lies was, of course, that a reformed white supremacy, even as a seemingly less malevolent practice in the North, could dispense racial justice.

Another contradiction that became very evident to numerous white students in 1965 that was less evident in 1964 was the role of whites in a black-led movement, a movement whose aim was increasingly for black self-determination. Conceding that whites often "monopolized leadership to the detriment of the local community," one University of Chicago student hoped for a diminished white role. Another SCOPE volunteer and civil rights veteran whose activism included the march on Washington, the Freedom Vote, and tutoring in a Freedom School in 1964 admitted that "many of us made the mistake of taking over too much ... instead of training other people to do what we were doing" (Project South interviews with Edith Black and Bob Billman).

I also brought that missionary sensibility into my work in helping to set-up a Freedom School in the Hill District in Pittsburgh. Nonetheless, in the process of tutoring and teaching young black students, I got to know black community activists. The knowledge I gained from that interaction was an antidote to any white paternalism and expedited the lifting of the veil of whiteness. Recognizing that I was, in fact, a part of a racialized order that oppressed blacks not just in the South but also throughout the country, I began to comprehend to a degree the invisible markers of whiteness. Going into black homes and churches for the first time in my life, I experienced both the openness of the community and its righteous frustration over issues such as inadequate and overpriced housing to irrelevant education.[5] Although working initially in an integrated environment, events were moving both locally and nationally towards Black Power within the activist civil rights organizations such as SNCC. It was during this turn to Black Power that whites in SNCC and Friends of SNCC were forced to confront our whiteness and its implications for our political involvement with civil rights.

A number of those white student activists with SNCC recognized their own form of "double consciousness" during their involvement with SNCC. Mary

---

4   By the end of the 1960s 40% of college students considered the U.S. a "sick society." See Anderson 1995: 251.
5   For an excellent study of the civil rights struggle in the North with all the attendant contradictions, see Sugrue 2008.

King highlighted this "double consciousness" and her sense of estrangement from the "white" world in the following manner: "If I stepped back and looked at myself from a distance, I saw someone sincere and committed, but also determined, reliable, tenacious, and dedicated. It came as a shock to my self-image suddenly to see myself through the eyes of our opponents: lawbreaker, "nigger lover," deviant, and radical" (King 1987: 115). In many respects, the threat of the "nigger lover" was more destabilizing to white supremacy than black insubordination.[6] Hence, white southern activists, like Bob Zellner, were the recipients of vicious attacks by white mobs (Zinn 2002: 167–189). On another level, Mary King's condition mirrored the socio-psychological situation analyzed by Kenneth Keniston in his study of young radicals of the 1960s. Among the characteristics that informed radical activists were "a confrontation with heretofore unexperienced aspects of American life, a growing disenchantment with existing institutions for social change, the development of a new interpretation of American life, (and) a feeling of personal responsibility for social and political change" (Keniston 1968: 124).

That growing disenchantment marked another kind of "double consciousness" that white student volunteers brought home with them after the summers of 1964 and 1965. One 1964 summer volunteer remarked "coming out of Mississippi and into the 'civilized white' world was hard. It was like cultural shock or something" (quoted in McAdam 1988: 135). A 1965 summer volunteer gave even further definition of that cultural shock: "When I returned home, white people looked 'funny': I had difficulty relating to them; and I didn't trust them. My skin was white – but I was not a white man. Attitudes and views that white acquaintances had now seemed to reek of bias and prejudice ... I was bitter. As if my whole value scheme, learned from infancy, was a lie" (quoted in Demerath et al. 1971: 164). Such a form of the "transvaluation of values" experienced by white students proved inimical to the social constructions of whiteness. Also, many of those white students involved in the black freedom struggle were to become even more dedicated, albeit driven, radicals in later 1960s and beyond (McAdam 1988: 161–240).

While Black Power became an extension of the civil rights agenda to achieve fundamental dignity and a sense of self-worth (Joseph 2006), for white student activists in the civil rights movement their confrontation with racial constructions became a challenge to their own identities. One interpreter of the impact on civil rights on white student activists suggests that "white and black partisans

---

6   Jon Daniels, a northern seminary student, was murdered in Lowndes County Alabama in August 1965 because he was considered a "nigger-lover" and, hence, "race traitor." See Eagles 1993: 260.

of the Black Freedom Struggle came to see that struggle was as much if not more about the meanings and prerogatives of whiteness as it was about black self-determination" (Martin 2002: 87). In what may be construed as a provocative statement, Stokely Carmichael (Kwame Ture) insisted that there were no "whites" in SNCC. However, in his elaboration, he clarified how "whiteness" was deconstructed by those "unusually conscientious and socially aware young people" who joined SNCC and accepted the role of black leadership. He further noted that when those white student activists with SNCC "experienced the full force of racist hostility from Southern white politicians, police, and public opinion, compounded by the indifference or paralysis of the national political establishment, whatever class and color privileges they might have taken for granted were immediately suspended" (Carmichael 2003: 308).

In the fall of 1966 my involvement as a student activist was in the process of a transition from civil rights work to anti-war work. Nonetheless, I participated in a campaign to bring Dr. Martin Luther King, Jr. to the University of Pittsburgh as a featured speaker. As part of that campaign, an interracial group to which I belonged forced the administration to change its original intent to have the Dean of Students by himself in his own compact car pick up Dr. King at the airport. Instead, as a consequence of our protest, the university's limousine drove to the airport with a few representative students, including myself. We made sure that the route from the airport to the campus would go through one of the black neighborhoods close-by the university, the neighborhood where, in fact, I worked as a tutor and organizer for our local Freedom School.

I was particularly excited and apprehensive about Dr. King's speech since I had been chosen to introduce him. In the overflowing ballroom of the Student Center, a stage had been fashioned to accommodate several local civil rights dignitaries, leaving me, as I recall, the only white person on the stage. When Dr. King finished his inspiring address, the African-American contingent on the stage, joined by a few others, linked arms and began to sing the well-known anthem of the civil rights movement – "We Shall Overcome." To those in the movement the proper way to link up for performing this stirring song was to cross one's arms and join hands with the person on either side. Although I knew this and had done this ritual previously, before I could enact the correct stance, my non-crossed arms were pulled in opposite directions. And, there I was, an ungainly white person, connected to a solid front of black civil rights activists, sheepishly singing "We Shall Overcome," embarrassed about how I must have appeared to those around me.

In some respects, my personal dilemma at that moment as a white appendage to a black vanguard mirrored the larger shifting political context for white supporters of the civil rights movement. Only recently, Stokely Carmichael, had enunciated the call for "Black Power," and SNCC had moved to urging its white cadre to leave the organization and go into the white community to combat racism. What civil rights activists were being asked to do was, in effect, to acknowledge that the new phase of the black freedom struggle required the pursuit of racial justice for African Americans inside the white community. In the process, white civil rights advocates and activists were compelled to confront the intransigence of white racism, but also to question their own racial constructions of whiteness. According to one critical study of this historical moment, "If whites did not understand their racialization, they would have to believe that their condition, relative to black people, was natural. Understanding their own racialization was the prerequisite to understanding the social relationships of their society" (Barber 2008: 21).

However, what was becoming more compelling to white student activists like myself was our relationship to the Vietnam War, especially those of us who were of draft age. In some respects, it was the escalation of the war in Vietnam that further alienated students like myself for whom whiteness and citizenship seemed thoroughly compromised. From the perspective of one of the most insightful historians of the impact of that war on Americans that led to anti-war activities: "the Vietnam War compelled millions of citizens to question the once widely held faith that their country is the greatest force for good in the world, that it always acts to advance democracy and human rights, that it is superior in both its power and virtue" (Appy 2015: xii).[7] It was that profound alienation from this national identity that led me in 1966 to sign the national "We Won't Go" statement that gave birth to the draft resistance movement (Foley 2003). Increasingly, my energies were focused on the war and the draft, so much so that by the summer of 1967, I became a full-time volunteer for the American Friends Service Committee's Vietnam Summer activities. By the time I got to grad school at the University of Minnesota in the fall of 1967, I worked exclusively on draft and anti-war issues. Yet, I was well aware that my schooling as an activist came out of my involvement with and understanding of civil rights. It was there that I gained a sense of becoming a historic agent for change and began the confrontation with my whiteness and privileged citizenship.

Taking responsibility for social and political change and, indeed, becoming historic agents of change drew students by the tens of thousands to become activists in the civil rights movement. During the Berkeley Free Speech Movement, Jack Weinberg, a CORE activist and campus radical asserted that

---

7 On the anti-war movement, see Small 2002 and Wells 1994. For a fine collection of activist voices from the anti-war movement, see Aguilar-San Juan and Joyce 2015.

"students have turned to the civil rights movement because they have found it to be a front on which they can attack basic social problems, a front on which they have some real impact" (quoted in Martin 2002: 87). Many white student activists gravitated toward SNCC because it offered the opportunity to address not only continuing racial inequities but also to engage their own visions of racial justice and human rights. As Debra Schultz contends in her study of the disproportionate number of Jewish women who went south to work as volunteers, "SNCC provided a home for white antiracist activists at a time when the very notion of white antiracism was all too rare for most Americans" (Schultz 2001: 2).

Whether "going South" or staying on and around the campus, white student activists pushed an antiracist agenda that would continue to inform the social movements of the 1960s (Evans 1980 and Thompson 2001). Through exhibiting a "common collective consciousness, historical understanding, and vision of necessary social change" students sought in the civil rights movement and black freedom struggle an outlet for their insistence on justice and freedom now! (Rogers 1993). In his recollections of his involvement in SNCC, Mendy Samstein provided what could stand as a tribute to the legacy of those white student activists: "I felt, yes, I'm in a black movement, I'm in a civil rights movement, but not just that I'm in a civil rights movement and not just that I'm in a certain struggle at a specific time, but I felt I was joining the human race, and this was what was so moving and continues to move me" (quoted in Greenberg 1998: 126).[8]

Although not extinguishing the contradictions of white privilege, white student activists in the black freedom struggle created a liminal space in which they challenged the privileges of white supremacy. In acknowledging the impact of the black freedom struggle on the "new left," Michael Harrington wrote that part of the gift of that struggle was "an existential, moralistic, and quite emotional critique of the entire society and, in particular, a sense that the self-proclaimed reformers and social changers were hypocrites for maneuvering within the framework of the possible when what the times called for was a nonviolent John Brown" (Harrington 1996: 12). The other part not acknowledged by Harrington was the degree to which black liberation was a catalyst for the "deconstruction of whiteness" (Winant 2001: 107–108) and the opening up of the possibility, still unrealized, of citizenship and democracy without racialized privilege (Olson 2004). Moreover, with their developing radicalization

---

8   In his study of white anti-racist activists, Mark Warren maintains "activists find that by participating in the struggle for equality and freedom they gain the opportunity to become more fully human" (Warren 2010: 110).

through the black freedom struggle, white students became conscious of the sickness of the system which actually predisposed them to question their own attachments to constructions of whiteness and its attendant dysfunctional consciousness before the alienation caused by the Vietnam War. Speaking at a February 1968 memorial for Malcolm X in Houston, white student activist and SDS leader, Bob Pardun summarized the lessons learned from his cohort's involvement with the civil rights movement and the attendant radicalization of white youth in the 1960s: "It is hard for white America to stand against the assumptions of white America. The idea that this is the best of all possible worlds for white people is taught to you every day in your life by the schools and mass media. It is hard to understand that this society exploits and regiments and destroys white people as well as black people – that it separates them from their brothers (and sisters) and keeps them from understanding what is happening to them. But we learned" (Pardun 2001: 225–226).

Obviously, the lessons learned by white student activists in the civil rights and black freedom movements varied according to a number of factors. One of the most critical factors was the initial confrontation with racism, whether in the South with its attendant vicious "displays of antipathy toward minorities," or in the North where "structured inequality (allowed) white people to remain self-satisfied and smug about their own innocence" (Lipsitz 2006: 46). Catching hell in the South certainly provided a different and more intense experience with racism than participating as allies in the struggle against the oppressive conditions facing African Americans in the North. Nonetheless, whether the veil of whiteness was ripped off by facing brutal violence or removed through a less intimidating and reflective manner, white student activists learned life-altering lessons about the invidiousness of the internal and external racial divide during their participation in the civil rights movement. In particular, the unveiling of their own whiteness revealed to them and to the nation that their aspirations to transcend the racial divide was an integral and necessary part of the deconstruction of whiteness. In turn, that deconstructing whiteness meant, in the profound and moving words of Mendy Samstein, "joining the human race."

CHAPTER 5

Exorcising the Ghosts of the Past: From Civil Rights Murders to Confederate Monuments

William Faulkner, the legendary Mississippi-bred writer who wrestled in his novels with the tortured legacies of the South, famously noted that "the past isn't dead; it isn't even past." Recognizing the absence of power and privilege in Faulkner's formulation, James Baldwin's searing indictment of Faulkner's failure to "exorcise a history which is also a curse" further asserts that the victims of history cannot "accept that history's arrogant and unjust judgment" (Baldwin 1998: 381). Contesting the curse embedded in the South's haunted past, whether through the re-trials of the murderers of civil rights activists or the deconstruction of Confederate monuments, entails both a re-framing of that past and a confrontation with the ghosts of that past. Such hauntings are, as Jacques Derrida reminds us, intimately connected to "the structure of every hegemony" (Derrida 1994: 37). In this case, the focus of this chapter will be on a white hegemony that inscribed in the law, public acts, and public spaces the arrogance and injustices of structural racism.

When Edgar Ray Killen died in prison on January 11, 2018, just a few days short of his ninety-third birthday, it seemingly ended the chapter on the notorious Klan murders of civil rights activists in Mississippi during the 1960s. Convicted of the planning and participation in the murders of James Chaney, Andrew Goodman, and Mickey Schwerner in June 1964, Killen was the last of those white terrorists and murderers who died in prison. Preceding him on November 5, 2006 was Sam Bowers, imprisoned for the firebombing and subsequent murder of Vernon Dahmer in January 1966. Also, dying in prison on January 21, 2001 after his long-awaited conviction for the assassination of Medgar Evers in June 1963 was Byron De La Beckwith. It took years after the crimes each committed to prosecute them successfully and send them to prison (Romano 2014: 9–12). In the aftermath of the 1994 conviction of De La Beckwith, the *Atlanta Constitution* opined, "an evil ghost has been exorcised, an ugly chapter has been closed, and Mississippi's changes for the better had been confirmed" (quoted in Romano 2014: 143).

However, while a chapter might have been closed, there is still the book on white supremacy that haunts not just Mississippi but also the whole national experience, especially in relationship to racial injustice. By examining in some detail the murder of Medgar Evers and the trials of Byron De La Beckwith, one might be able to comprehend not only the weaponized whiteness of the past, but also how white identity politics, defeated finally in one era, can, nonetheless, be resurrected to haunt the living in the present. Indeed, as the legendary leader of the Birmingham civil rights movement, Fred Shuttlesworth, asserted, "If you don't tell it like it was, it can never be as it ought to be" (quoted in Romano 2014: 183). Indeed, the struggle to achieve racial justice requires not only prosecuting the past criminal actions of white supremacists, but also contending with the persistence of the injustices of white identity politics. Hence, for Shuttlesworth and other racial justice activists, "refusing to recognize the legacies of past racial practices in the present (would be) another manifestation of racism" (Romano 2014: 184–185).

Certainly, the re-trials of those individuals who murdered civil rights advocates from the 1960s opened the possibility for a much more radical examination of institutional racism. After the October 1992 hearing before a Mississippi court to dismiss the trial against Byron De La Beckwith for the murder of civil rights leader, Medgar Evers, his long-suffering and eloquent widow, Myrlie Evers, defended the need to go forward with the trial. "We have to settle those dastardly acts of old," she said. "If we don't, we will live with ghosts that will haunt us forever" (quoted in Vollers 1995: 321). The Beckwith trial and eventual conviction in 1994 initiated a period of attempting to bring to justice those who plotted and carried out high-profile murders of civil rights activists. According to the Southern Poverty Law Center, close to 22 murder cases have been re-opened in the South since 1989, resulting in 25 arrests and 16 convictions. The three most significant cases (Beckwith, Bowers, and Killen) have been part of a decade long (1994–2005) effort to re-try those murder cases and achieve what the legal scholar, Margaret Russell calls "retrospective justice" (Russell 2003: 1225–1268). In effect, the legal hauntings of these cases, especially for the families of the victims, required judicial restitution if not racial reconciliation with the past.[1]

What this first part of Chapter 5 intends to explore, if not exorcise, are those ghosts of white supremacy that continue to haunt us as we attempt to reformulate the hegemonic ordering of race in the United States, especially the transformation and persistence of white supremacy and white identity politics. I intend to focus on the murder of Medgar Evers and the legal and racial hauntings that are attached to his murder, and the eventual conviction of his murderer, Byron De La Beckwith in 1994, after two mistrials in 1963 and 1964. I want to examine briefly the historical context of the civil rights movement that

---

[1] As of 2014 an account of those men sent to prison for racially motivated murders during the 1950s and 1960s was more than twenty. See Romano 2014: 2.

Medgar Evers was part of in Mississippi and the two initial murder trials. Then, I want to consider how the development of the retrial of Beckwith became part of an attempted reconciliation with the legal and racial hauntings of Mississippi, and, indeed, the nation's past.

In re-contextualizing the historical moment, one cannot escape the fact that the civil rights movement is still a contested and unfinished political project (Romano and Raiford 2006). Moreover, that movement and our continuing struggle around racial issues play significant roles in our national narrative, a narrative still imbued with white privilege which defines our national racial story as "the slow but inevitable triumph of reason over ignorance, of tolerance over intolerance and prejudice, and of equality of opportunity over discrimination" (Carlson 2004: 303). Central to that national narrative were and are the media constructions of Medgar Evers' murder and the 1994 retrial, especially the news media's coverage of the trial and the 1996 film, *Ghosts of Mississippi*. According to one critical review of both, the "journalistic coverage of Beckwith's trial and the *Ghosts of Mississippi* worked together to comprise a narrative that established Beckwith's conviction as the conclusion of the civil rights struggle" (Hoerl 2008: 63). The media constructions, such as those in the film, *Ghosts of Mississippi*, also managed to obfuscate the persistence of white supremacy, assuming that it had been cast in the shadows in the aftermath of the trial (Romano 2014: 161–165).

Re-examining the history of the civil rights struggle in Mississippi, the key role played in that struggle by Medgar Evers, and the resistance by the white power structure entails the necessary backdrop to understanding why there is neither closure in the narrative (the past not being dead) nor resolution of the inequities of a reformulated hegemonic ordering of white supremacy. The virulent and visible white supremacy confronted by Medgar Evers and the myriad foot soldiers of the civil rights movement in Mississippi is part of an extensive historical record (Dittmer 1994; Morris 2015; Payne 1995). Yet, the racial hauntings of the past certainly necessitate revisiting that past with a critical eye towards what may still be invisible to both memory and narrative. In turn, the deconstruction of white identity politics that informed one era still requires its exposition and analysis in later eras.

Medgar Evers was born and raised in Mississippi. While Beckwith moved to Mississippi the age of 5, both men were socialized in the virulent form of white supremacy that dominated Mississippi life in mid-century America. Both men served in World War II. Evers became, however, part of that cadre of black veterans who were prepared to challenge the very structures and strictures of white supremacy that Beckwith was, in turn, committed to upholding, even to the point of violent intimidation and murder. After graduating from Alcorn

College, where he met and married Myrlie Beasley, Evers stepped forward in 1953 as a volunteer to attempt to enter the University of Mississippi Law School. His rejection, nonetheless, brought him into the spotlight and led to an appointment as the Mississippi Director of the NAACP in 1954 at the very moment of the U.S. Supreme Court's historic rendering in Brown v. Board of Education. That case set off a wave of black activism and massive white resistance that in Mississippi led to outright murders and vicious repression from job dismissals to termination of loans to blacks. In the period from 1954–1959 there were at least ten African-American men murdered by whites, none of whom were ever found guilty. Included among the killers was Sheriff Lawrence Rainey who would later play an instrumental role in the 1964 murder of Chaney, Goodman, and Schwerner (Evers 1996; Massengill 1994; Nossiter 1994; Vollers 1995).

However, at least one of the murders, that of fourteen-year-old black Chicagoan, Emmett Till, would gain national and international attention, primarily because of the quiet insistence of Mamie Till, Emmett's mother, that justice should be served. Of course, justice was not served then as the two men responsible for killing Emmett Till were acquitted by an all-white jury (Tyson 2017). On the other hand, the incident aroused the passions and commitment of a younger generation of Mississippians, like Anne Moody. In her autobiography, she recounts how her mother tried to explain away the murder of Emmett Till as the work of an "Evil Spirit." But Anne and her high school compatriots in rural Mississippi came to a different realization, one of "the fear of being killed just because I was black" (Moody 1968: 121–125).

That fear was reinforced by the institutionalization of a white terrorist state. Beyond the violence of the KKK and White Citizens Councils in Mississippi, organizations to which Beckwith belonged, Mississippi created a vast spy network known as the Mississippi State Sovereignty Commission (Katagiri 2001). Even in the face of such terror and intimidation, black Mississippians and Medgar Evers, in particular, organized campaigns to confront segregation in all its many oppressive forms. Galvanized by the student sitins in 1960, black students in Mississippi, especially at Tougaloo, the premier historical black college in Jackson, became active. Voter registration drives were organized throughout the state with residents like Amzie Moore, another black WWII veteran, and outsiders like Bob Moses from SNCC taking the lead. By 1962 these campaigns were in full swing, confronting horrific repression. By May of 1963, the movement in Jackson became a mass movement with Medgar Evers heavily involved. Appearing, unbelievably, in late May on a local Jackson television station, Evers laid down the gauntlet of historical contestation: "Whether Jackson and the state choose to change or not, the years of change are upon us.

History has reached a turning point here and around the world" (Evers 1996: 268).

With all the activity in the Deep South reaching such a crescendo, President Kennedy could no longer remain above the fray. On the evening of June 11, Kennedy spoke to the nation about the moral challenge posed by segregation. Acknowledging that this moral issue was "as old as the Scriptures and ... as clear as the American Constitution," Kennedy promised to ask Congress "to make a commitment it has not fully made in this century to the proposition that race has no place in American life or law" (quoted in Weisbrot 1991: 75). (Much of Kennedy's speech would become part of the opening sequence in the film, *Ghosts of Mississippi*, a sequence that follows through crosscutting methods Medgar Evers and Byron De La Beckwith on the night of the murder.) Heralded as the opening salvo of a Second Reconstruction, there were many in the civil rights movement who were very wary, if not downright dismissive of Washington's intentions.[2]

However, only hours later another salvo was heard in the driveway of Medgar Evers home as he got out of his car. That volley came from the rifle of Byron De La Beckwith. The lyrics of the well-known Bob Dylan song, *Only a Pawn in Their Game*, written shortly after the murder provide a compelling rendering of the deed and its larger meaning: "A bullet from the back of a bush took Medgar Evers' blood/A finger fired the trigger to his name/A handle hid out in the dark/A hand set the spark/Two eyes took the aim/Behind a man's brain/ But he can't be blamed/He's only a pawn in their game." What followed was organized outrage at the assassination and the unfortunately predictable white supremacist injustice.

Evers's death and mass funeral mobilized over 5000 angry black Mississippians and led to increased tensions in Jackson, putting pressure on the ever-recalcitrant Mississippi authorities to find the killer. Byron De La Beckwith was arrested on June 23, 1963 and brought to trial in February of 1964. At that first trial, it was clear that the state of Mississippi was fully supportive of Beckwith, most evident when the former Governor of the State, Ross Barnet, crossed the courtroom to shake hands with Beckwith. Support poured into Beckwith's defense committee. The all-white jury, neglecting compelling evidence of Beckwith's guilt, split, seven for acquittal and five for conviction. A second trial

---

2   Among those skeptical of Washington's intentions was the Rev. Edwin King, the Methodist chaplain during the early 1960s at Tougaloo, a historic black college in Jackson Mississippi that was a hotbed of civil rights activism. See Salter 1987: vii–xxi.

in April of 1964, with another all-white jury, led to an eight to four decision for acquittal, apparently consigning the case to legal oblivion. However, this actually marked the beginning of the legal haunting that would persist for two more decades until a jury composed of eight blacks and four whites rendered a conviction (Evers 1996; Massengill 1994; Nossiter 1994).

Although Myrlie Evers and Mississippi blacks, including Charles Evers, the brother of Medgar and a controversial civil rights leader, tried to apply pressure to reopen the case, it was not until the late 1980s when a change in the political climate of Mississippi opened up the possibility of consideration. In 1987, a reform Democrat, Ray Maybus, won the governorship with 90% of the black vote and 40% of the white vote. That reform ticket included Dick Molpus as Secretary of State. Molpus's 1989 speech, promising to look into the "dark corners" of Mississippi's past, aided the efforts to re-open legal proceedings against those previously acquitted of civil rights murders. In addition, the formerly the insular and racist Jackson newspaper, the *Clarion-Ledger*, was taken over by Gannett and an African-American managing editor was installed. With investigative reporting coming from Jerry Mitchell at the *Clarion-Ledger*, revelations about jury tampering in the second trial put increasing pressure on the Jackson District Attorney, Ed Peters, to re-visit the case. Peters appointed his newly hired assistant DA, Bobby DeLaughter to look into the press allegations and determine what, if anything, could be done about the Evers case (Romano 2014: 66–73 and 103–118; Vollers 1995: 260–263).

DeLaughter soon became the focus of efforts to right the legal haunting. It is instructive, therefore, to consider the language used by DeLaughter in his later recounting of the re-trial of Beckwith for the murder of Medgar Evers. DeLaughter writes that he was "a white prosecuting attorney who tried to free himself of the shackles of the past." From DeLaughter's perspective he was required to perform an "exorcism of sorts" for the state of Mississippi. "With the world watching," reflects DeLaughter, "the state cast out many demons of racism that had possessed it for so many years." Aware that he "could not put the civil rights movement and the reaction of the State of Mississippi on trial" if he "wanted to win," DeLaughter followed standard legal practice to go after the dastardly perpetrator of the murder and to cast the victim as innocent and upright (DeLaughter 2001: 75 and 18). However, in following such a line of attack, DeLaughter not only helped to re-enact a melodrama of competing personalities, but also to reinforce the view that white supremacy was a product of individual beliefs and attitudes.[3]

---

3 On the tendency of Americans to "view racism and sexism as products of individual beliefs and attitudes," see Glenn 2002: 263.

By framing the issue of white supremacy in individualistic terms, the underlying racial dynamics become reified and relegated to an arcane past. In effect, as noted by George Lipsitz, "we have so demonized the white racists of 1960s Mississippi that we fail to see the ways in which many of their most heinous practices and policies have triumphed in our own day" (Lipsitz 1998: xv). Although by the 1990s Beckwith's attitudes did seem a relic of the past, white supremacy in a newer and invisible form, cast as anti-welfare attitudes and tough-on-crime drug sentencing, only added to the structural inequities that hid white supremacy under the covering of a "color-blind" society. The trials of Beckwith and other racist relics thus became contested space where "those who wanted to harness them to the project of declaring and celebrating the end of racism in a 'postracial' nation and those who saw in them a potential to challenge the denial of the significance of race that was at the foundation of a new racial order" (Romano 2014: 2–3).

Nonetheless, as the case for re-opening was being built by DeLaughter and pushed by local black activists, polarizing racial patterns re-emerged. One can find varying statements from local Mississippi residents, both black and white, that the trial was either "a useless dredging up on unpleasant memories" or it served a function as an important "community exorcism" (Vollers 1995: 330). In other words, this trial, and the other succeeding ones, became contested grounds for the meanings and memorializing of the past and the distance that Mississippi, in particular, and the nation, in general, had traveled to overcome the racial injustices of the past.

In her study of the media constructions of the re-trial, Kristen Hoerl found that major opinion-forming newspapers, the *New York Times,* the *Washington Post,* and USA *Today* all conformed to the view that the re-trial closed the book on the terrible Mississippi past. She contends: "By framing Beckwith as a relic from the past, reports positioned the state's trial against Beckwith as a sign of racial progress.... By embodying Mississippi's racist past with Beckwith, press reports positioned Beckwith as a scapegoat for Mississippi's history of violence against African-Americans and civil rights activists" (Hoerl 2008: 72–73). Beckwith in such media constructions becomes the exorcised spectral representation of that ghostly and ghastly past. In turn, Bobby DeLaughter becomes the white knight in shining armor whose battle with the ghostly and ghastly Beckwith is a vindication of the forces of right (and white) over the archaic white supremacy of the past.

Nowhere is this ideological media construction more evident than in the 1996 Rob Reiner film, *Ghosts of Mississippi.* Although paying homage at the beginning of the film to the civil rights struggle through the use of documentary footage, the film quickly develops into a courtroom drama and family melodrama with DeLaughter at the center. In focusing on DeLaughter,

Myrlie Evers is marginalized, becoming, in the words of one critic of the film, "a resigned bystander, waiting for a few good white men to come along and save the day" (quoted in Romano 2014: 160). This displacement, even more crudely constructed in the 1989 film about the murders of Chaney, Schwerner, and Goodman, *Mississippi Burning*, "gives us," in the critical review of the film by George Lipsitz, "a history that hides the present rather than illuminating it, that serves to protect social relations from examination, analysis, and critique" (Lipsitz 1998: 220).

As far as the family melodrama is concerned, it is made especially poignant because of the ghosts that DeLaughter has to combat, from his racist in-laws to white opponents of the trial who threaten his family. The exorcisms of these hauntings come to an interesting denouement in a crucial scene where DeLaughter must comfort his daughter's fears of ghosts. Earlier, he had sung "Dixie" to calm her fears. A second and later time, after his involvement in the retrial, when she requests "Dixie," he responds in a more enlightened manner: "Maybe Dixie's not the right song. Maybe that's why the ghost keeps coming back." Instead, he suggests the innocuous "Old MacDonald" (quoted in Hoerl 2008: 72–73). It seems that "Dixie" was no longer part of the repertoire that DeLaughter could sing or a song that could soothe the ghosts of the past. This redemptive move positions DeLaughter as someone who "had no understanding of the powerful presence of white supremacy in southern history to one who recognizes that the history of white racism still haunts the South" (Romano 2014: 164).

Although the film and other media constructions help to shape a new emergent national narrative that disposes of these racial ghosts through legal retribution, we must still face the persistent racial hauntings and the accompanying hegemonic reordering of white supremacy. These hauntings leave us with alternative contentious sensibilities that we have either successfully escaped the racial ghosts of the past through convictions of the white racist murderers or have merely extended another ideological cover to the persistence of white supremacy. In trumpeting how the convictions have closed a terrible chapter in U.S. history and led to an era of post-civil rights and color blindness, some of those associated with the trials and boosters of transformative changes in Mississippi may be committing another racial injustice. According to one of the most perceptive historians of the lingering effects of white supremacy, "to be truly color-blind in a nation that aggressively maintains structural racism and oppressive social hierarchies is to become blind to the reality and living consequences of American history" (Marable 2001: 96–97).

While the dead hand of the past and, indeed, dead victims of past racial injustices continue to haunt our present, the trials and commentary around these Mississippi court cases do require us to contend with the "living consequences of American history." It may be, as argued by Renee Romano, that "the legal format narrowed the scope of the inquiry into the actions of the defendants outside of a broader historical context in ways that minimized societal responsibility for the racial terror of the civil rights era, obscured the systemic nature of racial violence, and did little to address the relationship between the racial structures of the past and racial inequalities of the present" (Romano 2014: 202). If the ideological discourse found in these trials and the accompanying texts shed some significant light on the past, does that discourse ultimately help liberate us from what haunts us in the present? Perhaps, as argued by Dennis Carlson, "things have not changed as much as they seem on the surface, that whiteness only has taken on a new form, revising its narrative of the national history to make room for racial Others but still telling the story in ways that legitimate continued inequalities" (Carlson 2004: 363).

On the other hand, the regional narrative produced in the segregated South for over one hundred years was committed to upholding racial inequalities, especially in public space. Indeed, the monuments and memorials propagated by a white power structure invoked "the most deeply ingrained assumptions into self-justifying fables" (Savage 2018: xiii). These "self-justifying fables," part of the "curse of history" promulgated by white hegemony and white identity politics, have been unmasked in the recent efforts to remove Confederate monuments throughout the South (Schein 2018: 12). According to a 2019 study by the Southern Poverty Law Center (SPLC), entitled "Whose Heritage? Public Symbols of the Confederacy," the "deeply rooted but false narrative (Lost Cause mythology) is the result of many decades of revisionism in the lore and even textbooks of the South that sought to create a more acceptable version of the region's past. Confederate monuments and other symbols are very much a part of that effort" (SPLC 2019: 6).

The recent efforts by racial justice activists are aimed both at contesting this false narrative and challenging the structural racism that surrounds these symbols. The unmasking or deconstruction is not just a symbolic struggle over monuments and memorials, but also an effort to confront the ways in which white identity politics continues to inform how power and privilege is wielded not just in the South, but also throughout the nation. As a 2015 online petition for removal of prominent Confederate monuments in New Orleans by the grass-roots racial justice movement, "Take 'Em Down NOLA," argued: "The monuments and signs are so much more than symbols of bygone days. There are active parts of an abusive system in which intentionally unequal distribution of power and resources goes unchecked."[4]

---

4 The success of the pressure by "Take 'Em Down NOLA" and other activists and some sympathetic local politicians led to a several year process of removal of the most notorious of the four prominent Confederate and white supremacist monuments. See Meyerson 2017.

The impetus for the activism against Confederate monuments and symbols can be directly traced to a horrific crime committed on June 17, 2015 which shocked the sensibilities of the nation and underscored the vicious hate embedded in Confederate symbols. When a young white supremacist murdered nine members of the historic Charleston African-American church, the Emanuel A.M.E., while they were gathered in worship, the response went beyond shock and sorrow. His terrorist act initiated a wave of protest, especially in the aftermath of the surfacing of his photograph waving a Confederate battle flag. Beyond the removal of the Confederate flag in Charleston and at the South Carolina State House grounds, other cities and states in the South were immediately confronted with demands to demolish or remove Confederate monuments. Memphis responded by taking down a statue of Nathan Bedford Forrest, the infamous Confederate General who directed the wholesale slaughter of black Union soldiers and helped lead the post-Civil War Ku Klux Klan. According to the study of the Southern Poverty Law Center more than one hundred monuments and other Confederate symbols have been removed even though more than seventeen hundred still remain in public places mostly in the South (SPLC 2019: 3–5).

It is important to underscore, as does the Southern Poverty Law Center report, that most of the Confederate monuments were erected during specific eras when Jim Crow laws were being enacted, in the late nineteenth and early twentieth centuries, or under attack as in the 1950s and 1960s (SPLC 2019: 7–8). The earlier period witnessed private organizations, such as the United Daughters of the Confederacy, founded in 1894 and responsible for hundreds of monuments and memorials, gaining public funds to establish a white supremacist landscape throughout the South. As one of the leading historians of Southern history notes, the Confederate monuments "were ... the result of private groups colonizing public space." He gives the example of Confederate veterans in Durham, North Carolina lobbying the state legislature to use county taxes to underwrite the monument, pointing out that "black residents, who were denied the right to vote by Jim Crow laws, (were not asked) whether they supported spending their tax dollars on this public, political statement" (Brundage 2017).

There are several other egregious instances of the promotion of white supremacy through the establishment of such monuments during this time in the South. For example, a statue was erected of the former North Carolina Governor, Charles Brantley Aycock, who ran and governed as an extreme white supremacist. Among his white supremacist positions, Aycock promoted the disenfranchisement of African Americans in violation of the 15th Amendment to the U.S. Constitution.[5] Tying together the racist and imperialist agendas of

---

5 By the end of the 19th century *de jure* black disenfranchisement in the South was integral to the political rule of reigning Jim Crow. For example, by 1904 there were only 1,342 African

the times, Aycock opined: "If manifest destiny leads to the seizure of Panama, it is certain that it likewise leads to the dominance of the Caucasian. When the negro (sic) recognizes this fact we shall have peace and good will between the races" (quoted in SPLC 2019: 20). Another instance of such white supremacist ideology is to be found in the 1913 dedication of a Confederate monument on the University of North Carolina where one of the notable speakers, a white industrialist, "urged his audience to devote themselves to the maintenance of white supremacy with the same vigor that their Confederate ancestors had defended slavery" (Brundage 2017).

On the other hand, most Confederate monuments and markers are less explicit about the defense of slavery and white supremacy, especially those erected in the 1950s when segregation faced both legal and movement challenges. For example, in two small towns in Georgia the Historical Commission in that state in 1957 promoted markers that memorialized the final days of Jefferson Davis with the words "his hopes for a new nation, in which each state would exercise without interference its cherished 'Constitutional rights,' forever dead" (SPLC 2019). Nonetheless, this false narrative and the monuments that promulgate it have been protected by state laws, some enacted as recently as 2017. Indeed, the Alabama state attorney General relied on the 2017 Alabama Memorial Preservation Act, an act that forbid local governments "from removing, altering or renaming monuments more than 40 years old." He sued the city of Birmingham, with its black majority government, from concealing a Confederate monument under a tarp. The Governor of Alabama called such attempts to hide or remove Confederate monuments "politically correct nonsense" (SPLC 2019: 18).

On the other hand, there were some courageous Southern white politicians who not only took on the task of removing Confederate monuments but also contested the false narrative promoted and embedded in these monuments. For example, in New Orleans, Mayor Mitch Landrieu worked assiduously for years to build support for removal of monuments and statues in New Orleans that he argued "were created as political weapons, part of an effort to hide the truth, which is that the Confederacy was on the wrong side of humanity" (Landriue 2018: 3). In particular, his efforts to take down a monument erected in 1891, called the "White League Obelisk" that commemorated an 1874 revolt by white supremacist Democrats to topple the Republican Reconstruction government of New Orleans, faced a nasty backlash that required a militarized operation for its removal (Landriue 2018: 169–171 and 193). Landriue offered a

---

Americans registered to vote in Louisiana whereas the number in 1896 was 130,334. Black turnout in the 1904 Presidential election hardly registered any number. See Menand 2019: 20.

forthright denunciation of this White League Obelisk as a memorial to a "warped political movement by wealthy people supporting a mayor who was determined to regain power for white people, to reduce blacks to second class status, and to control how history was seen, read, and accepted by whites" (Landrieu 2018: 172).

Landrieu's unstinting efforts to remove these monuments had roots in his own experiences as the son of a former reformist mayor of New Orleans, Moon Landriue, his association with prominent New Orleanian African Americans, particularly the jazz musicians Wynton Marsalis and Terrence Blanchard, and the activist responses in the aftermath of the Charleston massacre. However, those activist responses, represented by groups like "Take 'Em Down NOLA," were often subsumed under the touting of his own political agenda, an agenda compromised by neoliberal policies that, among other courses of action, expedited the privatization of public schools in New Orleans.[6] Landrieu gives special attention to how his eyes were opened by Terence Blanchard to how the monument to General P.G.T. Beauregard, a New Orleans native who led the attack of Confederate soldiers on Fort Sumter in 1861, made Blanchard "feel less than" (Landrieu 2018: 38–39). Given the vitriolic response opposing removal of this and other statues, particularly the prominently displayed General Robert E. Lee monument, Landrieu invokes the courage demonstrated by John Lewis in the Selma march in 1965 and his resultant beating by the police as a reminder that others, especially African Americans, have faced more lethal attacks in their challenge to the white supremacist status quo (Landrieu 2017: 191).

Of course, many of the opponents of Confederate monument removal take refuge in the preservation of history, arguing that removing these monuments would be an act of "historical erasure." In rebuttal to such arguments, Southern historian, W. Fitzhugh Brundage, makes that case that "removing – or moving – Confederate monuments is not historical erasure. The same logic could have been used to justify maintaining, after 1964, signs that identified "Negro water fountains," "Colored waiting room," and other markers of Southern segregation" (Brundage 2017). On the other hand, Brundage recognizes that some of these monuments which have "aesthetic significance can and should be preserved in museums where they can be properly interpreted by curators and

---

6   Landrieu was seen, in particular, by the African-American activists in the "Take 'Em Down NOLA" movement as a Johnny-Come-Lately and opportunistic politician. For that perspective by one of the founders of the movement, see Moore 2018. For an overview of the New Orleans NAACP criticism of Landrieu's promotion of charter schools and their negative impact on black students, see Quigley 2017. For criticism of the neoliberal bent of Landrieu's policies, see Stein 2017.

docents. In such settings, they will serve as historical artifacts rather than civic monuments" (Brundage 2017).

Certainly, there is a range of positions concerning what should be done to "deconstruct" the Confederate monuments. Troy Duster, a professor emeritus of sociology at the University of California, argues that the statues should be left in place, but alongside monuments to Forrest or Lee could be those of abolitionists like William Lloyd Garrison, Charles Sumner, or Frederick Douglass. For Duster providing an alternative reading of this history could be a "source of informed dialogue about our past" (Duster 2017). Irrespective of the deconstructionist strategies for these monuments, it is imperative to emphasize that this fight over removal of Confederate monuments has not been "about history per se, but the commemoration of a history claimed in strategic and critical places in cities and communities which work normatively to reinscribe particular versions of what American life was and should be about by those with the power and social capital to do so" (Schein 2018: 12).

Exorcising the ghosts of the past will continue to plague the nation unless and until we truly comprehend the profound meanings of white supremacy and white identity politics, both in the past and the present. As Timothy Tyson contends in his conclusion to his compelling history of the Emmett Till murder: "To see beyond the ghosts, all of us must develop the moral vision and political will to crush white supremacy – both the political program and the concealed assumptions. We have to come to grips with our own history – not only genocide, slavery, exploitation, and systems of oppression, but also the legacies of those who resisted and fought back and still fight back" (Tyson 2017: 216). Indeed, deconstructing white supremacy and white identity politics requires more than just exorcising the ghosts haunting our past, albeit that is a necessary step on the road to racial justice. Making the "concealed assumptions" visible and contesting the "political program" of white identity politics in its present form means that whites must confront in the most rigorous manner how our own constructions of whiteness continue to impede the ultimate goal of justice for all.

CHAPTER 6

The Deconstructions of Whiteness in a "Post-racial" America

The election of Barack Obama in 2008 was touted by pundits and wishful-thinking citizens as the triumph of a "post-racial" America, a fulfillment of the dreams of Martin Luther King, Jr., and the conclusion to any lingering debts from an earlier civil rights era. However, in the aftermath of Obama's stunning electoral victory, what was seen as "post-racial" soon quickly morphed into what could be called "most racial" (Tesler 2016). As noted by historian Brian Ward, "the election furnished plenty of evidence of racism in America, and Obama's first two years in office saw so much racist and racially inflected invective directed against the new president from an incensed American right wing that by the time of the November 2012 elections, *postracialism* (author's emphasis) had virtually disappeared from political discussion and the public imagination" (Ward 2011: 330).

Indeed, during the Presidential elections in 2008 and 2012 one could see signs everywhere of the persistence of racism even in the face of liberal attempts to re-stitch the tattered ideological cloak of post-racialism. Obama's presidency became a lightning rod for white racial resentment. The misguided perception that Obama would seek retribution against a white power structure and turn on those who clung to whatever remnants persisted of white privilege not only reflected a white blind spot, but also underscored how white racial politics informed a national narrative. That narrative, whether shaped by residual white supremacist ideology or by the fantasies of post-racialism, nonetheless, exhibited how issues around race continued to dominate the political landscape (King and Smith 2011; Sugrue 2010; Tesler 2016).

Post-racialism, and an earlier iteration of colorblindness, emerged in the post-civil rights era as an ideological operation to shore up a contested white racial privilege. As argued by the authors of *Whitewashing Race*, "formal equality before the law coexists with *de-facto* white privilege and whites' resentment of race-conscious remedies" (Brown et al. 2003: 30). Substituting for an articulated white supremacy that was deeply embedded in the state and civil society before the long civil rights movement, the ideological function of post-racialism was "the ultimate redemption of whiteness – a sociocultural process by which whiteness is restored to its full pre-civil-rights value" (Cho 2009: 1596). A social order still based on racial hierarchy and oppression, while susceptible to crises and changes, nonetheless, endured (Feagin 2009; Roediger 2008). Even as it was modified by changing circumstances and the ideological projections of a post-racial society, whiteness retained, to a great extent, certain privileges. However, without acknowledging the continuing centrality of race and white identity politics, post-racialism became another impediment to challenging the white blind spot that occludes the role of racism in the United States.

Especially in the aftermath of the civil rights struggles of the 1960s, "racial discourse has been unable to function as a logic of racial superiority and justified exclusion. Therefore, it has been forced into rearticulations, representations, reinterpretations of the meaning of race and, perforce, of whiteness" (Winant 2004: 3).[1] Such rearticulations and representations of whiteness have been "interrogated," especially since the 1990s through the analyses of critical whiteness studies (Fishkin 1995). With roots in the crucial investigations of whiteness by black scholars (from W.E.B. DuBois to Harold Cruse) and writers (from Langston Hughes to James Baldwin to Toni Morrison), this interdisciplinary field traverses such disciplines as history (Theodore Allen, Noel Ignatiev, Matthew Jacobsen, George Lipsitz, David Roediger, and Judith Stein); sociology (Eduardo Bonilla-Silva, Teresa Guess, Michael Omi, and Howard Winant); philosophy (David Theo Goldberg and Charles Mills); anthropology (John Hartigan, Jr. and Frances Kendall); and feminist and cultural studies (Ruth Frankenberg and bell hooks). As noted in a review of critical whiteness studies, "the field now includes critiques of whiteness that examine the institutional arrangements, ideological beliefs and state practices that maintain white privilege even as those prerogatives are being challenged by anti-racist social movements, identity politics, multiculturalism and immigration" (Twine and Gallagher 2008: 5).

What I intend to interrogate and examine in this chapter is the intersection of these ideological beliefs with racial formations, discursive practices, and racial projects as they have developed over the last several decades, especially through the re-articulation of whiteness in a supposed post-racial America. Identifying contending ideological tropes along a political continuum suggests the following discursive practices and racial projects: (1) a right-wing backlash reflected in a form of "paranoid" whiteness (Martinot 2010: 106); (2) a convergence of neo-conservative and neoliberal "colorblind" whiteness; (3) a liberal multicultural and anti-racialist "post-racial" whiteness; and (4) a progressive/ radical anti-racist whiteness. Each of these ideological tropes and historically and socially specific constructions will be subjected to a form of deconstructive

---

1   With his co-author Michael Omi, Howard Winant has defined and situated racial formations and racial projects within a post WWII historical context. See Omi and Winant 2015.

and semiological decoding. In addition to situating and contextualizing such ideological tropes, the chapter, in keeping with the interdisciplinary filed of critical whiteness studies, will attempt "to strip whiteness of its historical and political power to produce, regulate, and constrain racialized others within the discursive and material relations of racial domination and subjugation" (Giroux 1997: 292).

While defensive or paranoid whiteness has resonances in the earliest settlement of the North American continent by Europeans fearful of Native Americans who they were eradicating and the Africans who they were enslaving, the recent re-articulations crystallized around a politics of white resentment in the racial backlash of the 1960s. Expressed through the ideological tropes of "law and order," politicians from George Wallace to Richard Nixon to Ronald Reagan nurtured a resentful right-wing white populism (Carter 2000; Edgar 1981). Later joined by such right-wing media pundits as Rush Limbaugh, Glenn Beck, and Fox News, the most contemporary articulations have emerged in the Tea Party movement, right wing state legislators, and the Republican presidential primaries (Walker 2011). Both Limbaugh and Beck have exploited the racial resentments of their white audiences around issues of immigration and public policies, such as healthcare reform. According to Beck, Obama's health care reforms were an attempt to "settle old racial scores" through a sneaky form of racial reparations. In addition to Beck's overt antagonism to Obama, alleging that the president has a "deep-seated hatred for white people or white culture," Beck relied on the paranoid projections of his white audience, nurtured by the politics of racial backlash, that the federal government has become of tool for "privileging" black interests (quoted in Wise 2010: 149 and 59).[2]

While the politics of racial backlash preceded Obama's presidency, finding their way often into the culture wars of the late 20th century, the fear of a black president, compounded by the very real economic and social dislocations of a dying empire, made Obama a target for the right-wing campaign of paranoid whiteness. During the nomination process of Sonia Sotomayor for the Supreme Court, Limbaugh lumped Sotomayor and Obama together as power-seekers who wanted "to use their power as a means of retribution." Continuing his rant, Limbaugh alleged that one got promoted in the Obama Administration "by hating white people ... (making) white people the new oppressed minority" (quoted in Wise 2010: 148). Limbaugh's ideological soul mates at Fox News, in turn, "conducted an unremitting campaign of racially inflected

---

2 For an extended analysis of the ways in which white racial resentments over Obamacare and government health programs also redounds to the detriment of working class whites, see Metzl 2019: 121–188.

criticism of the president's performance, politics, and personality ... (stoking) doubts about the legitimacy of Obama's birth certificate, his religious affiliations, and the sinister significance of his strange name and youthful experiences outside America" (Ward 2010: 355). The "othering" of Obama, in this and other instances during the 2008 campaign, was just a more hysterical variation on the defensive or paranoid whiteness that has informed right-wing politics over the last several decades (Anderson 2016: 154–158; Walker 2011; Ward 2010).

Some of most fantastic attacks on Obama made their appearance in the discursive practices and media representations of various Republican presidential candidates during the 2012 Republican presidential primary. Of particular note was a truly bizarre science fiction-inflected ad by the Rick Santorum campaign. Called "Obamaville," the ad used both the televisual conventions of *The Twilight Zone* and the ideological tropes of white Christian families under siege to project a devastated and dispirited America in 2014 after the re-election of Barack Obama. Playing on the fears of disintegrating white communities, the ad flashed images more familiar to those inhabiting the devastated and deindustrialized inner cities of the United States. Using a variety of stark images and icons from a baby's cradle to abandoned old people, "Obamaville" also subliminally made clear that Obama was an enemy of this country, especially as constructed and deconstructed as a white Christian nation. (Obama's face was, at one point, quickly crosscut with President Mahmoud Ahmadinejad and the "obvious" threat of a nuclear-armed Iran.) Deeply embedded in this media construction is what David Theo Goldberg has identified as a "fear of a black state (that) is linked to worries about a black planet, of alien invasion..., of a loss of local and global control and privilege long associated with whiteness" (Goldberg 2009: 337).

While the Santorum campaign ad clearly projected the spatial and temporal sense of loss and diminishing white power and privilege as a consequence of Obama's presidency, the candidate's own fervid pronouncements about the present and past politics of the United States revealed other articulations of explicit paranoid whiteness. Santorum's claim that America was a "great place before 1965," was, as asserted by Tim Wise, "a slap in the face to every person of color who resided here before that time" (Wise 2012: 108). Obviously tied to the racial backlash, the date of 1965 is particularly instructive because of the passage of the Voting Rights Act that year and the efforts that followed from that legislation to extend the franchise to African Americans in the South. It is not surprising that recent efforts to make voting difficult for people of color by requiring voter identification cards, especially but not limited to legislatures in the South, is reminiscent of pre-1965 racial apartheid policies of poll taxes. As noted by Howard Winant, "because of its willingness to exploit racial fears and employ racially manipulative practices, the new right has been effective in achieving much of its agenda for political and cultural reaction and social structural recomposition" (Winant 2004: 7).[3]

On the other hand, this defensive or paranoid whiteness is based on a shrinking racial and older constituency. A more effective discursive strategy for maintaining privilege and power is the colorblind whiteness of neo-conservative and neo-liberal racial projects. Building on the myth of racial progress and the appeals to race-less universalism, colorblind whiteness attempts to transcode the ongoing oppression of people of color into so-called reverse racism. As argued by Michael Omi, the "notion of 'color-blindness' has been strategically appropriated by conservatives seeking to dismantle the social policies designed to mitigate racial inequality. 'Civil rights' initiatives and court cases are now more likely to involve issues of discrimination against whites, calling into question so-called 'preferential policies' and claiming that it is whites, particularly white males, who are increasingly the victims of racism and racist practices" (Omi 2001: 268). While such appeals to alleged racial injustice against whites is less explicit in the neo-liberal discursive practice than in the neo-conservative, both ideological tendencies converge in the denial of the very real and ongoing institutional oppression of people of color (Winant 2004: 7–10).

Given the persistence of racial inequalities, such white colorblindness indeed becomes blind to the structural impediments facing people of color in contemporary America whether in employment, housing, health care, or a variety of other areas (Bonilla-Silva 2003). The maintenance of such structural racism to which many whites seem either indifferent or deliberately closed-minded about suggests a kind of disconnect to both history and contemporary reality (Marable 2002: 96–97). In addition, as Evelyn Nakano Glenn points out: "To the extent that Americans believe in independence and free choice, they deny interdependence and are blind to institutional constraints on choice. There is thus an overwhelming tendency to view racism and sexism as products of individual beliefs and attitudes" (Glenn 2002: 263). As a consequence of historical amnesia, social blinders, and socio-cultural constructs, "most white Americans are resistant to the idea that they have major privilege over other racial groups," and more readily blame the victim for persistent patterns of discrimination (Feagin and O'Brien 2003: 72 and 192). In Derrick Bell's damning critique of this discursive feature of white colorblindness, "the indolence of

---

3   For two studies of the connections between southern politics, racial backlash, and the new right, see Crespino 2007 and Lowndes 2008. On the national convergences between conservatism and racism, see Smith 2010.

blacks rather than the injustices of whites explains the socioeconomic gaps separating the races" (Bell 2004: 77–78).

For even those social scientists looking to structural transformations as explanations for the continuing inequities, there is a strong residue of references to cultural deficiencies among people of color. Beginning with the work of William Julius Wilson's *The Declining Significance of Race*, liberal policy analysts and policy-makers de-emphasized race and stressed class and universalist approaches to ending inequality (Wise 2010: 16). Linked to the ideological trope of post-racialism, this position "rejects the centrality of race as an organizing feature in American society and holds that policymakers formulate social and legal remedies best without any consideration of group identity, especially racial identity" (Cho 2009: 1603). Invariably, such a position turns its back on the need to continue race-based remedies in the face of racial inequities and highlights alleged pathologies among the poor and people of color.

It is this latter discursive representation that ironically (given the accusations of paranoid white reactionaries as opposed to the ideological orientations of neo-liberalism) informs the perspectives of Barack Obama and his multiculturalist allies. In fact, multiculturalism often occludes "the material conditions of racist practices and institutions" (San Juan, Jr. 2002: 9). Prior to his presidency and often in his presidential pronouncements, Obama referred to the cultural deficiencies of the inner-city even while acknowledging a legacy of racism. However, as one critic of Obama's eliding of racism and poverty notes, "it has been a common trope of post-racial liberalism from the beginning: pay homage to the stark history of racism, then switch gears and ruminate how the problems of poor people in so-called ghettos are now distant from the mistreatment that so often met their ancestors" (Wise 2010: 37). Obama's universalist prescriptions in his statements and legislative initiatives may indeed have been strategically based on concerns about keeping white support, but such ideological tropes are deeply embedded in his policy initiatives. Nevertheless, Obama faced constant hyperbolic criticism from the right that he is promoting affirmative action for blacks (Wise 2010: 56–61).

More perniciously, Obama's policies and failures to contend with deepening racial inequalities further reinforced the privileges of post-racial whiteness. For example, in putting together and passing an economic stimulus package, Obama did nothing to confront the very racially compromised construction industry that benefitted from federal funding. Some African-American progressives and radicals like Cornel West took to admonishing Obama's failures to even address economic and social dislocations that have fallen more heavily on people of color (as in the housing debacle). Indeed, in Obama's response to the murders of Michael Brown and Eric Garner, he continued to sidestep the structural racism that is especially embedded in the criminal justice system. Thus, one can find critiques emerging from within more radical African Americans as the following: "As much success as some African Americans have achieved, four million Black children live in poverty, one million Black people are incarcerated, and 240,000 Black people lost their homes as a result of the foreclosure crisis – resulting in the loss of hundreds of millions of dollars in Black savings. Never before in American history has a Black president presided over the misery of millions of Black people, the denial of the most basic standards for health, happiness, and basic humanity" (Taylor 2016: 193).[4]

Moreover, there have been moments when the Obama Administration cravenly caved in to the howls from the right, reinforcing, in the process, white racial resentment. From the firing of Van Jones after Glen Beck labeled him a black nationalist to the dismissal of Shirley Sharrod from her appointment in the Agricultural Department after a doctored video produced by Republican operatives cast her falsely as an "anti-white activist," Obama too often placated the right out of a putative commitment to the ideology of post-racialism. Glen Ford, the editor of *Black Agenda Report*, even criticized what he has called the "Obama Delirium Effect" on black America. "It makes black people see progress when they are actually facing disaster" (quoted in Street 2010).

It is precisely the symbolic and often limited aspects of racial progress that underlie the ideological trope of post-racialism with its target audience among young cosmopolitan whites who are tired of the racial arguments of the past and want to feel good about getting beyond race. According to bell hooks, "while today's youth are eager to live in a world where racism does not exist, they do not want to do the political work of changing themselves or society" (hooks 2000: 81).[5] Instead of a vigorous anti-racist program, some white intellectuals and multiculturalist critics have rallied around anti-racialism as a way to deflect a more radical critique of the persistence of the power and privilege of whiteness. Indeed, as argued by Alana Lentin, "the post-racial agenda is intimately related to the rise of diversity as a less discomforting way of admitting that full equality has not yet been secured" (Lentin 2011: 164). So, instead of arguments about affirmative action in hiring and education, liberals have relied on diversity as the key discursive strategy, ala the University of Michigan Law School case.

---

4 For an extended examination of the various illusions and policy failures of Obama's presidency, see Taylor 2016: 135–152; and Wise 2010: 36–61.
5 While generally true, this claim overlooks the involvement of young people in campaigns from anti-apartheid, anti-sweatshop, alternative globalization, and Occupy movements.

On the other hand, there are those progressive and radicals who are committed to an anti-racist discursive practice and political project. Such white anti-racism is not without its own contradictions and ideological tendencies. One such ideological position, advocated by those attached to the journal, *Race Traitor*, is a call to repudiate one's whiteness and the privileges that go along with it as a form of radical and contemporary abolitionism. For other anti-racists such a position is less political than it is moral (O'Brien 2001; Thompson 2001; Warren 2010). According to one of those critics, "stressing privilege as a strategy to engage whites seems to emphasize the wrong thing. It focuses on the narrow and short-term benefit whites receive from a racial hierarchy rather than the larger interest in a racially just future. Alone, it seems to engage shame and guilt rather than anger at injustice and hope for a better future." Wallowing in guilt, it is argued, will only impede "a willing acceptance of the responsibility to act" (Warren 2010: 85 and 225). From a similar perspective, Eduardo Bonilla-Silva maintains that "anti-racist whites cannot just be 'race traitors'; they must engage in struggles to end the practices and the ideologies that maintain white supremacy" (Bonilla-Silva 2003: 183).

Among those struggles are discursive strategies to "deconstruct" and "decenter" whiteness (Omi 2001: 290) and white racism and to articulate a kind of "color consciousness" attuned to the "*consequences* of color in a historically white dominated nation" (Wise 2010: 191). For Ruth Frankenberg, such white antiracism "is … a stance requiring lifelong vigilance" (Frankenberg 2001: 77). Although predictions concerning the end of a white majority in the United States point toward the year 2050, the death throes of a wounded white supremacy, white nationalism, and white identity politics may make such a transition both exceedingly difficult and disturbingly violent (Wise 2012). Certainly, the proliferation of white fears about immigrants and Islam demonstrates "an anxiety about the sanctity and coherence of white hegemony and its underlying white racialized identity" (Martinot 2010: 141). However, in order to realize racial justice and an inclusive democracy, whiteness will not only have to be deconstructed and decentered, but also thoroughly delegitimized.

On the other hand, such deconstructions, decenterings, and delegitimizing cannot occur on some abstract or moral level. The political philosopher Sally J. Scholz, in her book *Political Solidarity* (2008), examines how members of a privileged group can come to "an active acknowledgement of the experience of the oppressed" (167), achieving in the process the beginning of an active solidarity. Scholz deconstructs how privileged white identity can be overcome through stages of commitment. Those stages involve three steps: (1) renunciation of privilege, (2) understanding "the situation and experience of the oppressed," and (3) "participation in acts of resistance" (181). Analyzing the ambiguities and impediments of the "race traitor" position, Scholz makes clear that only though "mutually shared commitment to a cause" can political solidarity engender essential affective ties (184) and create transformative moments of solidarity.

Another perspective on renouncing white privilege and attaining solidarity can be found in Chip Smith's book, *The Cost of Privilege: Taking on White Supremacy and Racism* (2007). Announcing at the start of the book that "the system of (white) racial preferences is the main barrier to forming a broad movement that can fundamentally transform U.S. society" (6), the author follows the work of DuBois and Roediger in highlighting how a white blind spot led to "missed opportunities" for the labor movement, in particular. However, eschewing the "individualistic moralism" (148) of the race traitor position, Smith turns to a Marxist analysis of how the "fog of white consciousness ... is all around us" (312). In some sense, Smith's reading of political struggles and the betrayal of solidarity, especially within the labor movement, goes beyond the critique of the "psychological wages of whiteness" found in DuBois and Roediger. If at times mired in sloganistic references to a class-conscious vanguard, the author deserves much credit for his impressive marshalling of current and historical examples of why political solidarity failed and how it still can be realized.

Contesting the history and present reality of white identity politics will certainly require the understanding of its constructions and the active commitment to its deconstructions. Beyond such deconstructions lay the more difficult tasks of achieving political solidarity that crosses the deep racial divide that has marred such efforts at solidarity in the past. In confronting both the recent and long racist past, we must probe not only how white supremacy and white identity politics mobilizes racial resentments, but also the ways, as suggested by Scholz and Smith, to achieve an authentic multi-racial solidarity. As noted by Michael Bray, "we need to tell more, not less, coherent stories about racial history than the right, which means we need to openly confront its racist character and imagine not what keeps us from confronting it but what might allow us to work through it" (Bray 2017). And working through it means understanding its constructions and embracing its deconstructions.

CHAPTER 7

Challenging Weaponized Whiteness: Black Lives Matter

Weaponized whiteness has deep roots in institutionalized racism and its contemporary resonances, especially in the repressive apparatus of the racial state.[1] As demonstrated in the previous chapters, the terrors promulgated by white identity politics have been mitigated, to some extent, as a consequence of the historical struggles by African Americans and their white allies. On the other hand, white identity politics are still very evident in the ways in which policing and the criminal justice system have deliberately targeted communities of color. Whether in the passage of racially coded laws to punitive sentencing for minor offenses to everyday harassment and, finally and tragically, to the murder, in particular, of African-American youth, there remains the remnants of white supremacist oppression. "It is no exaggeration," writes the black scholar and activist, Keenga-Yamahtta Taylor, "to say that the men and women in blue patrolling the streets of the United States have been given a license to kill – and demonstrated a consistent propensity to use it. More often than not, police violence, including murder and attempted murder, is directed at African Americans" (Taylor 2016: 2).[2]

In response to some of the most outrageous murders of unarmed black youth around the county, especially since 2009, a national movement emerged out of all of the local protests. Rallying around the slogan of "Black Lives Matter," the focus initially may have been to highlight the continuing racial injustice perpetrated by the police against African Americans. However, over time that focus shifted to underscore the systemic oppression that inhibited the lives of communities of color through racist victimization. By embracing a new

---

1 This chapter is a revised and expanded version of my article, "Black Lives Matter: Constructing a New Civil Rights and Black Freedom Movement," *New Politics* (Summer 2015): 80–85.
2 Taylor cites (131) a ProPublica study on the disparity of police killings of black and white youth from 2010–2012, noting blacks were twenty-one times more likely to be killed than whites of the ages of fifteen to nineteen. Also, on the targeting of African Americans by the police, see McKesson 2018: 52–67. Moreover, according to an exhaustive survey of "ten thousand fatal police shootings by on-duty police officers between 2004 and 2014, just fifty-four officers had been charged with a crime – and just a handful of those cases were officers convicted" (Lowery 2016: 46).

freedom struggle against these systems of racial oppression, the Black Lives Matter movement created the context to contest racial injustices and the rule of white identity politics in all its myriad forms (Lowery 2016). Challenging the "connections between whiteness and citizenship" (Olson 2004: xxiii), this new African-American freedom struggle may also advance a more inclusive and just democracy (Lebron 2017).

In the articulations of the goals and objectives of the Black Lives Matter movement, one can discern another moment in the long black freedom struggle. Behind this slogan is a proliferation of new organizations and networks reflective of engaged millennial activists of color. These organizations and networks have utilized social media to mobilize large numbers of young people, primarily in protest against police killings. While such social media facilitate quick, intense, and extensive protests, these mobilizations, not unlike the Occupy demonstrations, are often, especially because of social media, transitory events (Demby 2014). Nonetheless, these organizations and networks are committed to eradicating racial injustices around a wide variety of issues. As Darsheel Kaur, a community organizer with the Ohio Student Association, contends: "It's more than just police brutality. It's about systems in place that continue to devalue the lives of black and brown people in different aspects including the prison industrial complex, economic and food systems, the housing market, voting rights. The energy that came together as this movement is a collective energy that has been building up through frustration about these many issues" (quoted in Chatelin 2015).

On the other hand, the most visible protests that galvanized this potentially new black freedom movement can be traced to a number of incidents of police and vigilante murders of young African Americans. Some view the killing of nineteen-year-old Oscar Grant in Oakland, California by a transit cop on January 1, 2009 as a signal event. As Grant lay pinned on the ground, this white cop deliberately shot him in the back. Caught on cell phones and quickly going viral, the angry and militant demonstrations that followed also became a national story. While the BART officer was indicted and found guilty of involuntary manslaughter, his lawyer convinced a jury containing no African Americans that the cop had mistakenly pulled out his gun instead of a taser. After serving only twenty months, the BART officer was released. (The story of Oscar Grant was later made into a brilliant and gripping film, *Fruitvale Station*.)

More of a catalyst to this national network was the murder of seventeen-year-old Trayvon Martin by George Zimmerman. (Zimmerman was eventually acquitted of manslaughter charges by relying on the notoriously racist "Stand Your Ground" laws.) As noted by Dante Barry, a digital organizer with the Center for Media Justice and Director of *Million Hoodies Movement for Justice*: "Our organization, *Million Hoodies*, was founded in large part due to the failure of the media to adequately report on the murder of Trayvon Martin in 2012. It took a full month before it became national news. Local media didn't want to report it, and context around the details concerning Trayvon's death weren't highlighted. *Million Hoodies* used social media to mobilize, amplify, and empower folks to take action" (Chatelain 2015). Given the eventual media prominence that Trayvon Martin's murder attained, even President Obama felt compelled to express sorrow about Martin's death without fully condemning the racism inherent in "Stand Your Ground" laws.

Another organization established in the immediate aftermath of the acquittal of George Zimmerman was *#BlackLivesMatter*. According to Alicia Garza, a Bay Area queer activist of color and Special Projects Director for the National Domestic Workers Alliance: "*BlackLivesMatter* is a unique contribution that goes beyond extrajudicial killings of Black People by police and vigilantes. It goes beyond the narrow nationalism that can be prevalent within some Black communities, which merely call on Black people to love Black, live Black, and buy Black, keeping straight cis Black men in the front of the movement while our sisters, queer and trans and disabled folk take up roles in the background or not at all" (Garza 2014). In its inclusive organizational approach, *#BlackLivesMatter* attempts to transcend the class and sexual barriers that often plagued prior black freedom movements. Indeed, Garza's vision of the transformative role that her organization wants to attain is profoundly revolutionary. "When we are able to end hyper-criminalization and sexualization of Black people and end the poverty, control, and surveillance of Black people, every single person in this world has a better shot at getting and staying free" (Garza 2014).

Garza, along with the other young organizers of color, recognizes that the movement they are trying to build is one that can learn from the past social movements while adopting new strategies that conform to current-day insights, especially those which emphasize intersectionality, or the interpenetration of race, gender, and class. Such a "radical politics of intersectionality insists not only that marginalized sectors of oppressed communities be included in any political calculus for liberation but that their suffering, interests, and aspirations be at the very center of any movement concerned with social transformation" (Ransby 2018). As noted by one of the leaders of Black Lives Matter, Darsheel Kaur, "intersectional organizing means creating spaces where we can bring all of our identities into the space" (Chatelain 2015). In the process of coalescing all of these counter-hegemonic identities, that intersectional space embodies an implicit rejection of the hegemonic order of white identity politics.

In addition, the organizational focus of Black Lives Matter also entails an emphasis on the kind of participatory democracy and group-centered leadership represented by the Student Nonviolent Organizing Committee (SNCC) during its heyday in the 1960s (Hogan 2007). Certainly, one of the formative influences on these new millennial generation organizations and their group-centered leadership was Ella Baker, a key mentor to SNCC. A former NAACP and SCLC organizer, Baker helped establish SNCC in 1960 in the aftermath of the waves of sit-ins that mobilized mostly African-American students in the South. Having worked for SCLC with its hierarchical and male dominated organization, Baker wanted to break "with the largely middle class male centered leadership of existing civil rights organizations, in order to strip away the class based and gender based notion of who should and could give leadership to the movement and black community" (Ransby 2003: 259).

Just as SNCC often came into conflict with the older generation of civil rights leaders and organizations, so some of the millennials of the new movement have confronted elements of the establishment civil rights groups. During Rev. Al Sharpton's National Action Network's march in Washington, DC, on December 13, 2014 to protest the lack of prosecutions of police killings of black youth, several organizers from Ferguson, angry at their exclusion and the exclusion of other young people from speaking, charged the stage. When they tried to speak, the microphones were cut off even as others in the crowd held signs saying: "We, the youth, did not elect Al Sharpton our Spokesperson." Other Ferguson organizers who didn't attend the march also took umbrage at Sharpton's exclusionary generational and class orientation (Taylor 2016: 170–173). "It was people like me who came out to march in Ferguson," asserted Tory Russell, organizer of the St. Louis area group *Hands Up United*. "I didn't see no suits, I didn't see no NAACP or National Action Network. It was people like me – poor black people – out there" (Demby 2014). Immediately after the DC demonstration, those Ferguson activists issued a declaration that spoke not only to their exclusion from the stage but also the broader point concerning the make-up and organizational focus: "This is a movement of and for ALL Black lives – women, men, transgender, and queer. We are made up of both youth AND elders aligned through the possibilities of new tactics and fresh strategies to offer our movement.... We do not cast any one of ours to the side in order to gain proximity to perceived power" (Taylor 2016: 172–173).

Obviously, those in power did try to seek ways to co-opt the movement. Just as President Kennedy tried to cool down the young activists of SNCC during the Freedom Rides of 1961 by meeting with a few SNCC activists, so President Obama gathered a group of the post-Ferguson activists at the White House in December 2014 (McKesson 2018: 121–126). According to Ashley Yates of *Millennial Activists United*, Obama seemed genuinely concerned about the issues raised at the meeting. On the other hand, as Yates noted, other Administration officials, "seemed like they were trying to quell the streets," even as they touted some reformist measures, like funding body cameras for police departments. Yet, Yates, recognizing the efficacy of their own protests, from die-ins to targeted civil disobedience, as well as the historical connections with the past civil rights movement, concluded: "The day we met with the president was December 1 – it was the 59th anniversary of Rosa Parks not getting up from her seat. We definitely realize that we're standing on the shoulders of the people who came before us" (Demby 2014).

But will the die-ins and other protest activities of the new black freedom struggle have the efficacy of the older movement? Do the new movement centers of the virtual world from *#BlackLivesMatter* to *MillionHoodiesMovement* have the same staying power as those Southern movement centers from the long civil rights movement, such as the Highland Folk School in Tennessee or Tougaloo College in Mississippi? If the new movement, as Dante Barry argues, "is about transforming power structures" (Chatelain 2015), what are the strategic levers they will use to operationalize that transformation? Moreover, will this new freedom movement finally be able to bury the ghosts of past white supremacy even as it contests new repressive policies emanating from the Trump White House?

Perhaps it is enough that these young activists of color have cast a brilliant light on the racial inequities of the criminal justice system. Hence, from Charles Blow's perspective: "In the same way that Occupy Wall Street forever elevated that concept of income inequality, the Black Lives Matter protesters have elevated the idea of inequity in policing as it relates to minority communities" (Blow 2015). On the other hand, the goals of this new movement, like those of Occupy, which seem so inchoate, are so far-reaching and multifaceted that a single issue, like racist police brutality, is too narrow a focus, albeit a compelling and immediate one. Indeed, it may be that a more sweeping focus on what critics like Michelle Alexander, Heather Thompson, and Marie Gottschalk, among others, call the "carceral state" is essential to the advocacy of transformative politics. As a system of punitive white power that incarcerates millions of people of color and the poor, marginalizing them, their families and communities, the carceral state results in what Marie Gottschalk refers to as "civil death" (Gottschalk 2014). Hence, the absolute need for restorative justice for people of color, especially those in the African-American community who have been disproportionately punished by the carceral state.

While police brutality has not been limited to the African-American community, it remains as a visible thread of deeply woven structures of ongoing racial injustices. As made very clear in the Department of Justice report on Ferguson policing and the court system, African Americans in that community were singled-out for a wide variety of punitive policies from attacks by police and police dogs to endless and expensive court citations. The DOJ report cites instance after instance of the violation by the criminal justice system of First, Fourth, and Fourteenth Amendment rights of the black citizens of Ferguson, reflective of clear patterns of racial bias.

While the DOJ report on Ferguson provides ammunition to the arguments for a more expansive civil rights agenda, it also underscores the fact that without massive demonstrations following the murder of Michael Brown and the failure to indict Darren Wilson such a report may not have even been issued, especially in light of so many other examples of lethal police action against African Americans and Latinos. Given the report's focus on the denial of Constitutional protections for the African-American citizens of Ferguson, it is instructive that the DOJ never bothered to investigate or condemn the millions of blacks and Latinos whose rights, especially the Fourth Amendment protection against unwarranted searches, were violated by the "stop-and-frisk" policies in New York City (Singh 2017: 70). Although struck down in court and abandoned by Mayor DeBlasio, the erratic role of the federal government and the Obama administration in dealing with racial justice issues highlights the importance of the Black Lives Matter movement.

Ferguson certainly sparked outrage within and outside the black community, inciting agitated responses not only in Missouri but elsewhere in the United States. As Robin Kelley has argued regarding these movements led by African-American organizers in Ferguson and around the country: "They remind us not only that Black lives matter – that should be self-evident – but that resistance matters. It matters because we are still grappling with the consequences of settler colonialism, racial capitalism, and patriarchy.... The young people of Ferguson continue to struggle with ferocity, not just to get justice for Mike Brown or to end police misconduct but to dismantle racism once and for all" (Kelley 2014). Hence, the agenda of Ferguson activists and Black Lives Matter goes beyond remedying the gaps in civil rights and civil liberties protections for African Americans (Taylor 2016: 153–170).

It is with the understanding of the necessity for such a black-led movement now to address the whole complex of institutional racism that Alicia Garza connects this movement to the black freedom and liberation movements of the past. "It is appropriate and necessary to have strategy and action centered around Blackness," Garza contends, "without other non-Black communities of color, or White folks for that matter, needing to find a place and a way to center themselves within it. It is appropriate and necessary for us to acknowledge the critical role that Black lives and struggles for Black liberation in inspiring and anchoring, through practice and theory, social movements for the liberation of all people. The women's movement, the Chicano liberation movement, queer movements, and many more have adopted strategies, tactics, and theory of the Black liberation movement. And if we are committed to a world where all lives matter, we are called to support the very movement that inspired and activated so many more. That means supporting and acknowledging Black lives" (Garza 2014).

Foregrounding the significance of Black lives in this historical moment, especially in challenging weaponized whiteness, still faces obvious difficulties and resistance. Among those resisting the slogan of "Black Lives Matter" are those whites who counter that "All Lives Matter," assuming that African Americans, in a spurious post-racial America, are no longer in need of specifically targeted policies which confront the persistence of racial injustices. As pointed out by George Yancy and Judith Butler, those who assert "All Lives Matter" "misunderstand the problem, but not because their message is untrue. It is true that all lives matter, but it is equally true that not all lives are understood to matter which is precisely why it is important to name the lives that have not mattered, and are struggling to matter in a way they deserve" (Yancy and Butler 2015). Only through calling out why black lives have not mattered in equal measure to whites can the possibility emerge of equal justice for all.

Another major impediment for the realization of equal justice for all that these young activists in Black Lives Matter confront is the embedded role of neo-liberalism in the economic and political policies of the state. Whereas the 1960s civil rights movement achieved its political victories in an era of an expanding welfare state and democratic rights, that state and those rights have been massively eroded by neo-liberalism and its penchant for privatization and corporate, rather than government, solutions. Moreover, postracial and colorblind ideologies have aided "dismantling the state's capacity to challenge discrimination" (Taylor 2016: 5). Added to this are the attacks on the public sector and their unions that have been sites for the advancement, in particular, of African Americans and women. Furthermore, as noted by those critics of the carceral state, it was not a coincidence that this state really emerges with a vengeance in the 1970s as a way to punish those radical challenges by blacks and others to the dominant power structure. Just as neo-liberalism gained ascendancy in the 1980s, so the carceral state further embedded its insidious punitive policies.

Certainly, seeking fundamental racial justice in this era requires both a new civil rights agenda and black freedom movement. On the other hand, it may be, as Malcolm X argued in the 1960s, demanding civil rights may be too constraining when the larger issue of needing fundamental human rights of both the economic and political kind seems even more necessary now. That necessity reflects a late stage of capitalism in the United States that may be consigning the majority of African Americans to a permanent marginalization, treating them no longer as viable producers or consumers, but rather as "surplus humanity" (Davis 2006: 174–198). The insistence, then, of "Black Lives Matter" becomes compelling not only as a necessary transformative social movement but also as an essential struggle for survival, a survival that is only meaningful if it is rooted in freedom and liberation. "Black liberation," notes Keenga-Yamahtta Talor, "implies a world where Black people can live in peace, without the constant threat of the social, economic, and political woes of a society that places almost no value on the vast majority of Black lives" (Taylor 2016: 194).

It was that insistence on "Freedom Now" that the civil rights movement of the 1960s drove its demands into the national conscience and agenda, albeit in the midst of myriad contradictions. Still one of the most profound discussions of the contradictions of achieving freedom can be found in James Baldwin's masterful essay, *The Fire Next Time*. Written during the civil rights movement with its critical challenge to white supremacy, Baldwin ruminates on the national myths that sustain not only white supremacy but also an illusory sense of innocence among the white citizenry of the country, an innocence still embraced by large segments of the white community. Baldwin, however, believes, along with Sam Cooke, that a "change is gonna come." For Baldwin, the change we seek is not a "change ... on the surface but in the depths." That change, nonetheless, "becomes impossible if one supposes things to be constant that are not" (Baldwin 1963).

During the arduous and lengthy struggle for civil rights in that time, the hard work of overcoming racial oppression in the economic, political, and personal spheres required many sacrifices while encountering numerous setbacks. An example of those minor setbacks came in the form of the acquittal by an Oxford, Mississippi federal jury in December 1963 of five defendants responsible for jailhouse beatings of civil rights activists. One of those activists, Lawrence Guyot, denounced the fraudulent verdict. Ella Baker, the inspiring godmother of numerous civil rights organizations, counseled Guyot to "look beyond this foolishness. Don't let it stop you" (quoted in Branch 1999: 193).

Whether the new black freedom movement of Black Lives Matter can "look beyond the foolishness" of the present era with its relentless racial injustices and engage in a campaign of continual resistance is open to question. However, it is a testament to the courage and tenacity on the young activists that they have awakened their fellow citizens to the need to address long-standing grievances around the criminal justice system with its perpetuation of racial profiling and biases. To carry the struggle forward will require the sort of persistence that Ella Baker and so many others in the older civil rights and black freedom movement embodied.

On the other hand, it will also require whites, especially those in the white working class, to reject white identity politics in favor of solidarity against the class system of oppression that has historically exploited both black and white workers, albeit with certain advantages made available to whites. However, as those advantages disappear in a time of increasing capitalist sponsored state austerity, there are openings for the recognition that whiteness is no longer the refuge it might have once been. And solidarity of the kind that existed in the past and has gained traction in the present may provide not just a deconstruction of white identity politics but also an affirmation of the power of a more authentic and inclusive solidarity (Taylor 2016: 209–216; Roediger 2017: 157–188).

Conclusion

One of the constants running throughout the prior seven chapters and the variety of subject matter covered therein is the impact of socio-historical change on both the constructions and deconstructions of white identity politics. As material conditions have changed, the enactment of white identity politics, under an institutional and ideological racialized system of domination and advantage known as white supremacy, has undergone certain transformations. Thus, the virulent strain of legal and constitutional white supremacy in the early republic condemned Native Americans and African Americans to a deadly regime of exploitation and even, especially in the case of the Indian Wars of the nineteenth century, extermination. While the Thirteenth, Fourteenth, and Fifteenth amendments to the Constitution ended slavery and granted citizenship rights to African Americans, the imposition of Jim Crow segregation, not only in the South, established barriers to freedom and dignity that would require both legal and political challenges throughout the 20th century. The defeat of *de jure* segregation, however, did not guarantee equality before the law, much less a recognition that racialized others, black, red, brown, and yellow, would be afforded fundamental justice. Hence, the struggles discussed in the second part of this book examined contesting those conditions that still impeded freedom and justice.

In the midst of these changes, however, certain continuities persist and certain patterns recur. Among these, in particular, are myths that flow specifically from the dominant "racial frame" (Feagin 2009) and inform how matters, such as national identity, immigration, and the gun culture are rendered through white identity politics. James Baldwin's insightful delineation of these myths remains a crucial component of why they continue to resonate. Writing over fifty-five years ago, Baldwin identified these "collection of myths to which white Americans cling: that their ancestors were all freedom-loving heroes, that they were born in the greatest country the world has ever seen, or that Americans are invincible in battle and wise in peace, that Americans have always dealt honorably with Mexicans and Indians and all other neighbors and inferiors" (Baldwin 1963: 101).[1] By denial and "collective forgetting" (Glaude Jr. 2016: 46–50) these myths retain their racialized renderings even as such racial framing is especially invisible to those who embrace white identity politics. In

---

1 The question of whether the United States is "invincible" in battle has been punctured by any number of critics, most forcibly by military and diplomatic historian, Andrew Bacevich. See Bacevich 2008.

refusing to recognize the white supremacist violence inherent in the foundational structures of the American polity, historical responsibility for their perpetuation in different forms can be overlooked and attributed to "aberrations from America's exceptionalist path" (Behdad 2005: 6).

Beyond affirming historical responsibility for past egregious aggressions, the continuing racial injustices and inequalities "at the heart of this nation" cannot also be seen as mere "aberrations" (Glaude Jr. 2016: 8–9). Indeed, "when we forget about the horrors of lynching, lose sight of how African Americans were locked into a dual labor market because of explicit racism, or ignore how we exported our racism around the world – we free ourselves from any sense of accountability" (Glaude Jr. 2016: 188). It is the desire for historical understanding and accountability that has animated my investigation of the constructions and deconstructions of white identity politics. Therefore, before turning to the ways in which we whites "can challenge our own racial reality" (DiAngelo 2018: 148) and eliminate the pernicious effects of white identity politics, I want to re-emphasize how our nation's "racial nationalism" (Singh 2017) has persisted, how immigration continues to be defined by the tropes of whiteness and white supremacy (Jacobson 1999), and how the gun culture "entitled (and continues to entitle) white nationalism, racialized dominance, and social control through violence" (Dunbar-Ortiz 2018: 25).

The persistence of racial nationalism is particularly evident in the ways that the United States built and maintained an empire, whether by direct imperial aggression or through so-called indirect and soft imperialism. "U.S. empire-building," as compellingly described by Zillah Eisenstein, "projects a racialized and masculinist form" (Eisenstein 2004: 1). Whether by the advocates for "manifest destiny" in 19th century or Theodore Roosevelt's "strenuous imperialism" (Slotkin 1993: 51–62) at the beginning of twentieth century or Chris Kyle's "reluctant" warrior in the twenty-first century, the projection of power by the United States is replete with racist imagery and masculinist militarism. In turn, the cultural conditioning about the "exceptional" nature of our national identity and its global projections "occludes both the fact of U.S. power and the effects of its exercise" (Young 202: 279). In fact, the occlusion of the effects of that racialized power provides an ideological covering for a warfare state that has been responsible and continues to be responsible for "succoring vicious regimes, bombing, shelling, contaminating, torturing and killing hundreds of thousands of innocents, and destroying enemy others" (Hixon 2008: 14).

That ideological covering is, in fact, reinforced by media representations of racialized "others" who appear to threaten the "security" of the American citizenry, whether in distant conflicts, at the borders, or even in domestic uprisings. As noted in one of the most incisive studies of these media representations in

American popular culture, the "more uncritical the kind of patriotism that rules popular imagination and public discourse, the more alone, insulated, special and different the American ethos makes people feel. The more it holds up a distorting mirror to itself and the rest of the world, the more incomprehensible the rest of the world becomes, full of inarticulate, hostile elements" (Sardar and Davies 2002: 140). This distorting mirror operates through network television programs and news disinformation that represent the rest of the world through jingoistic images and simplistic and blinkered media discourse (Sardar and Davies 2002: 15–38).

In addition, the construction of a national identity and with it the production of patriotism, is reinforced by militarized spectacles, from Air Force jet flights over stadium sporting contests to showcasing military "heroes" at any and all public events. The effect of such militarized spectacles diminishes the cognitive capacity of citizens of the United States to understand fully the imperial ventures carried out in their name while heightening the sense of a hostile world inhabited by racialized others. It is not surprising, therefore, that the Pentagon paid the owners of the National Football League (NFL), all wealthy white men, to have their teams, who are collectively about seventy percent black, stand for the National Anthem during pre-game ceremonies. When Colin Kaepernick and other African-American football players used this time to protest the ongoing murders of innocent youth of color by police, the outcry, stoked by the racist demagoguery of President Trump, was that this action and these players were "unpatriotic." The majority of NFL fans, eighty-three percent of whom are whites, appeared to share Trump's rabid denunciations of kneeling African-American football players, demonstrating, in the process, what Robin DiAngelo calls "white solidarity" (DiAngelo 2018: 57).

Such expressions of "white solidarity" are also evident when gauging the attitudes of whites towards policing people of color. When polled about whether African Americans are greater targets of police harassment and violence, the racial divide was glaring, especially by responses of whites living in more homogeneous racial enclaves. From their blinkered racial perspective, blacks were not the victims of excessive police harassment and intimidation (NORC Center for Public Affairs 2015).[2] Overlooking or denying ongoing racial injustice meted out by the state underscores how white identity politics operates as an integral component of national identity. Once again, national identity, reinforced by "militarized police ... conjoins police and military power as necessary to manage capitalism's unevenness across borders and within populations and

---

2 According to a wide variety of surveys cited in Feagin 2014, "a majority of whites do not have much empathy for the suffering of those who face racial discrimination" (228).

re-animates racial despotism as a vector of community protection" (Singh 2017: xiv-xv).

It is at the border, in particular, that a racialized ideology and policy obtain, reaching back towards a trope of savages at the gates. As argued by Matthew Frye Jacobson in his study of the impact of race on immigration, "That the 'savage' resides at the borders of our imagined national community has textured American political life from the Indian Wars to the Gulf War: debates over actual policies regarding actual 'savages' work a kind of homogenizing magic on the homefront ... (that) casts the racial character of citizenship in stark relief" (Jacobson 1999: 204). Further noting that "the idea of citizenship had become thoroughly entwined with 'whiteness'" (Jacobson 1999: 25), he and other critics of the racializing of border policy demonstrate how white identity politics has been deeply embedded in the rendering of how immigrants become citizens. Even "the myth of asylum ... has obscured the role of xenophobia in the construction of national identity.... So-called 'benevolence toward immigrants' actually obscures both the political desire to appropriate new territories and the economic need for labor" (Behdad 2005: 116). In turn, a manufactured "crisis of immigration," beyond the xenophobic rhetoric and policies of the Trump Administration, provides the state with its militarized disciplinary power along the border and within a national identity of whiteness (Behdad 2005: 142).

Going beyond this white national identity requires an engagement with what the political philosopher Wendy Farley calls the "eros" of empathy. For Farley, the "obliviousness of another's personhood" is part of the "illusions" or "ideologies that inform individuals, communities, and nations" (Farley 1996: 17–25). Noting that the "reality of other persons is effectively concealed by a dense cloud of lies, misleading images, and intonations of moral grandeur," Farley designates "eros" or the empathy of the heart, as a "nondominating proximity (that) permits an understanding of others to emerge that would otherwise be impossible" (Farley 1996: 30 and 69).[3] Even with an understanding of the non-white other, there are illusions of racial reconciliation that still may diminish "a more fundamental concern about racial justice" while implicating all of us as "complicit in racial injustice" (Glaude Jr. 2016: 184). By calling attention to "white advantage ... assumptions and stereotypes that block empathy" (Glaude Jr. 2016: 69) may allow empathy to emerge. Therefore, without "an analysis of racial privilege, the politics of inclusion cannot fall to grasp the full

---

3   The psychiatrist and sociologist, Jonathan Metzl, raises an important objection to relying on inducing empathy – "my analysis leads not to a call for individual empathy ... but for greater awareness of the health implications of particular policies, and for better policies and structural change" (Metzl 2019: 293).

scope of whiteness, which is not so much a problem of difference or exclusion as it is a problem of alliance" (Olson 2004: 66).

While several prior chapters have explored white alliances with black freedom movements, from civil rights to Black Lives Matter, I want to turn to one of the most recent social movements that is cognizant of an alliance between self-conscious whites and blacks. This is the campaign against gun violence, initiated by student survivors of the massacre at Marjory Stoneman Douglas High School in Parkland Florida in the immediate aftermath of the tragedy (Cullen 2019). These students, sharing the desire for forcing both legal and lifestyle changes, not unlike the students of the sixties, were, nonetheless, able to use the new instruments of social media, having been used previously by BLM, for mobilization and organizing purposes. Like those in the civil rights movement, these students were literally under the gun as a consequence of their constant post-Columbine reminder through school safety drills that their lives were on the line. Hence, they and their supporters around the country organized the "March for Our Lives" on March 24, 2018.

Prior to this march, students around the country had organized walkouts to highlight the issue of gun violence, not unlike the younger students who walked out in 1963 from their high schools, middle schools, and even elementary schools in Birmingham, Alabama and Jackson, Mississippi. The difference, of course, was that whereas over 2000 students were arrested in Birmingham, there were hardly any arrests at either the walkouts or the demonstrations on March 24. The estimates of the main event in Washington DC ranged from 200,000 to 800,000. Parkland students like Cameron Kasky, David Hogg, and the amazing Emma Gonzalez spoke movingly as well as students of color from high schools in Chicago and LA, a few of whom had lost siblings and friends to gun violence. All were articulate, even Naomi Wadler, an elementary school student from Alexandria, Virginia. Their stories and their courage, reinforced by social media and lauded by the corporate media (with the exception of Fox News) compelled state and local authorities to pass new legislation, including by the Florida legislature, one of the most intransigent and NRA-loving state governments. Indeed, according to the Giffords Law Center to Prevent Gun Violence, since Parkland and as of mid-July 2018, 26 states have since passed 55 new gun-control laws.

Although the focus shifted to the fall 2016 elections and getting students registered (not unlike the more dangerous voter registration campaigns in Mississippi during Freedom Summer), it is not clear where this movement will go now. Certainly, the kind of multicultural/multiethnic diversity exhibited by these students is now second nature to them unlike the difficult efforts in the 1960s to form and keep such multi-racial alliances. Nonetheless, white activists like David Hogg realize that in building the larger #NeverAgain movement it is "important ... (that we) recognize this (racial) inequality and work to solve it ... First, though, we much call it out and we must it call it for what it is, and that's racial bias towards us and many other people that's not only in the media, but that's in our society, too, as a whole" (Hogg quoted in Zornick 2018: 14). However, as one commentator on this movement pointed out while "a new intersectional gun-control movement can expand the political base agitating for change, ...it might also find itself in a trap in which gun violence can't be solved until racism and inequality are, too" (Zornick 2018: 15).[4]

On the other hand, a radical reckoning with gun violence must, of necessity, also confront the ways in which gun culture in the United States represents a literal enactment of weaponized whiteness. The fetishizing of the Second Amendment continues to occlude the long history of its targeting of racialized others whether in the use of the military to exterminate Indigenous peoples or through the deployment of white militias, vigilantes, and police to oversee the enslavement of African Americans and to enforce the oppressive regimes of institutionalized racism (Briggs 2017; Dunbar-Ortiz 2018). As a weapon of white "redemptive" violence, gun culture is deeply entrenched in the expansion of the frontier (Slotkin 1985 and 1993) and the fashioning of American character (Langman and Lundskow 2016: 157–193). Indeed, the "privileges of white gun ownership meant that firearms emerged as particular weapons of white male authority" (Metzl 2019: 63). It is not surprising, therefore, that given that history and the recent erosion of the authority and status of white men that there has been a proliferation of new legislation promoting permissive policies of gun ownership (open-carry, permitless-carry, stand-your-ground laws) in states around the country, reinforcing the privileges of weaponized whiteness (Metzl 2019: 69–71).

Indeed, the passage of such laws reflects a desire on the part of many white men (with the ideological assistance of gun manufacturers and the NRA) to compensate for the presumed loss of privileges and the ramping up of imagined threats from racialized others. According to one reading of the interface between white men and guns, they believe that "guns give (them) strength, status, power, and respect – exactly what many white men feel they have been hemorrhaging ever since the 1960s" (Steinhorn 2014). Ironically, the very same permissive gun laws have resulted in a dramatic rise in suicide rates for white men by their own weapons. Not only has there been an increase in suicide

---

4 As racial justice activist, Tim Wise, exclaims "those of us who have chosen the pact of antiracist allyship, and who 'get it' in many ways, still make mistakes regularly, fall into old patterns and inadvertently collaborate with injustices we oppose" (2012: 13).

among white men in states where guns proliferate, but also from "2009 to 2015, non-Hispanic white men accounted for nearly 80 percent of all gun suicides in the United States, despite representing less than 35 percent of the total population" (Metzl 2019: 47). Moreover, when comparing states, like Missouri, where lax gun laws have been ratified recently, to Connecticut, where gun control laws have been tightened, especially in the aftermath of the Sandy Hook massacre, there is a stark difference in both suicide by guns among whites and gun violence in general (Metzl 2019: 97–109). In drawing his conclusions from such stark data, Jonathan Metzl argues that "privilege itself becomes a liability" with white men becoming the "biggest threats to themselves" (109).

Nonetheless, the persistence of weaponized whiteness through gun culture reinforces a racial framing that still massively disadvantages and harms people of color. That long history of the privileged position of white men vis-à-vis African Americans, in particular, has created a "double standard through which society coded white gun owners as 'protectors' and black gun owners as 'threats'" (Metzl 2019: 27). The institutionalization of weaponized whiteness through legislation and racial framing of social practices guarantees continued racial inequality and injustice. "This notion of armed supremacy ... helped white populations feel like they circumscribed and protected themselves, while at the same time enforcing and justifying all sorts of imbalances and segregations" (Metzl 2019: 77).

Weaponized whiteness and white identity politics will remain threats to the nation's well-being not only because of the persistence of structural racism, but also as a consequence of the social construction of whiteness. Robin DiAngelo, recognizing that "white identity is inherently racist" calls for being less white and breaking with "white silence and white solidarity, to stop privileging the comfort of white people over the pain of racism for people of color, to move past guilt and into action." She further insists "(u)ltimately, I strive for less white identity for my own liberation and sense of justice, not to save people of color" (DiAngelo 2018: 149–150).[5] Another perspective that resonates with DiAngelo's search for justice is that of a New Orleans white community and labor organizer who remonstrates that "the only way I can live in this racist and oppressive society is to feel like I'm part of a struggle to build a more just world" (quoted in Warren 2010: 87).

It should be evident from the history highlighted throughout this book that contending with white supremacy, white identity politics, and whiteness, itself, has involved moments of possibility for transcending that history as

---

5 For an excellent analysis of DiAngelo's book "as one-part jeremiad and one-part handbook," see Roediger 2018.

well as being weighed down by it. While racial justice activist Tim Wise observes, "we aren't to blame for history – either its horrors or the legacy it has left us. But we are responsible for how we bear that legacy and what we make of it in the present" (Wise 2012: 23). Embracing that responsibility also necessitates nurturing "an ethics of care for the ways we are implicated in producing others' suffering" (Ioanide 2015: 112). In turn, we must also take responsibility to act to reject white identity politics and the social construction of whiteness, especially when it has been and continues to be the cause of so much suffering to others. We have an opportunity, difficult though it may be, to create the kind of multiracial and inclusive society envisioned by the young students of Parkland and other racial justice activists in the past and in the present. Indeed, we may, as white citizens in authentic alliance with people of color, "pave the way for new possibilities in which (white) privilege would be inimical to democracy rather than a functional part of it" (Olson 2004: xxii).

Epilogue

As we have seen, the constructions of white identity politics over a long history have caused immense suffering for racialized others. In turn, efforts to deconstruct white supremacy, white identity politics, and whiteness itself have produced significant changes in each of those racial constructions. However, the pernicious persistence of class and racial constraints, under a capitalist regime, has created a zero-sum game, especially, but not exclusively, for workers of color. This "Epilogue," divided into two related sections, will consider how deindustrialization, as part of the logic of capital, promotes both structural dislocations that have profound racial implications and socio-psychological injuries that flow from such structural dislocations. While these physical and psychological displacements result in damage to all workers, historically it has been people of color who have had to deal with the most invidious components of these dislocations and the attendant infusion of white identity politics.[1]

It has long been a feature of racial capitalism in the United States that African Americans had to contend with structural disadvantages that shaped their employment opportunities and, often, their very survival.[2] Even when they achieved some economic stability in the industrial sector through unionization struggles, their jobs were at risk at times because of their level of militancy that opened up new employment opportunities. While the impact of deindustrialization has caused dislocation and economic hardship to many workers, regardless of racial/ethnic backgrounds, African Americans in certain industries and specific geographic regions have suffered serious setbacks. Given the dominant role of the auto industry and race in Detroit's economic, social, and political development, this first part of the "Epilogue" will situate the trajectory of deindustrialization in the second half of the twentieth century by examining the intersection of auto dislocation and its repercussions especially for Detroit's African-American workers.

The particular historical focus will be on key moments in two five-year periods (1948–1953 and 1978–1983) in the wave of auto deindustrialization in Detroit. In between those two periods was an insurrectionary interlude from

---

1 The first section appeared in a slightly different form in *Perspectives on Global Development and Technology* 15 (2016) under the title of "Auto De(con)struction: The Spatial Fixes and Racial Repercussions of Detroit's Deindustrialization."
2 For a concise exposition of the meaning and relevance of racial capitalism, see Melamed 2015.

1968–1973 that was not only a high-water mark of worker militancy, particularly among black workers, and wildcat strikes in the auto industry in Detroit and the U.S., but also in other auto manufacturing sites around the globe. In each of these periods, specific labor and political conflicts informed the contours of deindustrialization of Detroit. Thus, the macro economic climate, corporate decisions, racial politics, and labor resistance in the auto industry shaped that deindustrialization.

In order to identify the underlying economic imperatives driving capital and the auto industry, one can turn to the work of David Harvey and Beverly Silver. According to David Harvey, "one of the central contradictions of capital (is)that it has to build a fixed space ... necessary for its own functioning at a certain point in its history only to have to destroy that space ... at a later point in order to make way for a new 'spatial fix'" (2001). As Harvey elaborates further on the "spatial fix" in his essays in *Spaces of Capital,* such spatial fixes often overlap with and interpenetrate technological and administrative fixes (2001). The long trajectory of deindustrialization, then, is embedded in the spatial, technological, and administrative fixes of capital. However, within the global auto industry spatial fixes have not been a permanent solution to "the problems of profitability and labor control, (rather) relocation has only succeeded in geographically relocating the contradictions from one site of production to another" (Silver 2003: 64).

Turning to the United States in the twentieth century, the "process of deindustrialization – the closing, downsizing, and relocation of plants and sometimes whole industries – accelerated throughout (this century). Advances in communication and transportation, the transformation of industrial technology, the acceleration of regional and international economic competition, and the expansion of low-wage regions ... reshaped the geography of American industrial cities" (Sugrue 1996: 127). However, as Thomas Sugrue and others have argued, capital moves are also about control over workers and their level of resistance to those mechanisms of control (Cowie 1991; and Silver 2003). Hence, any inclusive and critical analysis of Detroit's deindustrialization must contend with the dialectics of capital controls and labor resistance.

In the aftermath of World War II through the early 1960s, Detroit was the pre-eminent auto-manufacturing site not only in the US, but also in the world. Nonetheless, during that same period, Detroit started hemorrhaging manufacturing jobs, losing a total of 134,000 of those jobs between 1947 and 1963 (Sugrue 1996: 126). Detroit's largest employer by 1960 was Chrysler. During the late 1950s Chrysler laid off thousands of workers and used speed-ups and overtime to cull their work force (Geschwender 1977: 40–41). Other employment dislocation for Detroiters came as a consequence of the inability of small auto firms, such as Nash, Hudson, Studebaker, and Packard, to match the capital expenditures by the Big Three for the construction of newer facilities and more automated equipment. Both General Motors and Ford spent billions of dollars on decentralizing their plants. Such decentralization, or spatial fixes, resulted in other auto related manufacturers cutting their workforces. Often such reductions or relocations to suburban or rural sites were enacted in order to reduce labor costs. According to Sugrue, "corporations made decisions about plant location and employment policy in a specific political, cultural, and institutional context – in the case of postwar Detroit in the aftermath of the rise of a powerful union movement and in the midst of bitter shop-floor struggles over work rules and worker control" (Sugrue 1995: 116).

Nowhere was this shop-floor struggle more intense and significant than at the massive Ford Rouge plant in Dearborn, Michigan. By the end of World War II and in the aftermath of the bitter fight over unionization at the Ford Rouge facility, there were 85,000 workers employed there with one-third of those workers African Americans who predominantly resided in Detroit. However, as a consequence of aggressive automation and decentralization, the Rouge workforce was reduced to 54,000 by 1954 and further still to 30,000 by 1960, much of that reduction coming in areas where blacks had made historic inroads (Sugrue 1995: 117–120).[3] In addition, African Americans had become integral to the large Progressive Caucus of the left-led Local 600 and their efforts to combat the use of speed-ups, overtime, and automation at the Ford Rouge plant. Not only did these efforts have to contend with the reactionary Cold War policies of the national government during the late 1940s and early 1950s, but also Local 600 had to fight against the Reuther Administration of the UAW (Culture 2004; Edsforth 1995: 155–179; Stepan-Norris and Zeitlin 2003). Indeed, when Local 600 initiated a demand for a 30 hour work week to stem the decentralization plans of the Ford Motor Co. at the Rouge, Reuther not only rejected it, even refusing to sign onto a lawsuit undertaken in 1951 by Local 600, but denounced such plans in Cold War terms as a "sabotage" of the US economy (Babson et al. 2010: 206–219; Sugrue 1996: 157–162).

The convergence of Cold War anti-communism with reactionary policies in the federal government and the UAW was framed by the passage of Taft-Hartley in 1947. With its provisions for signing loyalty oaths and undermining inter-union solidarity, Taft-Hartley became a convenient instrument for waging ideological war against communists in the UAW and seeking accords with

---

3 On the pre-WWII role of African Americans in Ford Motor Co., especially at the Rouge plant, see Bates 2012.

management that would cede control over worker's shop floor autonomy and initiatives (Lichtenstein 2002: 114–118). Nonetheless, workers at the Ford Rouge plant, especially when faced with speed-ups in plastics, the foundry, and motor building in 1950 and 1951, fought back with dozen of wildcat strikes and continued to press for challenging Ford's decentralization policies (Sugrue 1996: 157–158). When the House Un-American Activities Committee undertook hearings in 1952 in Detroit that singled out the left-wing leadership at Local 600, it provided the ideological excuse by the Reuther Administration to put the local under trusteeship. In the process, the UAW ceded further control to management prerogatives that reinforced this initial deindustrialization of Detroit (Sugrue 1996: 161–163; Stepan-Norris and Zeitlin 2003: 124–125; Babson et al. 2010: 206–223).

On the other hand, the UAW fought during this period to salvage the seniority system even for those being dislocated or relocated. Unfortunately for black autoworkers, who mostly had only secured their positions during the end of WWII and the immediate postwar era in precisely those unskilled jobs that faced automation, racial inequalities guaranteed three times the rate of unemployment of white autoworkers. Along with entrenched discriminatory patters, black autoworkers had to contend with devastating deindustrialization. Especially in the recession of the late 1950s, African Americans disproportionately lost jobs in Chrysler where they occupied a significant percentage of Chrysler's Detroit workforce (Sugrue 1996: 144 and 162; Geschwender 1977: 40–41).

In the 1960s as the auto industry once again began hiring, Chrysler opened its Detroit plant doors to younger black workers who were, nonetheless, slotted into some of the dirtiest and most dangerous jobs in its increasingly dilapidated factories. By the mid-1960s blacks compromised the majority in Chrysler's Detroit factories where they faced discrimination and speed-ups (Georgakas and Surkin 1998: 28–29; Thompson 2001: 58–59). Given the persistence of white supremacy at the managerial and supervisory levels in Chrysler operations, especially at Dodge Main, it was not surprising that this plant became the site of Black Power inspired insurgency. When a wildcat strike broke out on May 2, 1968, started by white women with the participation of other white workers, it quickly became a mobilization of angry young black workers, the core cadre being committed Marxists. It was that cadre in the immediate aftermath of the wildcat that initiated the Dodge Revolutionary Union Movement (DRUM), a movement that would resonate throughout the late 1960s and early 1970s in auto plants throughout the Detroit metro area and into other parts of the country (Georgakas and Surkin 1998; Geschwender 1977: 87–187; Lewis-Colman 2008: 90–117; Thompson 2001: 103–127).

DRUM not only fought against Chrysler management at Dodge Main and other Detroit plants, but also declared war against what it saw as a racist and intransigent UAW hierarchy. According to the DRUM constitution, "we must gear ourselves in the days ahead toward getting rid of the racist, tyrannical, and unrepresentative UAW." When DRUM began challenging the UAW white leadership at Dodge Main through union elections, the UAW, haunted by its anti-communist struggles of the past, struck back at DRUM and the black militancy that informed it and the other radical formations inside and outside the factories in the late 1960s and early 1970s. In an interview with the *Detroit News*, UAW official Emil Mazey opined: "black militants in Detroit's auto factories pose a greater peril to the UAW than the communist infiltration did in the 1930s" (Thompson 2001: 123). When the UAW could not contain the growing dissidence among not only black militants in the plants but also young white autoworkers, it resorted to outright repression, most evident at the 1973 Mack Stamping Plant wildcat where a force of nearly 2000 older UAW members prevented the continuance of the strike by massing in front of the plant and intimidating striking workers (Georgakas and Surkin 1998: 191–193; Thompson 2001: 199–203).

Although DRUM had managed to spin off other RUMs and give birth to the League of Revolutionary Black Workers, its "rhetoric, style, and racially exclusive and ill-planned tactics," according to Heather Thompson, "too often saw the RUM struggle as a means to fulfill the destiny of 'black manhood,' (which) severely weakened these organizations over time" (Thompson 2001: 168). On the other hand, what emerged from the RUMs and the League of Revolutionary Black Workers were "objective improvements in the areas of safety, working conditions, election of blacks to positions of authority in local unions (and) increases in numbers of black foreman" (Geshwender 1977: 1). Even as the militancy of this insurrectionary interlude of 1968–1973 was institutionalized in specific gains, in particular, for black autoworkers, Chrysler and the other U.S. auto manufacturers began moving operations to the semi-peripheral regions of the South. By the late 1970s, with increased global competition, auto corporations sought out even lower wage and less troublesome regions for outsourcing (Silver 2003: 48–49).

The second wave of deindustrialization from 1978–1983 took place in the context of a global movement toward neo-liberal policies that promoted privatization, deregulation and sweeping pressure on unions to grant concessions. These policies hit manufacturing and auto in Detroit especially hard, leading to further weakening of the UAW in particular. The estimations of job losses in auto and related industries in the Detroit metro area during this period was close to 90,000, resulting in more plant closures (Harrison and Bluestone 1990;

Trachte and Ross 1985). When Chrysler faced possible bankruptcy in 1979, federal intervention, premised on wage and benefit concessions by Chrysler workers, rescued the corporation. However, the rescue proved to be a Trojan horse for Chrysler employees. Dodge Main closed in early 1980, laying off over 3000 workers, and other Chrysler factories continued the shutdowns through 1983. Hence, not only did these concessions not stem further plant dislocation, but other auto manufacturers and major industrial employers demanded more wage cuts and control over their workforce, especially in the aftermath of Reagan's firing of the PATCO workers in 1981. Indeed, in the wake of the Chrysler concessions, GM used the threat of moving some of its facilities to Mexico to re-open negotiations in 1982 (Lichtenstein 2002: 225–234; Milkman 1997: 79–92; Trachte and Ross 1995: 208).

Both the UAW and the city of Detroit desperately sought to boost employment in auto even as additional Detroit plants were closing in this period. One move by GM, in particular, proved controversial even as it cemented the relationship between corporations, public officials, and trade union leadership. Seeking to stem the tide of plant closures in Detroit, the city administration, under Mayor Coleman Young, acceded to GM's request to take an extensive parcel of land on Detroit's East Side near to the shuttered Dodge Main plant. Through the use of eminent domain and tax abatements the Young administration, in lockstep with GM and the UAW, moved to relocate the residents of the area known as Poletown. As one of the attorneys for the Poletown residents declared: "GM has arbitrarily insisted on enough acreage to accommodate a plant designed for a flat open area ... To force this design on this neighborhood and this city establishes the 'government/business partnership' as a one-way deal" (Wylie 1990: 75). Indeed, GM's spatial and administrative fix in this instance also contained a technological fix with the utilization of robotics at the new Poletown plant, leading to a workforce that at its height was no more than 2/3 of what had been promised. In turn, that workforce became more an instrument of new company practices, such as quality and team circles, eroding in the process the power and even presence of the union. As one worker in the new Poletown facility noted: "The role of the union has become limited or irrelevant compared to the past in relations to everyday problems in the plant" (Wylie 1990: 210).

While the Poletown plant remained in operation, it did so with only about 1500 employed. With the recent announcement by General Motors of its corporate decision to close the Poletown plant, once again the city of Detroit will be littered with the detritus of deindustrialization. Since 2000 and up through 2015, Big Three employment shrank from 435,000 in 2000 to only 171,200, albeit with continuing transnational auto spatial fixes, especially, with Toyota and

Honda, in the rural Midwest and South, and transnational expansion in production and sales, especially in China. However, as reported in a *New York Times Magazine* story, "as a consequence of the economic crisis (of 2008), 20,000 black autoworkers were either laid off or took buyouts from the Big Three ... with a disproportionate number of those coming from the Detroit area" (Mahler 2009). Although the Obama Administration's bailout of Chrysler and GM raised the promise of new jobs, the institutionalization of the two-tiered wage system and increased automation suggests a divided workforce and a weakened union within a much more limited role for auto manufacturing in Detroit's future (Ryan and Campo 2013).

For some proponents of post-industrial radical alternatives to auto and industrial civilization itself, Detroit is ironically on the leading edge of a new and necessary transformation in how we live our lives as fully unalienated and ecologically minded human beings. In the opening scene of *American Revolutionary*, the documentary film about the life of Detroit radical activist, Grace Lee Boggs, she is walking outside the ruined hulk of the former Packard auto plant in Detroit. Her startling comment that she "feels sorry for those who are not in Detroit" reveals her perspective on what fifty years of deindustrialization has wrought and where Detroiters might have to go in the future for real solutions to the economic and social crisis in the city.

In her new book, *The Next American Revolution: Sustainable Activism for the Twenty First Century*, Boggs contends that we need "to begin imagining work that frees us from being the appendages to machines that we have become because of our dependence on jobs. We need to encourage the creation of work that not only produces goods and services but also develops our skills, protects our environment, and lifts our spirits" (2012: xx). Perhaps Boggs penetrating perspective on Detroit's deindustrialization can provide a fitting dialectical post-industrial postscript: "Detroit's deindustrialization, devastation, and depopulation turned the city into a wasteland, but it also created the space and place where there was not only the necessity but also the possibility of creating a city based not on expanding production but on new values of sustainability and community ... we had been granted an opportunity to begin a new chapter in the evolution of the human race, a chapter that global warming and corporate globalization had made increasingly necessary. In its dying, Detroit could also be the birthplace of a new city" (2012: 110). From this perspective, Detroit could also be a site for overcoming racial capitalism and any accompanying operation of white identity politics.

On the other hand, in an era of economic distress for many, especially those in the multi-racial working class, the dilemmas and challenges of deconstructing and defeating the invidious effects of white advantage and white identity politics are bewildered by the intricacies of class and racial dynamics. Given the long history of how race has managed to transform class injuries into racial resentments, especially among the white working class, the possibility of confronting structural racism, let alone enabling a multi-racial solidarity, seems almost insurmountable. On the other hand, resistance to an inherently unstable racial regime, especially by its victims, has provided "cognitive and moral resources" for alternative readings and renderings (Singh 2017: xi). Indeed, one of the main objectives of this book has been to reveal or unveil how white identity politics are constructed and deconstructed in order to provide an honest and necessary assessment of the past and present complications of a weaponized whiteness. It seems appropriate, therefore, to conclude the book with one of the more insightful recent representations of how race, class, and gender might still confound our ability to overcome whiteness and white identity politics.

Lynn Nottage's 2017 Pulitzer-Prize winning play, *Sweat*, brings to the stage the harsh realities and contradictions that have wreaked havoc on working class lives over decades of deindustrialization in what used to be the manufacturing heartland of America (Nottage 2017 – All further references will be to this text). Set in Reading, Pennsylvania in the early years of the twenty-first century, the nine characters created by Nottage, based on two and a half years of research in the town, reflect the tensions embedded in racial divisions deeply rooted in the American experience. In examining how these characters illuminate what Richard Sennett and Jonathan Cobb have referred to as "the hidden injuries of class," one may be able better to understand the racial and gender dynamics generated in this historic moment (Sennett and Cobb 1972).

Having won a previous Pulitzer for her off-Broadway 2009 play, *Ruined*, about the impact of the civil war in the Congo on women, the Brown and Yale educated Nottage, a Brooklyn born and raised African-American woman, was attracted to the dynamics of dislocation represented in the deindustrialized city of Reading, PA. With 41.3% of its residents living at poverty levels, placing it among the lead with cities more than 65,000, and having lost manufacturing jobs in companies such as Hershey, AT&T, Lucent Technologies and Dana Corp, the playwright moved to Reading to excavate the human wreckage caused by such deindustrialization (Mazelis 2016). With a commission from the Oregon Shakespeare Festival where it was premiered on July 29, 2015, Nottage told the *Los Angeles Times* that she discovered "people who felt helpless, who felt like the American dream that they so deeply invested in had been suddenly ripped away. I was sitting with these white men, and I thought, you sound like people of color in America" (quoted in Shulman 2017: 30). In some respects, her insight mirrors what Justin Gest, in his study of the white working class in deindustrialized Youngstown, calls "minoritization" by which "he means a perception of decline in their numbers, a dramatic loss in their status, and a feeling that other ethnic and racial groups are gaining social advantage at their expense" (Hahn 2017: 31; Gest 2017).

On the other hand, while *Sweat* explores these ethnic and racial tensions, especially through the interactions of the play's white, black, and Hispanic characters, Nottage locates both the moments of working class solidarity and its explosive limitations. In particular, the performance that I saw at the Public Theatre in New York City in the fall of 2016 brought to the stage a riveting range of gender, class, and racial dimensions that I can only explore in a rather incomplete manner. Therefore, what I intend to do is to re-present *Sweat* through highlighting the two gender triadic relationships within which certain class and racial conditions and contradictions obtain, and a final commentary that highlights the very real injuries of class suffered by two other characters.

The three women characters, Tracey, a middle-aged white woman of German descent, Cynthia, a middle-aged African American, and Jessie, a middle-aged Italian-American, all were born in Berks County, PA, where Reading is the largest city and county seat. They also are co-workers in a fictional factory facing job losses and a potential shutdown. Added to this stress is the possibility of an opening for a supervisory position for which both Tracey and Cynthia apply. Even though Tracey and Cynthia have been friends for years, the promotion of Cynthia to what Tracey calls "a frigging cushion of a job" (48) produces a breach in their friendship, a breach further exacerbated by what Cynthia believes is Tracey's collusion with management and ultimate betrayal. As Sennett and Cobb note: "In turning people against each other, the class system of authority and judgment-making goes itself into hiding: the system is left unchallenged as people enthralled by the enigmas of its power battle one another for respect" (Sennett and Cobb 1972: 150.)

For Cynthia, however, her promotion to supervisor is based on the humiliation she feels she suffered over the years as a line-worker. Indeed, in her defense against the charges of betrayal from Tracey, Cynthia remonstrates: "I've stood on that line, same line since I was nineteen. I've taken orders from idiots who were dangerous, or even worse, racist. But I stood on line, patiently waiting for a break. I don't think you get it, but if I walk away, I'm giving up more than a job, I'm giving up all that time I spent standing on line waiting for one damn opportunity" (83). For Cynthia, the status and money provided by becoming a supervisor captures what Michele Lamont, writing about the differences between male white and black workers, identifies as "a passport that can trump their racial stigma" (Lamont 2000: 101). Nonetheless, the passport for Cynthia leads to a bitter dead-end.

As the play fast forwards from 2000, when this action takes place, to 2008, both Cynthia and Tracey are victimized by the displacement caused by the plant closing and its move to Mexico, a move that historians and social scientists of deindustrialization, like Jefferson Cowie and Beverly Silver, have tracked which reflects the "spatial fix" that David Harvey analyzes as an integral component of capitalism (Harvey 2001; Cowie 1999; Silver 2003). Those left behind, like Cynthia and Tracey, have to confront the hardships left by capital's spatial fix, either jobless poverty and opioid addiction as in the case of Tracey or work at two low-paying non-union jobs in the case of Cynthia.

The third woman in this triangle of wrecked friendship and lives is Jessie who represents the dreams of an escape never realized. Instead of fantasies of becoming an owner of a small business, something that social scientists studying male autoworkers highlight, Jessie's hippie-inflected global trek from an Indian ashram to "Istanbul, Tehran, Kandahar, Kabul, Peshawar, Lahore, Katmandu" reflects not only a lost personal opportunity, but, ironically, a lost world absent the conflicts that have engulfed all of the Middle Eastern and Asian cities cited by Jessie. In a wistful recollection of her aborted plans, Jessie laments: "I wish ... I had gotten to see the world. You know, left Berks, if only for a year. That's what I regret. Not the work, I regret the fact that for a little while it seemed like, I don't know, there was possibility" (56). For Jessie the possibility was eliminated by class and gender constraints and, then, reduced to alcohol-fueled reveries.

The three men captured by what will become an explosive triangle are Jason, the twenty-something son of Tracey, Chris, the twenty-something son of Cynthia, who both work at the same factory as their mothers, and Oscar, a twenty something Columbian-American who aspires to get a job in the same plant. His aspiration and realization of working in that factory will set off the fireworks of the dramatic confrontation pitting Jason and Chris against Oscar which results in a violent brawl that has unintended repercussions for the three, as well as for the bartender bystander, Stan.

When Oscar leaves his job at the bar to become a scab at the factory, Jason, pushed along by anti-immigrant and racial resentments, stoked, in turn, by his mom, vows to get "that fucking spic" (100). Egging on her son, Tracey, acting almost Lady-Macbeth like, denounces Oscar for "eating your dinner, your steak and potatoes, your fucking desert" (101). Capturing the anti-immigrant attitudes that would fuel the right-wing populism mobilized by Donald Trump, Jason later recognizes the "blind fury" that led to the violent confrontation, a fury that "I ain't been able to shake" (109), as he faces life as an ex-con and unemployed worker.[4] Jason's remorse is, nonetheless, awash in the kind of shame and self-blame that Victor Tan Chen identifies as informing the lives of unemployed working class men in America (Chen 2015: 207.)

While drawn into the dramatic violent scene at the bar, Chris seems motivated by another desire, one built on getting an education that will take him out of the factory and, perhaps, into a white collar occupation. Unfortunately, Chris, like Jason, has to contend with standing up to the factory bosses by joining his working class comrades in a strike to put a stop to any further concessions and job losses. As Chris expounds in his masculinist expression of class solidarity: "I'm not gonna be a punk-ass bitch! That's what they want" (88).

On the other hand, Oscar, who will become the object of Chris and Jason's wrath because of his strikebreaking, interprets his actions, also, through the lens of macho posturing, but one based on the ethnic/racial realities of discrimination and exclusion. "What they're offering is better than anything I've touched since I got outta high school. So yo, I ain't afraid to cross the line. Let me puff up their chest, but it don't scare me no more than walking through my hood. I know rough. I ain't afraid to roll in the dirt" (91). Unfortunately, for him "the roll in the dirt" has irreparable repercussions for all three young men and one other.

That other, Stan, a former factory worker who now manages the bar that is the meeting place for all in the year 2000 action of the play, is doubly victimized. His first injury is the result of the neglect by management of faulty machinery in the factory. Although angry at the lack of sympathy by management for his injury, Stan does see the benefit of leaving his twenty-eight years of factory work behind. "Getting injured was the best thing that ever happened to me. Got me out of the vortex. Three generations on the floor. Loyal as hell, I never imagined working anywhere else" (36).

Stan's recollections are part of a dialogue with Brucie, the father of Chris and another injured, more psychologically than physically, former worker at the plant. In the following soliloquy, Brucie highlights not only his family's historical struggle to gain a foothold in the American dream, but also the continuing divisive effects of the intra-working class racial "blame game": "Last week, I was at the union office signing up for some bullshit training and this old white cat, whatever, gets in my face talking about how we took his job. We? I asked him who he was talking about, and he pointed at me. ME? So, I said, if you ain't noticed I'm in the same fucking line as you. Hello?! You'd think that would shut

---

4 Trump won Berks County with 93,094 votes to Clinton's 75,169 votes. Obama won Berks County by almost the same amount in 2008. For an incisive analysis of Trump's appeal to a certain segment of the white working class in the Rust Belt, see Davis 2017.

him down. But, no. He's a scratch in the vinyl, going on and on about us coming here and ruining everything. Like I'm fresh off the boat or some shit. He don't know my biography. October 2nd, 1952, my father picked his last bale of cotton. He packed his razor and Bible and headed North. Ten days later he had a job at Dixon's Hosieries. He clawed his way up from the filth of the yard to Union Rep, fighting for assholes just like that cat" (37–38).

As Sennett and Cobb note, the "burden of class" creates a "logic of discontent (that) leads people to turn on each other rather than on the 'system'" (Sennett and Cobb 1972: 173). Certainly, the devastation wrought by changing material circumstances exacerbates this logic of discontent. *Sweat* not only exposes how economic distress and racial animosities can led to a range of intersectional injuries, but it highlights how white supremacy and white rage can turn deadly, claiming even the lives of its perpetrators like Tracey and Jason, both of whom end up either isolated by paralyzing shame or addled by drugs. In her reflections on the impact of white supremacy on the physical and mental health of whites, Jessie Daniels notes: "The lie of whiteness holds out a promise that being white will save you from social isolation and disconnection through materialism, individualism, and the satisfaction of superiority. When the world changes, it burns off those false promises like a flame melting wax and what is left may not seem like enough to go on" (Daniels 2018). The revealing staging of the burning off of those false promises in Lynn Nottage's *Sweat* rivets our attention, highlighting the drama of continuing racial resentments that have fueled a perpetuation of weaponized whiteness. If we truly value authentic equality and wish to embrace an inclusive and diverse democracy, let alone guarantee physical and mental health for all, we can no longer abide a white identity politics built on white racial resentments and racist hatred of and hostility towards people of color.[5]

---

5 On the historical impact of institutionalized white rage, see Anderson 2016. For an examination of how "whiteness itself" has become "a negative health indicator," see Metzl (2019: 9).

Afterword

Frank Joyce

Thanks to Fran Shor and others like him,[1] the truth is coming out. Humans with white skin are not superior to any other humans. The systems built around that premise are not the pinnacle of human achievement. They are a menace.

It is no small achievement to pierce the curtain that hides the machinery behind 500 years of white supremacy as Fran Shor's essays do. But such revelations are now happening fast.

That's why we can see ahead to the day when this book will be an artifact of a profound social change. Our centuries long nightmare of race-based human on human abuse can significantly decline. We can pass along a new and better reality to generations to come.

This will not happen by itself. And it won't be easy. But we live in a time of opportunity as never before.

1   Why Now?

The system of white male domination is vulnerable. The entire edifice of whiteness as an apex identity and the white way of *thinking* is coming apart. Evidence is there for those prepared to look.

Which is not to say that the signs are obvious. The election of Donald Trump, his Euro-Russian counterparts, Brexit and so on makes the idea look far-fetched. Through that lens, the theory and practice of white male supremacy appears more resilient than ever.

Many seem surprised by this. The surprise is itself revealing. As James Baldwin so eloquently pointed out decades ago, it reflects the numbing to the consequences the system causes to all those it touches. The surprise also reveals resistance to understanding that anything that lasts for over 500 years clearly has highly developed adaptive capacities.

How so? One factor is that sub-systems of the white way of thinking continuously adjust the information it presents. Events are routinely presented as fragments so as to prevent awareness of connections and patterns.

Modern mass media provides an example of this obfuscation. Suppose we were having the national argument about slavery now, instead of 160 years ago.

---

1 This afterword is adapted from a work in progress titled *Unlearning Whiteness*.

MSNBC would routinely feature stories about enslaved people who alleged mistreatment by their master.

Fox News would counter with reports that ridiculed the slaves who were claiming abuse. Fox anchors would attribute the accusations to "political" maneuvers financed by George Soros.

And for good measure, Fox pundits would extol the contributions of various slave owners to the wellbeing of their communities, the overall economy and even the enslaved themselves. They would then put a bow on it all by oozing shock and contempt that the ultraliberals could think otherwise.

None of that exactly matters. What does matter is that neither MSNBC nor Fox would acknowledge slavery as a *system*.

The #metoo movement provides a contemporary example. Despite vastly increased attention to sexual harassment and abuse, there has been no mainstream media discussion about patriarchy as a system – which is, by the way, far older than white supremacy.

This high functioning organism which addresses symptoms instead of underlying causes is itself highly evolved from the very roots of the white supremacy project. Here, I use the word *project* intentionally.

Yes, humans did deliberately and consciously organize white supremacy and they are doing so still. It's a nasty invention like nuclear weapons, Agent Orange, Styrofoam, and the Electoral College.

My purpose here is to help advance the project to *disassemble* the white supremacy system. That will require recognizing that just as the human body seeks to repair and heal itself following an injury, white male power does too.

Often it happens automatically, as when a small cut or bruise fixes itself. But when necessary, interventions are made. They are comparable to applying a cast to a broken limb or major surgery to remove a tumor or even replace a vital organ.

For example: After the Civil War, a modified structure of economic exploitation was installed. In addition to share-cropping, a wave of contrived mass incarceration created the foundation for leasing convict labor to employers. Simultaneously, KKK terrorism was enforcing Jim Crow segregation throughout the defeated Confederacy. The result was slavery by another name.

In the mid-20th century, as Richard Rothstein explains in his book *The Color of Law*, the federal government used legislation and regulation to create the nationwide system of residential segregation that exists to this day. Aided and abetted by banks, insurance companies, media and local governments, that sub-system alone still plays a crucial role in regenerating and protecting a broad range of racial disparities.

In the 21st century, the mass incarceration of African Americans is once again a major tool for perpetuating racial disparity. Black people continue to be at risk in encounters with the police. Schools are more racially segregated than ever. And at the risk of stating the obvious, the election of Donald Trump represented a structural correction to the presidency of Barack Obama.

For now though, let's suspend our assumption that the white supremacy system is invincible. Let's adopt the perspective expressed in the *New York Times* by Michelle Alexander:

> Those of us who are committed to the radical evolution of American democracy are not merely resisting an unwanted reality. To the contrary, the struggle for human freedom and dignity extends back centuries and is likely to continue for generations to come. In the words of Vincent Harding, one of the great yet lesser-known heroes of the black freedom struggle, the long, continuous yearning and reaching toward freedom flows throughout history 'like a river, sometimes powerful, tumultuous, and roiling with life; at other times meandering and turgid, covered with the ice and snow of seemingly endless winters, all too often streaked and running with blood.'
>
> Harding was speaking about black movements for liberation in America, but the metaphor applies equally well to the global struggle for human dignity and freedom.
>
> ALEXANDER 2018

Amen. Let's look for the counter-narrative instead.

2   A Snapshot of Change

When Kevin Gray burned a Confederate flag in front of the Capitol of South Carolina in 1992 he started a movement. Ever since, albeit slowly, Confederate monuments have been coming down. Tributes to white supremacy in the North, slavery and settler colonialism are also being removed. Columbus Day, for example, is being redefined as Indigenous People's Day.

The true history of white violence against people of color and the cover-up that comes with it is increasingly acknowledged. Mainstream media publishes articles on whiteness. A museum dedicated to African Americans and the victims of lynching has opened in Montgomery, Alabama.

In recent years, illuminating work has been contributed by Gerald Horne, Ta-nehisi Coates, Roxanne Dunbar-Ortiz, Ibram X Kendi, Richard Rothstein, Ned and Constance Sublette, Manisha Sinha and many more. Previous insights from W.E.B. Dubois, James Baldwin and others remain relevant. The analytical foundation from which to challenge the white male power system is stronger than ever.

3   Why Didn't I Know That?

The ability to change the narrative is essential. One of the reasons that whites often react so defensively in any discussion of racial bias is that they have been trained into a state of ignorance. Multiple studies confirm that whites and even many people of color are profoundly unaware and misinformed about the realities of violent settler colonialism, slavery, segregation and discrimination.

The curriculum of the education system and the lens of the media are designed to conceal, not reveal, even the existence of the white supremacy system – let alone its inner workings.

Shifts in language also matter a lot in this context. It is promising that accurate terms such as white supremacy and white nationalism are increasingly used in place of diversity, civil rights, racism, racial tensions, the racial divide, Native American and other euphemisms. (Admittedly, these gains are offset by other language crimes such as the widespread misuse of the word *tribal* to characterize various current political disputes.)

The granddaddy of all the racial weasel words is *conservative*. From this time forward, when you see or hear *conservative* please instantly translate it to white supremacist. Why? Because white male supremacy is what is being "conserved," that's why.

Likewise important is the understanding that the basis of identity itself is more fluid than we previously accepted. This is most obvious from the rapid achievements of the LGBTQ movement.

Beyond that, DNA testing, dubious science though it may be, is primarily *marketed* not as a way to establish racial purity, but the opposite. Many whites pursue such testing, apparently because they no longer accept at face value the stories they have been told about who they are and/or who they must be.

Even identity changes aggressively pursued by Amazon and other corporate interests in pursuit of shopping and brand loyalties are upsetting the prevailing identity applecart. Transformations in religious attachments are also detaching many from old ways of thinking.

Yes, "race" is a social construct. To be sure, it is not the first "othering" rationale that humans have come up with to justify hierarchy, exploitation and violence. But it is among the most pernicious.

The removal, reduction and replacement of the white supremacy construct is now both possible and necessary. The time has come to discuss what will replace whiteness as an apex identity.

Also expanding the possibility, indeed the necessity, of a new approach is this: Across the planet homo sapiens are realizing that the trajectory of existential threats to our species could send us off the cliff. Pollution, disease, economic collapse, war and every other form of violence endanger every life form. More and more white people understand that these risks apply to them too.

It is harder than ever to deny that there are serious costs and consequences *even for whites* that come with perpetuating the white way of thinking and the white way of acting. Further, there are shifts already underway in the ecosystem in which white supremacy has thrived up to now.

4 Decoupling the Whiteness from the Supremacy – Changing the Identity Hierarchy

The first instances of humans perceiving "racial" differences in other humans has disappeared into the mists of time. But white supremacy has a measurable history.

In his provocative book, *The Lies that Bind – Rethinking Identity* (2018), Kwame Appiah discusses the evolution of racial identity. By the eighteenth century, emerging science, religion, colonialism, the slave trade and slavery converged to create a coherent philosophy. External qualities were widely associated with internal and social qualities such as intelligence and character. "One illustrious discipline after another was recruited to give content to color," Appiah says.

In our time social scientists like the late Daniel Moynihan, Charles Murray and Steven Pinker have concocted theories to reinforce the white supremacist way of thinking.

For at least the near term, discernable differences of skin color, hair type, eye shape and so on will still be "race" signifiers in a common sense way in Western culture.

Is awareness of outward physical difference in and of itself necessarily a problem? No. After all, other noticeable characteristics carry little or no social stigma or advantage.

Maybe blondes do have more fun. And yes, traits such as left-handedness have been used for human-on-human abuse. But such qualities are not the basis of centuries of global exploitation and mistreatment.

Could they become so? Perhaps. Netflix probably already has a series with that premise under development.

Let's ignore that possibility for now. Because race is a social construct it should be obvious that it is not the skin tone – the lack of melanin, if you will – of whites that is the problem. Rather, it is the social, political and economic identity that is connected to it.

Put simply then, the goal of ending white supremacy is to end the supremacy part.

Does white identity itself come into play in that process? Yes. Just as we now recognize that sexual identity exists on a continuum and can be fluid, racial identity is too, although not in exactly the same way.

5   Once upon a Time

In its early days, whiteness had to compete to win a place on a hierarchy of identities. The elevation of whiteness required rearranging the importance of religion. Whites might once have considered their identity as a Protestant or Catholic of greater importance. It is worth noting that over the 500 year period in which white supremacy has grown and evolved, antagonism between different Christian denominations has sharply diminished.

Similarly, nationalism was emerging in Europe in the same period as white supremacy. Identity as German, not French or, Irish not Polish, Portuguese not Italian and so on was newly important in the identity soup.

The creation of what is now called the United States was a turning point in bonding the ideology of white supremacy and capitalism with the structure and identity of a modern nation state. In this regard, it's helpful to think about loyalty and patriotism.

Consider these two pledges:

> I pledge allegiance to the Flag ... and to the Republic for which it stands, one Nation under God, indivisible, with liberty and justice for all.

> I pledge allegiance to the world, to care for earth and sea and air, to cherish every living thing with peace and justice everywhere.

The first pledge is, of course, the pledge of allegiance to the United States. The second was composed by the late Lillian Genser, a lifelong peace activist from Detroit.

It is an act of white supremacy to pledge allegiance to the United States because it is a white nationalist country. This is why defenders of the status quo leap to oppose any sign of alleged disrespect to the flag, even when the protest is not directed at the flag itself.

The struggle of former San Francisco 49'ers quarterback Colin Kaepernick is a case in point. In 2016 Kaepernick and another player, Eric Reid, intensified their previous opposition to the frequent abuse of black people by the police. During the pregame ritual of the National Anthem, they knelt instead of standing. Other players in the National Football League followed suit.

White nationalists, including President Trump, saw an opportunity. They made hating on taking a knee a rallying cry for loyalty to the white nationalist flag and the government for which it stands.

The controversy is also a good illustration of how the white supremacy system renews itself. The history of the writing and popularizing of the U.S. Pledge of Allegiance is itself a study in the construction of white supremacy and white nationalism. Like a statue of Confederate General Robert E. Lee or KKK wizard Nathan Bedford Forrest, it is a white supremacist/white nationalist symbol.

According to a November 3, 2017 article by Christopher Petralla in the *Washington Post*:

> "The origins of the pledge trace to the late 19th century, the product of an expansionist American project. In 1891, the family magazine *Youth's Companion* asked 35-year-old Francis Bellamy, a former pastor of Boston's Bethany Baptist Church, to fashion a patriotic program for schools around the country to commemorate the 400th anniversary of Christopher Columbus's 'arrival in America' by 'raising the U.S. flag over every public school from the Atlantic to the Pacific.'"

Even earlier, the Star Spangled Banner was also originally written to celebrate white supremacy and white nationalism.

Because of the white nationalist nature of the United States, it should come as no surprise that Frederick Douglas, W.E.B. DuBois, Vincent Harding and other black intellectuals have proposed alternatives to blind loyalty to the U.S. state. "I am a citizen of a nation that does not yet exist," was a concept intrinsic to much of Dr. Harding's work.

Indigenous people have their own statements to make about the illegitimacy of the United States of America. In developing a vision that furthers the decoupling of the whiteness from the supremacy, it will be essential to incorporate the perspective of Indigenous people and nations.

The meaning of the word citizen will also need to be examined.

6 The Concept of Quitting

Some whites have already written I quit letters. The idea is to overtly reject the standard issue way of thinking into which whites are trained and educated.

Following are two excerpts from one such letter. It was published in 2006 by someone calling themselves Conceptual Guerilla:

I Hereby Resign From The White Race

...being "white" is a Faustian bargain if ever there was one. Behold, the "heritage" of the white man. That mode of self-identification never did anything for "white" people, except to the extent that it led them to whip the slaves, kill the Indians, horde the gold, fence in the land, break the strikes, tear gas the marchers, bomb the churches, napalm the peasants, and do all of the other dirty little chores the ruling class requires, all in exchange for that California ranch style on a quarter acre. Being "white" is nothing more than an excuse to do the killing and stealing that wealthy elites, as with everything else, need someone to do for them. Which means that the only thing you will ever get from those jokers for being "white," is a job doing their dirty work. Beyond that, being "white" doesn't mean a god damn thing.

This will work, if you will help me. Sign the resignation. I need tens of thousands, and preferably millions of people to put their name to it. I need every "white" person in America to become aware of it. I need every "white" person in America presented with this same "moment of truth." I need every "white" person, who denies his bigotry, even as he clings to his "heritage" – such as it is – to be presented with this simple alternative. This corrosive American bigotry has stagnated this country, turned us into an international pariah, impoverished people around the world, even as it is impoverishing us.

Another "I quit" example is from an old and dear friend of mine. Referencing a time of pain and turmoil within his reasonably affluent family, it is an eloquent "I quit" statement in the form of a poem.

Here is its concluding stanza:

> All hail narcotic suburbia
> Where safety rules, for things but not people
> Where retreat and consume doth reign
> How beauty-full the home, how empty those within
> The welcome mat reads
> "Bitter Fruit of White Privilege"
> MARK SILVERBERG, November 2017

A 2019 tweet from Brian Edwards Tiekert reinforces the value for whites of considering their whiteness in a thoughtful way: "Us white folks were taught to think of racism as something you sign up for, instead of something you learn to do without even thinking about it. So we think not wanting to be racist is the same thing as not being racist."

African-American scholar Marc Lamont Hill made a similar point in an Instagram post on February 13, 2019. He was responding to the hackneyed claim of presidential aspirant Howard Schulz that he doesn't "see" race.

> A message to Howard Schultz and other "color blind" white people ... Please stop saying you don't see color. (1) you DO see color. It's a natural human response to recognize difference. What these differences MEAN, however, are entirely shaped by the social world. (2) there's nothing wrong with seeing my color. The problem is when you assign white supremacist meanings and values to my color. In other words, it's ok to notice I'm black. It's NOT ok to assume that I'm lazy, dumb, or immoral because of my blackness. (3) instead of pretending you don't see difference, focus on how to spotlight and celebrate those differences. Figure out how to love me AND my blackness. The goal shouldn't be a post-racial world. The goal should be a post-RACIST one.

The concept of quitting the white supremacy part of whiteness may seem somewhat less farfetched when viewed in a nonracial context. Who doesn't know someone who very deliberately left the Catholic Church, Scientology or some other religion that had once been a vital component of their identity?

Similarly, there is a reason that it's newsworthy when prominent public figures switch parties. Perpetual loyalty is the default expectation of religion, politics and other institutions. Changing political parties is a big deal, not just in an individual's life but also within the electoral system itself.

7 In Praise of Rachel Doležal

Over my decades of doing anti-racist work, I have occasionally been accused of being a "traitor to my race." That very concept reveals one of the many ways by which white supremacy is enforced.

Enter Rachel Doležal who now calls herself Nkechi Amare Diallo. In 2015 the nation was briefly fascinated by her story. Her offense was that although "white," she had been presenting herself as Black. At the time she was "outed," she was the President of the NAACP chapter in Spokane Washington. Rachel didn't just quit the supremacy part of being white. She repudiated being white itself.

From the beginning, I had trouble understanding what the fuss was all about. There is much to admire about Black culture. There is much that is repulsive about white culture. Why not switch? Why should these boundaries be so rigid?

It's true, her actions invite legitimate questions about whites taking responsibility to help educate and change other whites. Other issues around cultural appropriation have also been raised. At the very least though, her decisions are proof that questions of racial identity are not, pun intended, as black and white as they have been in the past.

Any deviation at all from total commitment to white superiority is intolerable to some. In an act of white supremacy at its most toxic, Dylan Roof murdered nine Black people in a bible study class at a church to express his loyalty to the white race. Make no mistake though. Pat Buchanan, Steve Bannon, Iowa Congressman Steve King, Donald Trump and other self-proclaimed defenders of white civilization enabled him.

My point is that the significant reduction of the supremacy part of white supremacy is not just about reforming public policy, or removing statues of Christopher Columbus, Confederate leaders, racist elected officials and such. It's about a profound shift in our self-identity *and* our social identity.

In my view Rachel Doležal was courageous in deciding to become Black. Nkechi Amare Diallo is courageous in defending and maintaining that choice.

And before you become indignant about Rachel/Nkechi, consider another instance of making a racial choice, Barack Hussein Obama, "I ceased to advertise my mother's race at the age of twelve or thirteen, when I began to suspect that by doing so I was ingratiating myself to whites" (2004: page 23).

In the story following that quote from the "Introduction" to his 1994 autobiography, Barack Obama returns frequently to his conscious decision to be Black. Over the centuries, many lighter skin Blacks have had such choices and made such decisions.

In a 2019 high profile professional golf tournament rising young star Cameron Champ created a sensation with a bold identity statement. He wore a black shirt and white pants to openly celebrate his racially mixed heritage. Lest anyone miss the point, he also wore one white shoe and one black shoe. For the record, all were branded with the Nike symbol.

Fluidity and choice when it comes to racial identity is also revealed in shifting language preferences. Today the term African American is more common than Negro or Black. Counter-intuitive, or controversial, as it may seem, whites have racial identity and racial language choices too.

That's the way it is with social constructs.

8 Identity in Flux

White identity is already scrambled by all sorts of forces. Many of them are commercial.

My wife and I joke that our Sunday worship often takes place at Costco. We see lots of other parishioners there. The same is true at Walmart.

Joking aside, Drew Austin explains in a September 2018 article in the online magazine Real Life, entitled "The Constant Consumer":

> Amazon similarly merges the customer and the user within its own optimized environments, letting these subjects exist at the center of an ever-expanding system. Imagine an avid Amazon customer's typical day living with a near future iteration of the platform: He wakes up and speaks his first words of the morning to his Amazon Echo in the kitchen, asking Alexa to order toothpaste after noticing he was running low. Upon checking his email, he gives Alexa a few more instructions, adding social engagements and reminders to his calendar, checking the weather, and finally opening the garage door once he's ready to leave for work. At the office throughout the day, idle shopping fills his distracted moments. He browses books, clothing, and even furniture, placing orders within seconds, many of which automatically appear in his shopping cart based on patterns from his activity history (he even knows that some of what he buys

will be waiting at home tonight). During the evening commute another Alexa-enabled device in his car prompts him to send his sister a birthday card, an action he asks Alexa to do for him. He stops by Whole Foods to pick up groceries – as an Amazon Prime member, it's always the most cost-effective option in his neighborhood. He arrives home to find a variety of Amazon packages stacked neatly on the living room coffee table, delivered throughout the day by part-time contractors who let themselves into the house via the smart lock on the front door. The soundtrack to his entire day is provided by Amazon Music, in which his Prime membership has automatically enrolled him for a small monthly fee. Few parts of this hypothetical day, which is already within the realm of possibility, remain untouched by Amazon's user experience.

Amazon, as much as any single company, is transforming the environments in which we live and embedding itself within the fabric of daily existence.

Step aside whiteness. Amazon has a better idea.

Here's another example of the evolution of commercialized identity. African-American basketball megastar Michael Jordan is a famous symbol of the Nike brand. His Air Jordan shoes are popular and expensive. When asked why he wasn't more supportive of Black causes, Jordan replied "Republicans buy shoes too."

Political party identity is also ascendant on the identity hierarchy. So too is the complexity of so many available identities. Young people today especially are overwhelmed with social media options, gender options, video game loyalties and a plethora of other components for defining who they *are*.

As mentioned previously, the fad of DNA ancestry testing and its marketing also speaks to the current fluidity of identity. Yes, the tests themselves are modern day snake oil. But the attraction to them attests to curiosity about family histories and options. People are not necessarily taking for granted the validity of the stories they have been told.

Sometimes they are shocked to learn that they have non-white ancestors. Sometimes, as in the notorious case of Senator Elizabeth Warren, they use them to "prove" that they do.

Another example of the unstable nature of identity is embedded within ideas about immigration. Many variables are at work here.

At any given moment, some employers want more immigrants, some want less. Some employers want high tech immigrants. Some want very low wage workers for jobs in agriculture, food processing; hotel housekeeping or other such sectors of the economy. Some employers want "legal" immigrants, some prefer "illegals."

Employment is not the only factor. Immigrant communities themselves have their own interests. There are profound differences from place to place within the Unites States over immigrant populations, experiences and polices.

The term immigrant itself has not and does not always have the same meaning. Under various circumstances, the word can have a positive or negative connotation. Sometimes immigrants are urged to preserve and celebrate their heritage. Sometime they are pressured to "assimilate."

Immigrant status is invariably linked to skin color, with "white" immigrants always privileged in various ways over people of color. Immigration is frequently a focus of political demagoguery although the target shifts. Irish, Chinese, Mexicans, Japanese and more have been interred, deported and otherwise demonized and abused at various times in U.S. history.

Almost always, immigrants are portrayed as attracted to the U.S. because of alleged opportunities. Only occasionally is attention paid to the forces pushing humans out of the places from which they come. The assumption that immigration to the U.S. is always more "pull" than "push" embodies the dominant culture of white supremacy and white nationalism.

It is worth noting an exception that proves this rule. When whites emigrate from multi-racial cities to all white suburbs it is often explained as them being pushed out.

9   The Three Choices and the Three Stages

White people have three options. One is to *actively* support white supremacy. Donald Trump and those around him exemplify this cohort. So do many others in local politics, religion, media, business, labor and every other sphere of the system.

Another choice is to *passively* support the status quo. Saying, I am not political, does not mean that you are not political. To be clear, passive support does not always mean doing nothing. To the contrary, when the white supremacy system is thought to have been destabilized or in danger of becoming so, whites work to *fix* it.

The third possibility is to actively oppose white supremacy. There are degrees of opposition from micro affirmative action to organizing for systemic change.

At the risk of some oversimplification, there are three stages of becoming an anti-white supremacist.

Stage one involves understanding/awakening. I get it why sometimes the idea of being "woke" is mocked. But I like the term. Awakening to the reality of white supremacy is a process. There are big and small epiphanies that people go through.

Once "awake," the learning process never ends. People become more open, even hungry for new information and insight. When the pupil is ready, the teacher appears, as the saying goes.

Phase two is deciding. What am I to do with this new awareness? Am I going to become an anti-white supremacist in my daily life?

If yes, then comes stage three: action. Here again there is a continuum of possibilities. Nineteenth century abolitionists are touchstones for this emerging new movement. In our time, Tim Wise, David Roedigger, James Loewen, Fran Shor and other whites have fought the ideology of white supremacy.

Clearly, issues of white identity call for further thought and research. But if we are serious about decoupling the whiteness from the supremacy, it is work worth doing.

And it is but one element of thinking big, thinking strategically and thinking long term in confronting the vulnerable white supremacy/white nationalism system. School curriculums, both religious and secular, are another. So are myriad public policies that sustain white male domination in real estate, finance, media, politics, the job system, war making and every other component of the current system.

In the spirit of John Brown, the Grimké sisters, Frederick Douglas, William Lloyd Garrison, Elijah Lovejoy, and other 19th century abolitionist activists, let's get it on.

References

Alexander, Michelle. 2018. "We Are not the Resistance." *New York Times*, September 21, 2018.

Appiah, Kwame Anthony. 2018. *The Lies that Bind: Rethinking Identity*. New York: Liveright, p. 118.

Austin, Drew. 2018. "The Constant Consumer." *Real Life magazine*. https://reallifemag.com/the-constant-consumer/.

Conceptual Guerilla. 2006. "I Hereby Resign From The White Race" *Daily Kos*. https://www.dailykos.com/stories/2006/6/6/216512/-.

Dolezal, Rachel. 2017. *In Full Color: Finding My Place in a Black and White World*. Dallas, TX: BenBella Books.

Obama, Barack. 2004. *Dreams of My Father*. New York: Three Rivers Press, p. 23.

Marc Lamont Hill – Marc Lamont Hill Instagram, February 13, 2019. https://www.instagram.com/p/BtozEcqAlfo/.

Bibliography

Abramsky, Sasha. 2017. *Jumping at Shadows: The Triumph of Fear and the End of the American Dream.* New York: Nation Books.

Achen, Christopher H. and Larry M. Bartels. 2016. *Democracy for Realists: Why Elections Do Not Produce Responsive Government.* Princeton, NJ: Princeton University Press.

Aguilar-San Juan, Karin and Frank Joyce, eds. 2015. *The People Make the Peace: Lessons from the Vietnam Antiwar Movement.* Charlottesville, VA: Just World Books.

Anderson, Carol. 2016. *White Rage: The Unspoken Truth of Our Racial Divide.* New York: Bloomsbury.

Anderson, Terry H. 1995. *The Movement and the Sixties.* New York: Oxford University Press.

Appy, Christian. 1993. *Working Class War: American Combat Soldiers and Vietnam.* Chapel Hill: The University of North Carolina Press.

Appy, Christian. 2015. *American Reckoning: The Vietnam War and Our National Identity.* New York: Viking.

Atwood, Paul L. 2010. *War and Empire: The American Way of Life.* New York: Pluto Press.

Babson, Steve, et al. 2010. *The Color of Law: Ernie Goodman, Detroit, and the Struggle for Labor and Civil Rights.* Detroit: Wayne State University Press.

Bacevich, Andrew. 2008. *The Limits of Power: The End of American Exceptionalism.* New York: Metropolitan Books.

Baldwin, James. 1963. *The Fire Next Time.* New York: Vintage.

Baldwin, James. 1971. "An Open Letter to My Sister, Miss Angela Davis." *The New York Review of Books*, January 7, 1971. https://www.nybooks.com/articles/1971/01/07/an-open-letter-to-my-sister-miss-angela-davis.

Baldwin, James. 1998. *Collected Essays.* New York: Library Of America.

Baptist, Edward E. 2014. *The Half Has Never Been Told: Slavery and the Making of American Capitalism.* New York: Basic Books.

Barber, David. 2008. *A Hard Rain Fell: SDS and Why It Failed.* Jackson: The University Press of Mississippi.

Bates, Beth Tompkins. 2012. *The Making of Black Detroit in the Age of Henry Ford.* Chapel Hill: The University of North Carolina Press.

Bauman, Zygmunt. 2003. *Liquid Love: On the Frailty of Human Bonds.* Cambridge: Polity Press.

Behdad, Ali. 2005. *A Forgetful Nation: On Immigration and Cultural Identity in the United States.* Durham, NC: Duke University Press.

Belfrage, Sally. 1990. *Freedom Summer.* Charlottesville: University Press of Virginia.

Bell, Derrick. 2004. *Silent Covenants: Brown v. Board of Education and the Unfulfilled Hopes for Racial Reform.* New York: Oxford University Press.

Berman, Ari. 2017. "Rigged: How Voter Suppression Threw Wisconsin to Trump," *Mother Jones* (November/December). https://www.motherjones.com/politics/2017/10/voter-suppression-wisconsin-election-2016.

Blow, Charles M. "Beyond 'Black Lives Matter.'" *New York Times*, February 9, 2015. https://www.nytimes.com/2015/02/09/opinion/charles-blow-beyond-black-lives-matter.html.

Boggs, Grace Lee. 2012. *The Next American Revolution: Sustainable Activism for the Twenty First Century*. Berkeley: University of California Press.

Bonilla-Silva, Eduardo. 2003. *Racism without Racists: Color-Blind Racism and the Persistence of Racial Equality in the United States*. Lanham, MD: Rowan & Littlefield.

Branch, Taylor. 1989. *Parting the Waters: America in the King Years, 1954–1963*. New York: Touchstone.

Branch, Taylor. 1999. *Pillar of Fire: America in the King Years, 1963–1965*. New York: Touchstone.

Branch, Taylor. 2006. *At Canaan's Edge: America in the King Years, 1965–1968*. New York: Simon & Schuster.

Bray, Michael. 2017. "The 'White Working Class' Does Not Exist: Thinking Through Liberal Postracialism." *Historical Materialism*, September 20, 2017. http://www.historicalmaterialism.org/blog/white-working-class-does-not-exist-thinking-through-liberal-postracialism.

Breines, Wini. 1992. *Young, White, and Miserable: Growing Up Female in the Fifties*. Boston: Beacon Press.

Briggs, William. 2017. *How America Got Its Guns: A History of the Gun Violence Crisis*. Albuquerque: University of New Mexico Press.

Brown, Michael, et al. 2003. *Whitewashing Race: The Myth of a Color-blind Society*. Berkeley: University of California Press.

Brundage, W. Fitzhugh. 2017. "I've Studied the History of Confederate Statues. Here's What to Do About Them." *Vox*, August 18, 2017. https://www.vox.com/the-big-idea/2017/8/18/16165160/confederate-monuments-history-charlottesville-white-supremacy.

Burner, Eric. 1994. *And Gently He Shall Lead Them: Robert Parris Moses and Civil Rights in Mississippi*. New York: New York University Press.

Bush, Melanie. 2004. *Breaking the Code of Good Intentions: Everyday Forms of Whiteness*. Lanham, MD: Rowman & Littlefield.

Cagin, Seth and Philip Dray. 1988. *We Are Not Afraid*. New York: Macmillan.

Carlson, Dennis. 2004. "Narrating the Multicultural Nation: Rosa Parks and the White Mythology of the Civil Rights Movement." In *Off White: Readings on Power, Privilege, and Resistance*, second edition, edited by Michelle Fine et al., 302–311. New York: Routledge.

Carmichael, Stokely (with Ekwueme Michael Thelwell). 2003. *Ready for Revolution.* New York: Scribner.

Carson, Clayborne. 1982. *In Struggle: SNCC and the Black Awakening of the 1960s.* Cambridge, MA: Harvard University Press.

Carter, Dan. 2000. *The Politics of Rage: George Wallace, the Origins of the New Conservatism, and the Transformation of American Politics.* Baton Rouge: Louisiana State University Press.

Chappell, David L. *Inside Agitators: White Southerners in the Civil Rights Movement.* Baltimore, MD: The Johns Hopkins University Press.

Chardy, Alfonso. 2016. "Record Number of Deportations Took Place on Obama's Watch." *Miami Herald*, December 25, 2016. https://www.miamiherald.com/news/local/immigration/article122715474.html.

Chatelain, Marcia. 2015. "Black Lives Matter: An Online Roundtable with Alicia Garza, Dante Barry, and Darsheel Kaur," *Dissent*, January 19, 2015. http://www.dissentmagazine.org/blog/blacklivesmatter-an-online-roundtable-with-alicia-garza-dante-barry-and-darsheel-kaur.

Chen, Victor Tan. 2015. *Cut Loose: Jobless and Hopeless in an Unfair Economy.* Oakland: University of California Press.

Cheung-Miaw, Calvin and Max Elbaum. 2019. "Trumpism's Global Strategy." *Organizing Upgrade*, February 7, 2019. https://organizingupgrade.com/trumpisms-global-strategy/.

Cho, Sumi. 2009. "Post-Racialism." *Iowa Law Review* 94:5 (July): 1589–1649.

Cleaver, Eldridge. 1968. *Soul on Ice.* New York: McGraw-Hill.

Coates, Ta-Nehisi 2017. "The First White President." *The Atlantic,* October 2017. https://www.theatlantic.com/magazine/archive/2017/10/the-first-white-president-ta-nehisi-coates/537909.

Coaston, Jane. 2018. "The Scary Ideology Behind Trump's Immigration Instincts." *Vox*, January 18, 2018. https://www.vox.com/2018/1/18/16897358/racism-donald-trump-immigration.

Cohen, Robert and Reginald E. Zelnik, eds. 2002. *The Free Speech Movement: Reflections on Berkeley in the 1960s.* Berkeley: University of California Press.

Cowan, Paul. 1970. *The Making of an Un-American.* New York: The Viking Press.

Cowie, Jefferson. 1999. *Capital Moves: RCA's Seventy-Year Quest for Cheap Labor.* Ithaca, NY: Cornell University Press.

Crespino, Joseph. 2007. *In Search of Another Country: Mississippi and the Conservative Counterrevolution.* Princeton, NJ: Princeton University Press.

Cullen, Dave. 2019. *Parkland: Birth of a Movement.* New York: HarperCollins.

Culture, Jonathan. 2004. *Labor's Time: Shorter Hours, the UAW, and the Struggle for American Unionism.* Philadelphia: Temple University Press, 2004.

Cunningham, Phyllis. 1964. "Project Report from Hattiesburg." In Stuart Ewen Papers, MSS 531, Box 1, State Historical Society of Wisconsin, November 1964.

Curry, Constance, et al. 2000. *Deep in Our Hearts: Nine White Women in the Freedom Movement.* Athens: The University of Georgia Press.

Daniels, Jessie. 2018."White Supremacy is Deadly for Everyone." *Huffington Post*, September 14, 2018. https://www.huffingtonpost.com/entry/opinion-white-suicide-addiction-death_us_5b903737e4b0511db3dea162.

Davis, Mike. 2006. *Planet of Slums.* New York: Verso, 2006.

Davis, Mike. 2017. "The Great God Trump and the White Working Class." *Jacobin*, February 7, 2017. https://www.jacobinmag.com/2017/02/the-great-god-trump-and-the-white-working-class.

DeLaughter, Bobby. 2001. *Never Too Late: A Prosecutor's Story of Justice in the Medgar Evers Case.* New York: Scribner.

Demby, Gene. 2014. "The Birth of a New Civil Rights Movement." *Politico*, December 31, 2014. http://www.politico.com/magazine/story/2014/12/ferguson-new-civil-rights-movement-1139.

Demerath, W.J. III, Gerald Maxwell, and Michael T. Aiken. 1971. *Dynamics of Idealism: White Activists in a Black Movement.* San Francisco: Jossey-Bass, Inc.

Derrida, Jacques. 1994. *Specters of Marx,* translated by Peggy Kamuf. New York: Routledge.

DiAngelo, Robin. 2018. *White Fragility: Why It's So Hard for White People to Talk About Racism.* Boston: Beacon Press.

Dittmer, John. 1994. *Local People: The Struggle for Civil Rights in Mississippi.* Urbana: University of Illinois Press.

Donnelly, John, and Robert Schlesinger. 2003. "Military Criticized for Type of Ordnance." *Boston Globe*, April 2, 2003. http://www.commondreams.org/headlines03/0402-7htm.

Dower, John W. 2017. *The Violent American Century: War and Terror Since World War II.* Chicago: Haymarket Books.

Drinnon, Richard. 1997. *Facing West: The Metaphysics of Indian-Hating and Empire-Building.* Norman: University of Oklahoma Press.

DuBois, W.E.B. 1961. *The Souls of Black Folk.* Greenwich, CT: Fawcett Premier.

Dudziak, Mary L. 2000. *Cold War Civil Rights: Race and the Image of American Democracy.* Princeton, NJ: Princeton University Press.

Dunbar-Ortiz, Roxanne. 2014. *An Indigenous Peoples' History of the United States.* Boston: Beacon Press.

Dunbar-Ortiz, Roxanne. 2018. *Loaded: A Disarming History of the Second Amendment.* San Francisco: City Lights Books.

Duster, Troy. 2017. "What to Do with a Man on Horseback." *The Chronicle of Higher Education*, August 14, 2017. https://www.chronicle.com/article/What-to-Do-With-a-Man-on/240923.

Eagles, Charles W. 1993. *Outside Agitators: Jon Daniels and the Civil Rights Movement in Alabama.* Chapel Hill: University of North Carolina Press.

Edgar, David. 1981. "Reagan's Hidden Agenda: Racisms and the New American Right." *Race & Class* 22:3 (January): 221–238.

Edsforth, Ronald. 1995. "Why Automation Didn't Shorten the Work Week: The Politics of Work Time in the Automobile Industry." In *Autowork*, edited by Robert Asher and Ronald Edsforth, 155–179. Albany: State University of New York Press.

Eisenstein, Zillah. 2004. *Against Empire: Feminisms, Racism, and the West.* New York: Zed Books.

Engelhardt, Tom. 1995. *The End of Victory Culture.* New York: Basic Books.

Estes, Nick. 2019. *Our History is the Future.* New York: Verso.

Evans, Sara. 1980. *Personal Politics: The Roots of Women's Liberation in the Civil Rights Movement and the New Left.* New York: Vintage Books.

Evers, Myrlie. *For Us, the Living.* 1996. Jackson: University Press of Mississippi.

Ewen, Stuart. 1990. "The Intellectual New Left." In *History and the New Left, Madison, Wisconsin, 1950–1970*, edited by Paul Buhle. Philadelphia: Temple University Press.

Fager, Charles E. 1967. *White Reflections on Black Power.* Grand Rapids, MI: William B. Eerdmas Publishing, Co.

Farber, David. 1994. *The Age of Great Dreams: America in the 1960s.* New York: Hill and Wang.

Farley, Wendy. 1996. *Eros for the Other: Retaining Truth in a Pluralistic World.* University Park: The Pennsylvania State University Press.

Farrell, James J. 1997. *The Spirit of the Sixties: The Making of Postwar Radicalism.* New York: Routledge.

Feagin, Joe and Eileen O'Brien, 2003. *White Men on Race: Power, Privilege, and the Shaping of Cultural Consciousness.* Boston: Beacon Press.

Feagin, Joe R. 2009. *The White Racial Frame: Centuries of Racial Framing and Counter-framing.* New York: Routledge.

Feagin, Joe R. 2014. *Racist America: Roots, Current Realities, and Future Reparations*, third edition. New York: Routledge.

Fields, Barbara Jean. 1990."Slavery, Race, and Ideology in the United States of America." *New Left Review* 181 (May-June): 95–118.

Fishkin, Shelley Fisher. 1995. "Interrogating 'Whiteness,' Complicating 'Blackness': Remapping American Culture." *American Quarterly* 47:3 (September): 428–466.

FitzGerald, Frances. 1972. *Fire in the Lake: The Vietnamese and the Americans in Vietnam.* New York: Vintage Books.

Flacks, Richard. 1988. *Making History: The Radical Tradition in American Life.* New York: Columbia University Press.

Foley, Michael S. 2003. *Confronting the War Machine: Draft Resistance During the Vietnam War.* Chapel Hill: The University of North Carolina Press.

Foreman, James. 1985. *The Making of Black Revolutionaries*. Seattle: University of Washington Press.

Formisamo, Ronald. 2017. *American Oligarchy: The Permanence of the Political Class*. Urbana: University of Illinois Press.

Four Arrows. 2019. "Violence Against Indigenous People is Rising Across the World." *Truthout*, January 26, 2019. https://truthout.org/articles/violence-against-indigenous-people-is-rising-across-the-world.

Fraga, Bernard, et al. "Why Did Trump Win?" *Washington Post*, May 8 2017. https://www.washingtonpost.com/news/monkey-cage/wp/2017/05/08/why-did-trump-win-more-whites-and-fewer-blacks-than-normal-actually-voted/?utm_term=.2b85dc7e1a92.

Frankenberg, Ruth. 1993. *White Women, Race Matters: The Social Construction of Whiteness*. Minneapolis: University of Minnesota Press.

Frankenberg, Ruth. 2001. "The Mirage of an Unmarked Whiteness." In *The Making and Unmaking of Whiteness*, edited by Birgit Brander Rasmussen et al., 72–96. Durham, NC: Duke University Press.

Franchetti, Mark. 2003. "Slaughter at the Bridge of Death." *London Times*, March 31, 2003. http://counterpunch.org/franchetti03312003.html.

Garza, Alicia. 2014. "A History of the #*BlackLivesMatter* Movement." *The Feminist Wire*, October 7, 2014. http://www.thefeministwire.com/2014/10/blacklivesmatter-2.

Georgakas, Dan and Marvin Surkin. 1998. *Detroit I Do Mind Dying*. Cambridge, MA: South End Press.

Geschwender, James. A. 1977. *Class, Race, and Worker Insurgency: The League of Revolutionary Black Workers*. New York: Cambridge University Press.

Gest, Justin. 2016. *The New Minority: White Working Class Politics in an Age of Immigration and Inequality*. New York: Oxford University Press.

Gibson, William. 2000. *The Perfect War: Technowar in Vietnam*. New York: Atlantic Monthly Press.

Giroux, Henry A. 1997. "Rewriting the Discourse of Racial Identity: Towards a Pedagogy and Politics of Whiteness." *Harvard Educational Review* 67:2 (Summer): 285–320.

Giroux, Henry A. 2018. *The Public in Peril: Trump and the Menace of American Authoritarianism*. New York: Routledge.

Giroux, Henry A. 2018. "Neoliberal Fascism and the Echoes of History." *Truthout*, August 8, 2018. https://truthout.org/articles/neoliberal-fascism-and-the-echoes-of-history/.

Gitlin, Todd. 1989. *The Sixties: Years of Hope, Days of Rage*. New York: Bantam.

Glaude, Eddie S., Jr. 2016. *Democracy in Black: How Race Still Enslaves the American Soul*. New York: Crown Publishers.

Glenn, Evelyn Nakano. 2002. *Unequal Freedom: How Race and Gender Shape American Citizenship and Labor.* Cambridge, MA: Harvard University Press.

Golash-Boza, Tanya Maria. 2016. *Immigration Nation: Raids, Detention, and Deportation in Post 9/11 America.* New York: Routledge.

Goldberg, David Theo. 2002. *The Racial State.* Walden, MA: Blackwell Publishers.

Goldberg, David Theo. 2009. *The Threat of Race: Reflections on Racial Neoliberalism.* Walden, MA: Blackwell.

Gottschalk, Marie. 2014. *Caught: The Prison State and the Lockdown of American Politics.* Princeton, NJ: Princeton University Press.

Graebner, William. 1990. *Coming of Age in Buffalo: Youth and Authority in the Postwar Era.* Philadelphia: Temple University Press.

Grandin, Greg. 2007. *Empire's Workshop: Latin America, the United States and the Rise of the New Imperialism.* New York: Holt Paperbacks.

Grandin, Greg. 2019. *The End of the Myth: From the Frontier to the Border Wall in the Mind of America.* New York: Metropolitan Books.

Grandin, Greg. 2019. "The Border Patrol Has Been a Cult of Brutality Since 1924." *The Intercept,* January 12, 2019. https://theintercept.com/2019/01/12/border-patrol-history/.

Greenberg, Amy S. 2005. *Manifest Manhood and the Antebellum American Empire.* New York: Cambridge University Press.

Greenberg, Cheryl Lynn, ed. 1998. *A Circle of Trust: Remembering SNCC.* New Brunswick, NJ: Rutgers University Press.

Grenier, John. 2005. *The First Way of War, 1607–1814.* New York: Cambridge University Press.

Hadden, Sally E. 2001. *Slave Patrols: Law and Violence in Virginia and the Carolinas.* Cambridge, MA: Harvard University Press.

Hahn, Steven. 2017. "The Rage of White Folk." *The Nation,* October 16, 2017.

Hankes, Keegan and Alex Amend. 2018. "The Alt-Right is Killing People." *Salon,* February 11, 2018. https://www.salon.com/2018/02/11/the-alt-right-is-killing-people_partner.

Harley, Shirley. 2001. "'Chronicle of a Death Foretold': Gloria Richardson, the Cambridge Movement, and the Radical Black Activist Tradition." In *Sisters in the Struggle: African American Women in the Civil Rights-Black Power Movement,* edited by Bettye Collier-Thomas and V.P. Franklin, 174–196. New York: New York University Press.

Harrington, Michael. 1966. "Introduction." In Jack Newfield, *A Prophetic Minority.* New York: Signet.

Harrison, Bennett and Barry Bluestone. 1990. *The Great U-Turn: Corporate Restructuring and the Polarizing of America.* New York: Basic Books.

Hartigan, John Jr. 1999. *Racial Situations: Class Predicaments of Whiteness in Detroit.* Princeton, NJ: Princeton University Press.

Harvey, David. 2001. *Spaces of Capital: Towards a Critical Geography.* New York: Routledge.

Harvey, David. 2005. *The New Imperialism.* New York: Oxford University Press.

Hinton, Elizabeth. 2016. *From the War on Poverty to the War on Crime.* Cambridge, MA: Harvard University Press.

Hixon, Walter L. 2008. *The Myth of American Diplomacy: National Identity and U.S. Foreign Policy.* New Haven, CT: Yale University Press.

Hochschild, Arlie Russell. 2016. *Strangers in Their Own Land: Anger and Mourning on the American Right.* New York: The New Press.

Hoerl, Kristen. 2008. "Mississippi's Social Transformation in Public Memories of the Trial Against Byron De La Beckwith for the Murder of Medgar Evers." *Western Journal of Communication* 72:1 (Jan/March): 62–82.

Hogan, Wesley C. 2007. *Many Minds, One Heart: SNCC's Dream for a New America.* Chapel Hill: The University of North Carolina Press.

Hohle, Randolph. 2015. *Race and the Origins of American Neoliberalism.* New York: Routledge.

Holt, Len. 1965. *The Summer That Didn't End.* New York: William Morrow & Co.

Hooks, Bell. 2000. *Where We Stand: Class Matters.* New York: Routledge.

Horne, Gerald. 2018. *The Apocalypse of Settler Colonialism.* New York: Monthly Review Press.

Horsman, Reginald. 1981. *Race and Manifest Destiny: The Origins of American Racial Anglo-Saxonism.* Cambridge, MA: Harvard University Press.

International Labor and Working Class History Forum. 2001. "Whiteness and the Historians Imagination." *ILWCH* 60 (Fall): 1–92.

Ioanide, Paula. 2015. *The Emotional Politics of Racism: How Feelings Trump Facts in an Age of Colorblindness.* Stanford, CA: Stanford University Press.

Isaacs, Arnold R. 2019. "A Cruel War on Immigrants." *TomDispatch*, February 7, 2019. http://www.tomdispatch.com/post/176524/tomgram%3A_arnold_isaacs%2C_a_catalog_of_heartlessness.

Jacoby, Susan. 2009. *The Age of American Unreason.* New York: Vintage.

Jacobson, Matthew Frye. 1999. *Whiteness of a Different Color: European Immigrants and the Alchemy of Race.* Cambridge, MA: Harvard University Press Paperback.

Jardina, Ashley. "White Identity Politics Isn't Just About White Supremacy." *Washington Post,* August 16, 2017. https://www.washingtonpost.com/news/monkey-cage/wp/2017/08/16/white-identity-politics-isnt-just-about-white-supremacy-its-much-bigger/?utm_term=.48e1333a46c5.

Jean-Pierre, Karine. 2018. "The Problem Isn't That Trump is Racist. It's That He Keeps Acting on His Racism." *Commondreams*, January 12, 2018. https://www.commondreams.org/views/2018/01/12/problem-isnt-just-trumps-racist-its-he-keeps-acting-his-racism.

Johnson, Walter. 2013. *River of Dark Dreams: Slavery and Empire in the Cotton Kingdom*. Cambridge, MA: The Belknap Press of Harvard University Press.

Joseph, Peniel E. 2006. *Waiting 'Til the Midnight Hour: A Narrative History of Black Power in America*. New York: Holt.

Jung, Moon-Kie. 2015. *Beneath the Surface of White Supremacy: Denaturalizing U.S. Racisms Past and Present*. Stanford, CA: Stanford University Press.

Katagiri, Yasukiro. 2001. *The Mississippi State Sovereignty Commission: Civil Rights and State Rights*. Jackson: University Press of Mississippi.

Katznelson, Ira. 2005. *When Affirmative Action was White: An Untold History of Racial Inequality in Twentieth-Century America*. New York: W.W. Norton & Co.

Kaufman, Brett Max. 2018. "Trump is Unshackling America's Drones Thanks to Obama's Weakness." *The Guardian*, September 17, 2018. https://www.theguardian.com/commentisfree/2018/sep/17/the-cia-is-back-in-the-drone-business-trump-is-unshackling-americas-drones-thanks-to-obamas-weakness.

Keefe, Patrick Radden. 2019. "Winning." *The New Yorker*, January 7, 2019.

Kelley, Robin D.G. "Why We Won't Wait." *CounterPunch*, November 25, 2014. http://www.counterpunch.org/2014/11/25/75039/.

Kellner, Douglas. 1992. *The Persian Gulf TV War*. Boulder, CO: Westview Press.

Keniston, Kenneth. 1968. *Young Radicals: Notes on Committed Youth*. New York: Harcourt, Brace, and World.

Kennedy, Paul. 2017. *Vampire Capitalism: Fractured Societies and Alternative Futures*. London: Palgrave McMillan.

King, Demond S. and Rogers M. Smith. 2011. *Still a House Divided: Race and Politics in Obama's America*. Princeton, NJ: Princeton University Press.

King, Mary. 1987. *Freedom Song: A Personal Story of the 1960s Civil Rights Movement*. New York: William Morrow & Co.

King, Mike. 2017. "Aggrieved Whiteness: White Identity Politics and Modern American Racial Formation." *Abolition Journal*, May 4, 2017. https://abolitionjournal.org/aggrieved-whiteness-white-identity-politics-and-modern-american-racial-formation.

Klein, Naomi. 2017. *No is not Enough: Resisting Trump's Shock Politics and Winning the World we Need*. Chicago: Haymarket Books.

Knowles, Eric D. and Linda R. Tropp. 2016. "Donald Trump and the Rise of White Identity in Politics." *The Conversation*, October 20, 2016. https://theconversation.com/donald-trump-and-the-rise-of-white-identity-in-politics-67037.

Kuttner, Robert. 2018. *Can Democracy Survive Global Capitalism*. New York: W.W. Norton.

Lahte, Janne. 2017. *Wars for Empire: Apaches, the United States, and the Southwest Borderlands*. Norman: University of Oklahoma Press.

Landrieu, Mitch. 2018. *In the Shadow of Statues: A White Southerner Confronts History*. New York: Viking.

Lamont, Michele. 2000. *The Dignity of Working Men: Morality and the Boundaries of Race, Class, and Immigration*. New York: Russell Sage Foundation.

Lamont, Michele, et al. 2017. "Trump's Electoral Speeches and His Appeal to the American White Working Class." *The British Journal of Sociology*, 68 (November): 153–180.

Langman, Lauren and George Lundskow. 2016. *God, Guns, Gold and Glory: American Character and its Discontents*. Chicago: Haymarket Books.

Lebron, Christopher J. 2017. *The Making of Black Lives Matter*. New York: Oxford University Press.

Lentin, Alana. 2011. "What Happens to Anti-Racism When We Are Post Race?" *Feminist Legal Studies* 19:2 (August): 159–168.

Leonard, Natasha. 2018. "Attack on the Immigrant Poor." *The Intercept*, September 26, 2018. https://theintercept.com/2018/09/26/public-charge-immigration-green-card.

Lewis-Colman, David M. 2008. *Race Against Liberalism: Black Workers and the UAW in Detroit*. Urbana: University of Illinois Press.

Levy, Peter B. 2003. *Civil War on Race Street: The Civil Rights Movement in Cambridge, Maryland*. Gainesville: University Press of Florida.

Lichtenstein, Nelson. 2002. *State of the Union: A Century of American Labor*. Princeton, NJ: Princeton University Press.

Lipsitz, George. 1990. *Time Passages: Collective Memory and American Popular Culture*. Minneapolis: University of Minnesota Press.

Lipsitz, George. 2006. *The Possessive Investment of Whiteness: How White People Profit from Identity Politics*. Philadelphia: Temple University Press.

Lindorff, Dave. 2014. "More Americans Killed by Police Than by Terrorists." *Alternet*, September 25, 2014. https://www.alternet.org/civil-liberties/more-americans-killed-police-terrorists-crime-down-why-police-aggression.

Louis, Debbie. 1970. *And We Are Not Saved: A History of the Movement as People*. GardenCity, NJ: Doubleday & Co.

Love, Eric. T.L. 2004. *Race Over Empire: Racism and U.S. Imperialism, 1865–1900*. Chapel Hill: The University of North Carolina Press.

Lowery, Wesley. 2016. *"They Can't Kill Us All": Ferguson, Baltimore, and a New Era in America's Racial Justice Movement*. New York: Little, Brown and Co.

Lowndes, Joseph E. 2008. *From the New Deal to the New Right: Race and the Southern Origins of Modern Conservatism*. New Haven, CT: Yale University Press.

Mahler, Jonathan. 2009. "General Motors, Detroit, and the Fall of the Black Middle Class." *New York Times Magazine*, June 24, 2009.

Marable, Manning. 2001. *The Great Wells of Democracy: The Meaning of Race in American Life*. New York: Basic Civitas Books.

Martin, Waldo. 2002. "Holding One Another: Mario Savio and the Freedom Struggle in Mississippi and Berkeley." In *The Free Speech Movement: Reflections on Berkeley in the 1960s*, edited by Robert Cohen and Reginald E. Zelnik, 83–102. Berkeley: University of California Press.

Martinot, Steve. 2010. *The Machinery of Whiteness: Studies in the Structure of Racialization*. Philadelphia: Temple University Press.

Massengill, Reed. 1994. *Portrait of a Racist: The Man Who Killed Medgar Evers?* New York: St. Martin's Press.

Mayer, Jane. 2017. *Dark Money: The Hidden History of the Billionaires Behind the Rise of the Radical Right*. New York: Anchor Books.

Mazelis, Fred. 2016. "*Sweat*: An Honest Depiction of the American Working Class." World Socialist Website. December 30, 2016. https://www.wsws.org/en/articles/2016/12/30/swea-d30.html.

McAdam, Doug. 1988. *Freedom Summer*. New York: Oxford University Press.

McKesson, DeRay. 2018. *On the Other Side of Freedom*. New York: Viking.

McWhorter, Diane. 2001. *Carry Me Home*. New York: Simon & Schuster.

Melamed, Jodi. 2015. "Racial Capitalism." *Critical Ethnic Studies* 1 (Spring): 76–85.

Menand, Louis. 2019. "In the Eye of the Law." *The New Yorker*, February 4, 2019.

Metzl, Jonathan M. 2019. *Dying of Whiteness: How the Politics of Racial Resentment is Killing America's Heartland*. New York: Basic Books.

Meyerson, Collier. 2017. "Inside the Fight to Take Down the Confederate Monuments in New Orleans." *The Nation*, June 19, 2017. https://www.thenation.com/article/inside-the-fight-to-take-down-the-confederate-monuments-in-new-orleans/.

Michel, Gregg L. 2004. *Struggle for a Better South: The Southern Student Organizing Committee, 1964–1969*. New York: Palgrave Macmillan.

Milkman, Ruth. 1997. *Farewell to the Factory: Auto Workers in the Late Twentieth Century*. Berkeley: University of California Press.

Miller, James. 1994. *"Democracy is in the Streets": From Port Huron to the Siege of Chicago*. Cambridge, MA: Harvard University Press.

Miller, Laura. 2013. "Death of an American Sniper." *Salon*, February 7, 2013. https://www.salon.com/2013/02/07/death_of_an_american_sniper.

Moody, Anne. 1968. *Coming of Age in Mississippi*. New York: Laurel.

Moore, Michael Quess? 2018. "How Black Activism is Coopted and Deflated by Liberal Politicians Like NOLA's Mayor Landrieu." *RaceBaitr*, May 3, 2018. https://racebaitr.com/2018/05/03/how-black-activism-is-coopted-and-deflated-by-liberal-politicians-like-nolas-mayor-landrieu.

Moreton-Robinson, Arleen. 2015. *The White Possessive: Property, Power, and Indigenous Sovereignty.* Minneapolis: University of Minnesota Press.

Morgan, Edmund P. 1991. *The Sixties Experience: Hard Lessons about Modern America.* Philadelphia: Temple University Press.

Morris, Aldon D. 1984. *The Origins of the Civil Rights Movement.* New York: The Free Press.

Morris, Tiyi. M. 2015. *Womanpower Unlimited and the Black Freedom Struggle in Mississippi.* Athens: The University of Georgia.

Muhammad, Ashahed M. 2012. "Above the Law? Extrajudicial Killings of Blacks Are Increasing." *The Final Call,* July 17, 2012. https://www.finalcall.com/artman/publish/National_News_2/article_9045.shtml.

Mutz, Diana C. 2018. "Status Threat, not Economic Hardship, Explains the 2016 Presidential Vote." *PNAS,* April 23, 2018. https://www.pnas.org/content/115/19/E4330.

NORC Center for Public Affairs. 2015. "Law Enforcement and Violence: The Divide Between Black and White Americans." http://www.apnorc.org/projects/Pages/law-enforcement-and-violence-the-divide-between-black-and-white-americans.aspx.

Nossiter, Adam. 1994. *Of Long Memory: Mississippi and the Murder of Medgar Evers.* Reading, MA: Addison & Wiley.

Nottage, Lynn. 2017. *Sweat.* New York: Theatre Communication Group.

Nugent, Walter. 2009. *Habits of Empire: A History of American Expansion.* New York: Vintage Books.

Obineme, Ejike. 2018. "Too Afraid to Enter an Arena of Ideas? The Debate Over Cornel West's Critique of Ta-Nehisi Coates." *Truthout,* January 4, 2018. https://truthout.org/articles/too-terrified-to-enter-an-arena-of-ideas-the-debate-over-cornel-west-s-critique-of-ta-nehisi-coates.

O'Brien, Eileen. 2001. *Whites Confront Racism: Antiracists and their Paths to Action.* Lanham, MD: Rowman & Littlefield.

Olson, Joel. 2004. *The Abolition of White Democracy.* Minneapolis: University of Minnesota Press.

Olson, Lynne. 2001. *Freedom's Daughters: The Unsung Heroines of the Civil Rights Movement from 1830 to 1970.* New York: Scribner.

Omi, Michael. 2001 "(E)racism: Emerging Practices of Antiracist Organizations." In *The Making and Unmaking of Whiteness,* edited by Birgit Brander Rasmussen et al., 266–293. Durham, NC: Duke University Press.

Omi, Michael and Howard Winant. 2015. *Racial Formation in the United States,* third ed. New York. Routledge.

Osnos, Evan. 2018. "Ghost in the Machine," *The New Yorker,* September 17, 2018.

Page, Benjamin and Martin Gilens. 2018. *Democracy in America? What Has Gone Wrong and What We Can Do About It.* Chicago: University of Chicago Press.

Palast, Greg. 2019. "In Venezuela, White Supremacy is a Key Driver of the Coup." *Truthout*, February 7, 2019. https://truthout.org/articles/in-venezuela-white-supremacy-is-a-key-driver-of-the-coup/.

Pardun, Robert. 2001. *Prairie Radical: A Journey Through the Sixties* (Los Gatos, NM: Shire Press).

Patterson, Richard North. 2018. "Donald Trump Has Put White Identity Politics on Steroids," *Boston Globe*, June 5, 2018. https://www.bostonglobe.com/opinion/2018/06/05/donald-trump-has-put-white-identity-politics-steroids/VVo4fUc6EavsBgOvQS9EnI/story.html.

Payne, Charles M. 1995. *I've Got the Light of Freedom: The Organizing Tradition and the Mississippi Freedom Struggle.* Berkeley: University of California Press.

Perusek, Glenn. 2017. "Class, Race, and Political Strategy in the Rust Belt." *Stansbury Forum*, May 30, 2017. http://stansburyforum.com/class-race-and-political-strategy-in-the-rust-belt.

Piketty, Thomas. 2014. *Capital in the Twenty-First Century*. Cambridge, MA: Harvard University Press.

Polletta, Francesca. 2002. *Freedom is an Endless Meeting: Democracy in American Social Movements*. Chicago: The University of Chicago Press.

Quigley, Bill. 2017. "Major Challenges of New Orleans Charter Schools." *CounterPunch*, April 25, 2017. https://www.counterpunch.org/2017/04/25/major-challenges-of-new-orleans-charter-schools-exposed-at-naacp-hearing.

Ransby, Barbara. 2003. *Ella Baker and the Black Freedom Movement*. Chapel Hill: The University of North Carolina Press.

Ransby, Barbara. 2018. *Making All Black Lives Matter.* Oakland: University of California Press.

Rashid, Ahmed. 2008. *Descent into Chaos: The United States and the Failure of Nation Building in Pakistan, Afghanistan, and Central Asia.* New York: Viking.

Riverbend. 2005. *Baghdad Burning: Girl Blog from Iraq*. New York: Feminist Press at the City University of New York.

Robnett, Belinda. 2002. "External Political Change, Collective Identities, and Participation in Social Movement Organizations." In *Social Movements: Identity, Culture, and the State*, edited by David S. Meyer, Nancy Whittier, and Belinda Robnett, 266–285. New York: Oxford University Press.

Roediger, David. 1994. *Towards the Abolition of Whiteness.* New York: Verso.

Roediger, David R. 2010. *How Race Survived U.S. History.* New York: Verso.

Roediger David R. 2017. *Class, Race, and Marxism.* New York: Verso.

Roediger, David R. 2018. "On the Defensive: Navigating White Advantage and White Fragility." *Los Angeles Review of Books*, September 6, 2018. https://lareviewofbooks.org/article/on-the-defensive-navigating-white-advantage-and-white-fragility/#.

Rogers, Kim Lacy. 1993. *Righteous Lives: Narratives of the New Orleans Civil Rights Movement*. New York: New York University Press.

Rogin, Michael Paul. 1976. *Fathers and Children: Andrew Jackson and the Subjugation of the American Indian*. New York: Vintage Books.

Romano, Renee C. and Leigh Raiford., eds. 2006. *The Civil Rights Movement in American History*. Athens: The University of Georgia Press.

Romano, Renee C. 2014. *Racial Reckoning: Prosecuting America's Civil Rights Murders*. Cambridge, MA: Harvard University Press.

Rosen, Deborah. 2015. *Border Law: The First Seminole War and American Nationhood*. Cambridge, MA: Harvard University Press.

Rosenfield Seth. 2012. *Subversives: The FBI's War on Student Radicals and Reagan's Rise to Power*. New York: Farrar, Straus & Giroux.

Rossinow, Doug. 1998. *The Politics of Authenticity: Liberalism, Christianity, and the New Left in America*. New York: Columbia University Press.

Rothschild, Mary Aickin. 1982. *A Case of Black and White: Northern Volunteers and the Southern Freedom Summers, 1964–1965*. Westport, CT: Greenwood Publishing.

Rothstein, Richard. 2017. *The Color of Law*. New York: Liveright.

Roy, Arundhati. 2004. *An Ordinary Person's Guide to Empire*. Cambridge, MA: South End Press.

Russell, Margaret M. 2003. "Cleansing Moments and Retrospective Justice." *Michigan Law Review* 101:5: 1225–1268.

Ryan, Brent D. and Daniel Campo. 2013. "Autopia's End: The Decline and Fall of Detroit's Automotive Manufacturing Landscape." *Journal of Planning History* 12:2 (May): 95–132.

Sale, Kirkpatrick. 1974. *SDS*. New York: Vintage Books.

Sally Belfrage Papers, Micro 599, Reel 1, State Historical Society of Wisconsin.

Salter, John R. 1987. *Jackson, Mississippi: An American Chronicle of Struggle and Schism*. Malabar, FL: Robert E. Krieger Publishing.

San Juan, E., Jr. 2002. *Racism and Cultural Studies: Critiques of Multiculturalist Ideology and the Politics of Difference*. Durham, NC: Duke University Press.

Sardar, Ziauddin and Meryl Wyn Davies. 2002. *Why Do People Hate America?* New York: The Disinformation Co.

Savage, Kirk. 2018. *Standing Soldiers, Kneeling Slaves: Race, War, and Monument in Nineteenth-Century America*. Princeton, NJ: Princeton University Press.

Schein, Richard. 2018. "After Charlottesville: Reflections on Landscape, White Supremacy, and White Hegemony." *Southeastern Geographer* 58:1 (Spring): 10–13.

Scholz, Sally J. 2008. *Political Solidarity*. University Park, PA: The Pennsylvania State University Press.

Schultz, Debra L. 2001. *Going South: Jewish Women in the Civil Rights Movement*. New York: New York University Press.

Sellars, Cleveland. 1973. *The River of No Return: The Autobiography of a Black Militant and the Life and Death of SNCC*. New York: William Morrow & Co.

Sennett, Richard and Jonathan Cobb. 1972. *The Hidden Injuries of Class*. New York: Alfred A. Knopf.

Shulman, Michael. 2017. "The Listener." *The New Yorker*, March 27, 2017.

Silver, Beverly. 2003. *Forces of Labor: Workers' Movements and Globalization Since 1870*. New York: Cambridge University Press.

Singh, Nikhil Pal. 2017. *Race and America's Long War*. Oakland: University of California Press.

Slotkin, Richard. 1985. *The Fatal Environment: The Myth of the Frontier in an Age of Industrialization, 1800–1890*. New York: Atheneum.

Slotkin, Richard. 1993. *Gunfighter Nation: The Myth of the Frontier in Twentieth Century America*. New York: HarperPerennial.

Small, Mel. 2002. *Antiwarriors: The Vietnam War and the Battle for America's Hearts and Minds*. Wilmington, DE: Scholarly Resources.

Smith, Chip. 2007. *The Cost of Privilege: Taking On the System of White Supremacy and Racism*. Fayetteville, NC: Camino Press.

Smith, Robert C. 2010. *Conservatism and Racism, and Why in America They Are the Same*. Albany: State University of New York Press.

Soberon, Lennart. 2017. "The Old West in the New Middle East: *American Sniper* and the Global Frontier of the Western Genre." *European Journal of American Studies* 12:2 (Summer): 1–32. https://journals.openedition.org/ejas/12086#entries.

Southern Poverty Law Center. 2019. "Whose Heritage? Public Symbols of the Confederacy." February 1, 2019.

Stein, Michael. 2017. "Democrats Deserve Better Than Mitch Landrieu." *The New Republic*, August 24, 2017. https://newrepublic.com/article/144446/democrats-deserve-better-mitch-landrieu.

Steinhorn, Leonard. 2014. "White Men and Their Guns." *Huffington Post*, February 16, 2014. https://www.huffpost.com/entry/white-men-and-their-guns_b_4419903.

Stepan-Norris, Judith and Maurice Zeitlin. 2003. *Left Out: Reds and America's Industrial Unions*. New York: Cambridge University Press.

Stevenson, Bryan. 2017. "A Presumption of Guilt: The Legacy of America's History of Racial Injustice." In *Policing the Black Man*, edited by Angela Davis, 3–30. New York: Pantheon Books.

Stoper, Emily. 1989. *The Student Nonviolent Coordinating Committee: The Growth of Radicalism in a Civil Rights Organization*. New York: Carlson Publishing, Inc.

Street, Paul. 2010. "Is Barack Obama Bad for Racial Justice." *Black Agenda Report*, October 6, 2010. https://www.blackagendareport.com/content/barack-obama-bad-racial-justice.

Sugrue, Thomas J. 1995. "'Forget about Your Inalienable Right to Work': Deindustrialization and Its Discontents at Ford, 1950–1953." *International Labor and Working Class History* 48 (Fall): 112–130.

Sugrue, Thomas J. 1996. *The Origins of the Urban Crisis: Race and Inequality in Postwar Detroit.* Princeton, NJ: Princeton University Press.

Sugrue, Thomas J. 2008. *Sweet Land of Liberty: The Forgotten Struggle for Civil Rights in the North.* New York: Random House Paperbacks.

Sugrue, Thomas J. 2010. *Not Even Past: Barack Obama and the Burden of Race.* Princeton, NJ: Princeton University Press.

Sutherland, Elizabeth, ed. 1965. *Letters from Mississippi.* New York: McGraw-Hill.

Takaki, Ronald. 2008. *A Different Mirror: The Making of Multicultural America.* New York: Back Bay Books.

Taylor, Keeanga-Yamahtta. 2016. *From #BlackLivesMatter to Black Liberation.* Chicago: Haymarket Books.

Tesler, Michael. 2016. *Post-Racial or Most-Racial: Race and Politics in the Obama Era.* Chicago: The University of Chicago Press.

Thompson, Becky. 2001. *A Promise and A Way of Life: White Antiracist Activism.* Minneapolis: University of Minnesota Press.

Thompson, Heather Ann. 2001. *Whose Detroit? Politics, Labor and Race in a Modern American City.* Ithaca, NY: Cornell University Press.

Torres, Sasha. 2003. *Black, White, and In Color: Television and Black Civil Rights.* Princeton, NJ: Princeton University Press.

Trachte, Kent and Robert Ross. 1985. "The Crisis of Detroit and the Emergence of Global Capitalism." *The International Journal of Urban and Regional Research* 9:2 (June): 186–217.

Turse, Nick. 2017. *Kill Anything That Moves: The Real American War in Vietnam.* New York: Metropolitan Books.

Twine, France Winddance and Charles Gallagher. 2008. "The Future of Whiteness: A Map of the 'Third Wave.'" *Ethnic and Racial Studies* 31:1 (January): 4–24.

Tyson, Timothy B. 2017. *The Blood of Emmett Till.* New York: Simon & Schuster Paperbacks.

Vollers, Maryanne. 1995. *Ghosts of Mississippi: The Murder of Medgar Evers, the Trials of Byron De La Beckwith, and the Haunting of the New South.* Boston: Little, Brown & Co.

Walker, Alice. 1976. *Meridian.* New York: Washington Square Press.

Walker, Clarence E. 2011."We're Losing Our Country: Barack Obama, Race, and the Tea Party." *Daedalus* 140:1 (Winter 2011): 125–130.

Wallerstein, Immanuel. 2003. *The Decline of American Power: The U.S. in a Chaotic World.* New York: The New Press.

Ward, Brian. 1998. *Just My Soul Responding: Rhythm and Blues, Black Consciousness, and Race Relations*. Berkeley: University of California Press.

Warren, Mark R. 2010. *Fire in the Heart: How White Activists Embrace Racial Justice*. New York: Oxford University Press.

Watson, Bruce. 2010. *Freedom Summer*. New York: Viking.

Weisbrot, Robert. 1991. *Freedom Bound: A History of America's Civil Rights Movement*. New York: Plume.

Wells, Tom. 1994. *The War Within: America's Battle over Vietnam*. New York: Henry Holt and Co.

West, Cornell. 2018. "America is Spiritually Bankrupt. We Must Fight Back." *The Guardian,* January 14, 2018. https://www.theguardian.com/commentisfree/2018/jan/14/america-is-spiritually-bankrupt-we-must-fight-back-together.

Williams, Joan C. 2017. *White Working Class: Overcoming Class Cluelessness in America*. Boston: Harvard Business Review Press.

Williams, William Appleman. 1982. *Empire as a Way of Life*. New York: Oxford University Press.

Winant, Howard. 2001. "White Racial Projects." In *The Making and Unmaking of Whiteness*, edited by Brigit Brander Rasmussen, et al., 97–112. Durham, NC: Duke University Press.

Winant, Howard. 2004. "Behind Blue Eyes: Whiteness and Contemporary U.S. Racial Politics." In *Off White: Readings on Power, Privilege, and Resistance*, second ed., edited by Michelle Fine et al., 3–16. New York: Routledge.

Wise, Tim. 2010. *Color-Blind: The Rise of Post-Racial Politics and the Retreat from Racial Equity*. San Francisco: City Lights Books.

Wise, Tim. 2012. *Dear White America: Letter to a New Minority*. San Francisco: City Lights Books.

Wise, Tim. 2018. Interview by Chauncey Devega,. *Salon*, September 5, 2018. https://www.salon.com/2018/09/05/author-and-activist-tim-wise-the-republican-party-is-a-white-identity-cult.

Wright, Kai. 2017. "On White Identity Politics and American Terrorism." *The Nation,* September 12, 2017. https://www.thenation.com/article/on-white-identity-politics-and-american-terrorism.

Wu, Frank H. 2002. *Yellow: Race in America Beyond Black and White*. New York: Basic Books.

Wylie, Jeanie. 1990. *Poletown: Community Betrayed*. Urbana: University of Illinois Press.

Yancy, George. 2004. *What White Looks Like*. New York: Routledge.

Yancy, George and Judith Butler. 2015. "What's Wrong with 'All Lives Matter.'" *New York Times*, January 12, 2015. http://opinionator.blogs.nytimes.com/2015/01/12/whats-wrong-with-all.

Young, Marilyn B. 2002. "The Age of Global Power." In *Rethinking American History in a Global Age*, edited by Thomas Bender, 274–294. Berkeley: University of California Press.

Zellner, Bob (with Constance Curry). 2008. *The Wrong Side of Murder Creek: A White Southerner in the Freedom Movement*. Montgomery, AL: New South Books.

Zinn, Howard. 2002 (originally published in 1964). *SNCC: The New Abolitionists*. Cambridge, MA: South End Press.

Zinn, Howard. 1995. *A People's History of the United States*, rev. ed. New York: HarperPerennial.

Zornick, George. 2018. "How the #NeverAgain Movement is Disrupting Gen Politics." *The Nation*, April 30/May 7, 2018.

Name Index

Abramsky, Sasha 34, 37
Adams, John Quincy 10, 11–12
Ahmadinejad, Mahmoud 84
Alexander, Michelle 94, 121, 132
Allen, Ralph 49
Allen, Theodore 82
Anderson, Carol 26, 62, 84, 118
Appiah, Kwame 123, 132
Aycock, Charles Brantley 77–78

Babson, Steve 109, 110
Bacevich, Andrew 99
Baker, Ella 93, 97
Baldwin, James 20, 21, 52, 53, 68, 82, 97, 99, 119, 122
Ballard, Hank 52
Bannon, Steve 128
Barry, Dante 91, 94
Beauregard, P.G.T. 79
Beck, Glenn 83, 87
Beckwith, Byron de la 5, 68, 69, 70, 71, 72, 73, 74
Belfrage, Sally 55, 57, 59
Bell, Derrick 85, 86
Bellamy, Francis 125
Blanchard, Terrence 79
Blow, Charles 94
Bluestone, Barry 111
Boggs, Grace Lee 113
Bond, Julian 51
Bonilla-Silva, Eduardo 82, 85, 88
Bowers, Sam 68, 69
Bray, Michael 89
Brown, John 132
Brown, Michael 28, 29, 86, 95
Browning, Joan 51
Brundage, Avery 77, 78, 79, 80
Brundage, Fitzhugh 79
Buchanan, Pat 128
Burlage, Dorothy Dawson 51
Bush, George H.W. 15
Bush, George W. 15, 16, 49, 72
Butler, Judith 96

Calhoun, John 12
Calley, William 14

Carlson, Dennis 70, 76
Carmichael, Stokely (Kwame Ture) 64
Chaney, James 29, 55, 68
Chen, Victor Tan 117
Cleaver, Eldridge 52
Clinton, Hillary 1, 117
Coates, Ta-Nehisi 32, 122
Cobb, Jonathan 114, 115, 118
Columbus, Christopher 125, 128
Cooke, Sam 97
Cowie, Jefferson 108, 116
Cruse, Harold 82
Curry, Constance 51, 56

Dahmer, Vernon 68
Daniels, Jessie 118
Daniels, Jon 63
Davis, Jefferson 78
Davis, Mike 42
de Blasio, Bill 95
de Tocqueville, Alexis 11
DeVos, Betsy 37
Del Pozzo, Theresa 56
Diamond, Dion 56
DiAngelo, Robin 2, 5, 100, 101, 105
Doležal, Rachel 128, 132
Douglass, Frederick 12, 125, 132
Drinnon, Richard 9, 10, 14
DuBois, W.E.B. 48, 82, 89, 122, 125
Dudziak, Mary 49
Dunbar-Ortiz, Roxanne 10, 22, 23, 100, 104, 122
Duster, Troy 11, 80
Dylan, Bob 72

Eastwood, Clint 17
Eisenstein, Zillah 100
Englehardt, Tom 14
Estes, Nick 43
Evers, Charles 70, 73
Evers, Medgar 5, 54, 68, 69, 70, 71, 72, 73
Evers, Myrlie 69, 73, 75
Ewen, Stuart 56, 57

Farley, Wendy 102
Faulkner, William 68

NAME INDEX

Feagin, Joe 3, 49, 82, 85, 99, 101
Fields, Barbara Jean 22
Fitzgerald, Frances 14
Fletcher, Bill 40
Ford, Christine Blasey 38
Ford, Glen 87
Forman, James 57, 58
Forrest, Nathan Bedford 77
Franchetti, Mark 17
Frank, Thomas 34
Frankenberg, Ruth 38, 48, 49, 82, 88
Futterman, Craig 28, 29

Garner, Eric 86
Garrison, William Lloyd 80, 132
Garza, Alicia 92, 95, 96
Georgakas, Dan 110, 111
Geschwender, James 108, 110, 111
Gest, Justin 39, 115
Giroux, Henry 2, 25, 31, 32, 34, 35, 36, 37, 83
Glaude, Eddie Jr. 2, 99, 100, 102
Glenn, Evelyn Nakano 85
Goldberg, David Theo 3, 82, 84
Gonzalez, Emma 103
Goodman, Andrew 29, 58, 55, 68, 71, 75
Gottschalk, Marie 94
Grant, Oscar 91
Gray, Kevin 121
Grier, Bobby 53
Guyot, Lawrence 97

Harding, Vincent 121, 125
Harrington, Michael 66
Hartigan, John 49, 82
Harvey, David 31, 33, 108, 116
Hill, Marc Lamont 127
Hochschild, Arlie 33, 37, 40
Hoerl, Kristen 70, 74, 75
Hofstadter, Richard 36
Hogan, Wesley 47, 48, 93
Hogg, David 103, 104
Holder, Eric 30
hooks, bell 82, 87
Horne, Gerald 22, 122
Hughes, Langston 82

Ignatiev, Noel 82

Jackson, Jimmy Lee 60
Jacobson, Matthew Frye 12, 13, 82, 100, 102
Jefferson, Thomas 10, 23
Jones, Van 87

Kaepernick, Colin 41, 101, 125
Kaur, Darsheel 91, 92
Kavanaugh, Brett 38
Keller, Brigitt 29
Kelley, Robin 95
Kendall, Frances 82
Keniston, Kenneth 63
Kennedy, John F. 54, 72, 93
Kennedy, Paul 33
Killen, Edgar Ray 68
King, Edwin 72
King, Martin Luther 64, 66, 81, 92
King, Mary 50, 62, 63
King, Mike 38
King, Steve 128
Klein, Naomi 32, 42
Kuttner, Robert 33
Kyle, Chris 17, 18, 20, 100

Lahte, Janne 9
Lamont, Michele 31, 39, 115, 116
Landrieu, Mitch 78–79
Landrieu, Moon 79
Lawson, James 51
LeBron, Christopher 91
Lee, Robert E. 79, 125
Lentin, Alana 87
Leonard, Natasha 3
Lewis, John 79
Limbaugh, Rush 83
Lipsitz, George 74, 75, 82
Liuzzo, Viola 60
Loewen, James 132
Lovejoy, Elijah 132
Lowenstein, Allard 54

Maher, Bill 113, 122
Malcolm X 67, 96
Manning, Chelsea 18
Marsalis, Wynton 79
Martin, Trayvon 91, 92
Maybus, Ray 73
Mayer, Jane 36
Mazey, Emil 111

NAME INDEX

McAdam, Doug 55, 57, 58, 59, 63
McKesson, DeRay 2, 28, 90, 93
Metzl, Jonathan 6, 31, 37, 40, 83, 102, 104, 105, 118
Milkman, Ruth 112
Miller, Dorothy 17, 47, 51
Mills, Charles 82
Mitchell, Jerry 73
Molpus, Dick 73
Moody, Anne 71
Moore, Amzie 71
Moreton-Robinson, Arleen 10
Morrison, Toni 82
Moses, Bob 54–56, 58, 59, 61, 71
Moynihan, Daniel 123
Mueller, Robert 35
Murray, Charles 123

Nash, Diane 56, 109
Nielsen, Kirstjen 24
Nixon, Richard 1, 37, 83
Nottage, Lynn 6, 114, 115, 118
Nugent, Walter 9, 13

Obama, Barack 32, 37, 81, 84, 86, 121, 128, 129, 132
Olson, Joel 5, 43, 49, 51, 66, 91, 103, 106
Omi, Michael 82, 85, 88

Pardun, Bob 60, 67
Parks, Rosa 53, 94
Patch, Penny 51
Perdew, John 54
Piketty, Thomas 33
Pinker, Steven 123
Postman, Neil 34

Rabinowitz, Lynne 50, 51
Reagan, Ronald 83, 112
Reeb, James 60
Reid, Eric 125
Reiner, Rob 74
Richardson, Gloria 54
"Riverbend" 19–20
Robnett, Belinda 60
Roediger, David 3, 38, 49, 82, 89, 98, 105, 132
Romano, Renee 26, 27, 29, 60, 68, 69, 70, 73, 74, 75, 76
Roof, Dylan 128

Roosevelt, Theodor 13, 100
Rothstein, Richard 4, 27, 120, 122
Roy, Arundhati 16
Rumsfeld, Donald 16
Russell, Margaret 69
Russell, Tory 93

Samstein, Mendy 66, 67
Santorum, Rick 84
Savio, Mario 58, 59
Saxton, Alexander 38
Scholz, Sally J. 88, 89
Schultz, Debra 50, 51, 66
Schultz, Howard 127
Schwerner, Mickey 55, 68
Sellers, Cleveland 47
Sennett, Richard 114, 115, 118
Sessions, Jeff 24
Sharpton, Al 93
Sharrod, Shirley 87
Shirah, Sam 50, 59
Shuttlesworth, Fred 69
Silver, Beverly 108, 111, 116
Silverberg, Mark 127
Singh, Nikhil Pal 3, 4, 9, 11, 16, 22, 28, 30, 33, 42, 95, 100, 102, 114
Sinha, Manisha 122
Slotkin, Richard 9, 11, 12, 13, 14, 26, 100, 104
Smith, Chip 89
Soros, George 120
Sotomayor, Sonia 83
Stanford, Leland 11, 54–55
Steiber, Josh 18
Stembridge, Jane 50, 51
Stevenson, Bryan 26
Strong, Josiah 12
Sublette, Constance and Ned 122
Sugrue, Thomas 37, 62, 81, 108, 109, 110
Sumner, Charles 80

Takaki, Ronald 3, 38
Taylor, Keeanga-Yamatha 2, 28, 90, 97
Thompson, Heather 49, 66, 88, 94, 110, 111
Tiekert, Brian Edwards 127
Till, Emmett 71, 80
Till, Mamie 71
Torres, Sasha 53
Turse, Nick 14, 15
Tyson, Timothy 71, 80

Van Buren, Martin 23

Wadler, Naomi 103
Walker, Alice 50
Wallace, George 83
Ward, Brian 52, 81, 84
Warren, Mark 50, 66
Warren, Elizabeth 42, 130
Weinberg, Jack 65
West, Cornel 35–36, 43, 86
Williams, Joan 37
Wilson, Darren 29, 95

Wilson, William Julius 86
Winant, Howard 49, 66, 82, 84
Wise, Tim 1, 84, 104, 132

Yancy, George 10, 96
Yates, Ashley 93, 94
Young, Coleman 112

Zellner, Bob 50, 51, 63
Zimmerman, George 91, 92

Subject Index

abduction 19, 23
abolitionism, contemporary 88
abolitionists 12, 80
Abu Ghraib 17, 20
abuse 25, 120
   frequent 125
   human 119
   human-on-human 124
acquittal 72, 73, 92, 97
activism 48, 59, 62, 77
activists 1, 48, 50, 61, 62, 65, 66, 76, 90, 92, 97
   post-Ferguson 93
   white anti-racist 66
   white Southern 51, 63
   young 93, 94, 96, 97
advocacy 11, 94
affirmative action 86, 87, 98, 131
Afghanistan 4, 9, 13, 15, 16, 20, 40
African Americans 3, 4, 5, 26, 27, 28, 29, 52, 90, 95, 96, 99, 107, 109, 121
   community 6, 27, 94
   freedom struggles 5
   students 47, 93
   youth 90
agenda 43, 58, 79, 85, 95, 97
   antiracist 66
   post-racial 87
   transformative 43
   vindictive 37
   white supremacist 16
Agent Orange 120
agents 25, 35
   becoming historic 65
   conscious 2
aggression 4, 40
   direct imperial 100
   escalating 30
Alabama 23, 51, 53, 54, 60, 78, 103, 121
   Memorial Preservation Act 78
   state attorney 78
alienation 50, 52, 65, 67
allies 27, 57, 67
   multiculturalist 86
America 23, 26, 61, 81, 84, 114, 117, 121, 126

   contemporary 85
   mid-century 70
   postwar 52
America First 40
American Sniper 17–18
American Revolutionary 113
annexation 11
antagonism 37, 124
anti-apartheid 87
anti-colonial struggles 49
anti-immigrant 116
anti-intellectualism 36
anti-racist 51, 82, 87, 88
   activism 51
   allyship 104
   discursive practice 88
   work 128
anti-war activities 65
Apache nation 9
Arabs 31
arrests 53, 55, 69, 103
arrogance 3, 40, 68
articulations 84, 91
   contemporary 83
assassination 19, 54, 68, 72
   extra-legal 30
assault 9, 35
asylum 24, 102
   seeking 24
Atlanta 47, 51
Atlanta Constitution 68
atrocities 13, 14, 20
attitudes 17, 55, 57, 60, 63, 73, 85, 101
   anti-immigrant 31, 116
   anti-welfare 74
   missionary 57
attorneys 30, 112
   prosecuting 5
   white prosecuting 73
authorities 24, 30, 104, 111, 115
   federal 30, 56
   legal 23
   local 103
   national 28

auto   107, 109, 111, 112, 113
   corporations   111
   deindustrialization   107
   dislocation   107
   firms   108
   industry   107, 108, 110
   manufacturing sites   108
   plants   110
autobiography   17, 18, 71, 129
automation   109, 110

Baghdad Burning   19–20
bankruptcy   112
   forced   34
   spiritual   35
bans   41, 43
Baptist ministers   50
barbarism   13, 25
battle   5, 74, 99
beatings   55, 56
   jailhouse   97
beliefs   9, 73, 85
   religious   51
Berkeley   47, 58, 59
   campus   58
   Free Speech Movement   59, 65
   revolt   59
Berks County   115, 117
betrayal   57, 89, 115
   ultimate   115
biases   63, 97
   implicit   29
   racial   95, 104, 122
bigotry   31, 37, 126
Birmingham   53, 54, 69, 78, 103
birtherism   32
Black Agenda Report   87
Black
   activists   1, 74
   autoworkers   110, 111, 113
   children   87
   communities   27, 28, 34, 92
   culture   51, 52, 128
   freedom movements   49, 67, 90, 96, 97, 103
   intellectuals   125
   -led movement   62, 95
   liberation movement   96
   manhood   111

migration   26
militants   111
Mississippians   58, 71, 72
nationalist   87
neighborhoods   64
scholars   82, 90
self-determination   62, 64
struggle   5, 47, 49, 50, 63, 64, 65, 66, 67, 121
students   47, 51, 54, 57, 62, 71, 79
suburban history   28
turnout   78
urban history   28
vanguard   64
workers   108, 110, 115
youth   57, 90, 93
   struggle   5, 47, 49, 50, 63, 64, 65, 66, 67, 121
Black Lives Matter   5, 43, 90, 92, 94, 96, 97
Blackness   48, 95, 127
   partisans   63
Black Power   28, 60, 62, 63, 65, 110
Blacks   26, 39, 40, 53, 71, 73, 79, 86, 90, 95, 96, 101, 103, 109, 111
   marginalized   59
   mid-1960s   110
   oppressed   62
   southern   54
   unarmed young   28
blind   20, 75, 85
   eye   27
   fury   116
   loyalty   125
Blue Wave   42
bombings   15, 16, 54, 55, 100
   indiscriminate   15
   strategy   15
   shock and awe   16
bombs   15, 126
   anti-personnel fragmentation   15
   cluster   15, 16, 20
border   13, 24, 25, 41, 100, 101–2
   agents   25
   crisis   25
   enforcement   25
   management   25
   militarized southwestern   4
   policy   102
   southwest   24, 26, 27
Border Patrol   25

SUBJECT INDEX 157

Boston 47, 58
boundaries 128
　socio-cultural 9
Brexit 119
brutality 11, 13, 25
　methods 28
　nature 14
bully pulpit 41
burnings 27, 118
bus boycott 53
business 116, 131
　operations 34
　venture 35

cadre 70, 110
California 11, 80, 91
　Native Americans 11
Cambodia 14, 15
campaigns 10, 18, 54, 64, 71, 84, 87, 97, 103
　voter registration 103
　organized 71
　presidential 32, 35, 36
　primary 24
　right-wing 83
campus 48, 54, 56, 58, 64, 65, 66
　activists 58
　activity 60
　appearances 56
capital 33, 107, 108
　contemporary 34
　contemporary global 33
　corporate 6
　cultural 35
　political 35
　social 80
　transnational 33
capitalism 31, 33, 96, 98, 116, 124
　finance 33
　global 41
　racial 95, 107, 113
　unevenness 101
　vampire 33
　vulture 33, 34
catalyst 49, 66, 91
Catholic Church 124, 127
Caucasian 12, 78
Central America 24, 25, 41
challenges 4, 52, 113
　implicit 5

legal 3
political 43, 99
radical 5, 96
change 2, 5, 31, 54, 55, 64, 65, 71, 73, 97, 104, 121, 122, 128
　enacting transformational 1
　political 42, 63, 65
　socio-historical 99
　structural 102
　systemic 131
　transformative 31
Charleston massacre 77, 79
Cherokee 11, 23
　removal 23, 24
Chicago 27, 28, 103
Chicano liberation movement 96
Chickasaw 23
children 13, 14, 17, 21, 23, 24, 25, 53
　brown 30
　kidnapping 25
　young 24
　young immigrant 25
China 40, 113
Chinese 27, 131
Choctaw 23
Christian 9, 39, 50
　denominations 124
　existentialism 51
Chrysler 108, 110, 111, 112, 113
　concessions 112
　employees 112
　factories 112
　management 111
　operations 110
　workers 112
churches 62, 126, 128
　Black 51
　historic Charleston African-American 77
CIA 30
cities 16, 20, 34, 43, 53, 77, 78, 80, 112, 113, 114
　deindustrialized 114
　industrialized inner 84
　multi-racial 131
citizens 20, 65, 101, 102, 125
　fellow 2, 97
citizenship 5, 12, 49, 65, 66, 91, 102
　privileged 49, 65
　racialized 49
　second-class 27, 28

civic illiteracy 2, 35, 36
civil disobedience 94
civilians 13, 14, 15–16, 18
   casualties 14, 16
   deaths 15, 16
civilization 9, 11, 13, 14, 17
   industrial 113
civilizing mission 4, 13, 17, 22–23
civil liberties, suppressing 33
civil liberties protections 95
civil rights 4–5, 49, 50, 52, 53, 54, 55, 56, 58, 59, 60, 61, 62, 63, 97
   activism 48, 50, 52, 72
   activists 47, 53, 55, 56, 65, 68, 69, 74, 97
   agenda 55, 58, 63
   campaigns 54
   campus activists 58
   demonstrations 53, 54
   era 5, 76, 81
   groups 93
   initiatives 85
   leaders 5, 69, 93
   organizations 62, 93, 97
   protests 47
   struggle 53, 59, 62, 70, 74, 82
   veterans 58, 62
   work 57, 64
   workers 29
civil rights movement 47, 48, 49, 50, 51, 53, 55, 57, 58, 60, 63, 64–67, 69, 70, 97
   early 52
   long 81, 94
   modern 4
civil rights murders 5, 29, 68, 69, 71, 73, 75, 77, 79
Clarion-Ledger, Jackson 73
class 6, 37, 38, 39, 48, 64, 92, 93, 107, 114, 115, 116, 128
   burden of 118
   injuries 6, 114
   matters 43
   orientation 93
   privilege 38
   resentments 41
   ruling 126
   solidarity 117
   status 79
   system 6, 98, 115

class-conscious vanguard 89
cluster bomblets 16
   left-over 16
Cold War 49, 52, 54, 109
collective forgetting 99
college 51, 54, 57, 71
   degree 39
   education 37
   environment 53
   historic black 71–72
   liberal arts 54
   students 62
Colombia 30
colonialism 123
   settler 95, 121
colonialist 10
colonies 22
color 22, 29, 31, 36, 39, 40, 84, 85, 86, 92, 94, 101, 105, 107, 127
   communities of 90
   privileges 64
color blind 5, 75, 81, 85, 127
   multi-cultural 5
color consciousness 88
Columbia 30
Columbus Day 121
commitment 1, 5, 47, 50, 53, 60, 71, 72, 88
   active 89
   moral 58
   putative 87
   shared 89
   total 128
commodities 34
communities 2, 59, 62, 80, 94, 102, 113, 120
   Black 27, 53, 93, 95
   dominant WASP 52
   imagined national 102
   local 62
   minority 94
   oppressed 92
   university 60
companies 112, 114, 130
   insurance 120
Conceptual Guerilla 126, 132
concessions 112, 117
Confederacy 76, 77, 78
   ancestors 78
   and white supremacist monuments 76

SUBJECT INDEX 159

battle flag   77
defeated   120
leaders   128
monument removal   79, 80
soldiers   79
symbols   77
veterans   77
Confederate Monuments   5, 68, 69, 71, 73, 75, 76, 77, 78, 79, 80, 121
and markers   78
and symbols   77
in New Orleans   76
removing   78
contradictions   4, 5, 11, 28, 36, 38, 47, 49, 57, 62, 66, 88, 108, 114, 115
control   3, 15, 26, 79, 92, 108, 110, 112
cede   110
democratic   37
global   84
mechanisms   2
social   3, 100
worker   109
convergence   40, 42, 82, 109
convictions   14, 68, 69, 72, 73, 75
CORE (Congress of Racial Equality)
activists   58, 65
organizer   55
corporations   109, 112
interests   122
media establishment   36
corruption   34
political   36
Cost of Privilege, The   89
cotton   23, 118
counterinsurgency techniques   28
county   90, 117
seat   115
taxes   77
coup   24, 40
courage   79, 97, 103
courts   23, 24, 95
cases   85
citations, expensive   95
crimes   36, 43, 68, 77, 90
criminal   29
criminalization   3
criminalizing   24
potential   29

crises   3, 41, 81
economic   113
foreclosure   87
social   113
critiques   1, 75, 82, 85, 87, 89
emotional   66
radical   87
cruelty   9, 12, 23–25
extraordinary   25
fascist   25
malignant   32
culture   28, 32, 34, 109
appropriation   128
assumptions   52
black popular   52
chauvinism   18
conditioning   100
conformist   52
deficiencies   86
dominant   131
economic   39
emergent youth   52
mass-mediated   20
national   48
political   22, 35
reaction   85
wars   37, 83

Daily Kos   132
Dallas   54, 132
damage   31, 107
collateral   15
untold   6
DC demonstration   43, 47, 93
Dearborn   109
death   11, 15, 30, 54
civil   94
penalty   32
squads   19
throes   88
debts   18, 81
decentralization   88, 109
plans   109
decisions   73, 109, 128, 129
corporate   108, 112
Declining Significance of Race, The   86
deconstructions   5, 42, 68, 76, 80, 88, 89, 107, 113

deconstructions (*cont.*)
    of white identity politics   4, 45, 70,
      98–100
    of whiteness   5, 51, 58, 66, 67, 81, 83, 85,
      87, 89
    strategies   80
Deep South   51, 72
deindustrialization   39, 107, 108, 110, 111, 112,
    113, 114, 116
    initial   110
    Youngstown   115
de jure segregation   99
democracy   33, 36, 49, 65, 66, 91, 106, 118
    advanced   5
    authentic   49
    ethos   35
    imperialist   10
    inclusive   49, 88
    inclusive pluralist   6
    participatory   47, 92
    political   36
Democratic Party   35, 60
    establishment   42
    regular   59
demonstrations   43, 58, 60, 91, 103
denial   74, 85, 87, 95, 99
    climate change   42
Denmark   47
Department of Justice   57
    report on Ferguson policing   94
depleted uranium   20
deployment   17, 36, 41, 104
deportations   24, 30
deregulation   111
destiny   12, 111
    manifest   12, 78, 100
detentions   19, 24, 30
    camps   23
    centers   24, 25
Detroit   27, 28, 34, 107, 108, 109, 110, 111, 112,
    113, 125
    African-American   107
    area   113
    auto factories   111
    city of   112
    deindustrialization   107, 108, 113
    East Side   112
    metro area   110, 111
    plants   111, 112

postwar   109
dialogue   117
    informed   80
die-ins   94
differences   3, 103, 115, 127, 131
    discernable   123
    physical   123
    racial   123
dignity   43, 99, 121
    fundamental   63
    human   121
dilemmas   4, 5, 45, 113
    existential   56
disciplinary power   26
    internalizes   26
    militarized   102
discourse   34, 76
    blinkered media   101
    political   37
    public   101
    racial   82
    racist populist   37
discrimination   70, 85, 96, 110, 117, 122
    hiring practices   58
    racial   53, 101
discursive practices   82, 84
    strategies   88
disenfranchisement   39, 77
dislocations   107, 114
    contemporary economic   6
    social   38, 83, 86
    structural   107
displacement   24, 75, 116
disposability   34
dispossess   3, 10, 11, 13, 24, 33, 49
    indigenous peoples   10
distance   21, 63, 74
    historical   48
distorting mirror   101
diversity   87, 122
    multicultural/multiethnic   103
Dixie   75
DNA   1, 122
    ancestry   130
    national   2
Dodge Main   110, 111, 112
Dodge Revolutionary Union Movement
    (DRUM)   110–111
dominance   39, 78

SUBJECT INDEX   161

racial   48
racialized   100
social   26
domination   2, 9, 12, 99
    racial   83
    white male   119, 132
draft resistance movement   65
dramas   52, 118
    courtroom   74
dreams   81, 116, 132
drugs   27, 118
    dealer   29
Durham   77
dynamics   114
    explosive   51
    racial   74, 114
    social psychological   6

economy   120, 130
    circumstances   41
    climate   108
    distress   42, 113, 118
    globalist elite   36
    hardship   107
    interests   36
    motivations   9
    national   49
    spheres   3
    stability   107
    turbulence   33
education   3, 36, 37, 53, 62, 71, 87, 117
    average   55
    political   56, 60
    public   33, 37
    system   122
election   35, 55, 81, 103, 111, 119, 121
    rolls   39
    union   111
electoral   33, 39
    victory   1, 4
Electoral College   120
    slaveholding-rooted   1
elites   33, 40
    professionals   37
El Salvador   24
eminent domain   112
empathy   34, 35, 101, 102
    blocked   102
    inducing   102

empire   22, 83, 100
    building   100
employers   120, 130
    industrial   112
    largest   108
employment   85, 112, 131
    dislocation   108
enemies   37, 84, 100
    racial   11
    uncivilized brown   14
enslavement   22, 104
    Africans   23
    imported   22
environment   26, 31, 113, 130
    comfortable   57
    integrated   62
    lethal   19
    optimized   129
    political   36
    protections   33
    repressive   56
    semiotic   35, 52
equality   33, 56, 66, 70, 87
    formal   81
    guarantee   99
    racial   48, 53
Equal Justice Institute   2
era   2, 27, 69, 70, 77, 96, 113
    postwar   110
    present   97
escape   41, 70, 116
establishment   3, 9, 15, 59, 77, 93
    liberal   59
estrangement   63
    growing   60
Europeans   83, 124
    settlements, earliest   9
    settlers   22
events   25, 29, 48, 53, 54, 59, 60, 61, 62, 103, 119
    dramatic   53, 58, 60
    pivotal   59
    public   101
    signal   91
    transitory   91
    watershed   60
evolution   113, 123, 130
    radical   121
exclusion   22, 25, 93, 103, 117

executions   19, 20
executive order   25, 30
   first   41
expansion   4, 9, 11, 12, 22, 24, 42, 55, 56, 104, 108
   transnational   113
exploitation   22, 80, 99, 123
   economic   120
   global   124
   shameless   36
extermination   11–13, 14, 24, 99
   attacks   11
   Indigenous peoples   104
extradition   18
extrajudicial killings   28, 92
   murder   29
   sanctioning   30
   terror engagements   30

Facebook   35
facilities   109, 112
   overcrowded   25
   segregated   47
factory   111, 116, 117
   bosses   117
   closings   6
   dilapidated   110
   fictional   115
   work   117
Fallujah   16, 20
families   19, 24, 25, 56, 69, 75, 94, 117
   affluent   127
   desperate   24
   gatherings   15
   histories   130
   immigrant   25
   melodrama   74, 75
   member   24
   refugee   25
   separation   25
fantasies   81, 116
   restorative   40
fathers   12, 17, 50, 117, 118, 132
fear   13, 17, 18, 34, 37, 71, 75, 83, 84
   racial   30, 84
federal funding   86
federal intervention   112
Ferguson   30, 93, 95

activists   93
   activists and Black Lives Matter   95
   organizers   93
   police department   29
   police officer Darren Wilson   28
   policing   94
Filipinos   13
film   17, 18, 70, 72, 74–75, 91
   documentary   113
   popular   17
Fire Next Time, The   97
fixes
   administrative   112
   spatial   107, 108, 109, 112, 116
   technological   112
flag   124, 125
   white nationalist   125
Florida   10, 40
   legislature   103
forces
   global   48
   political   29
   state police   30
Ford Motor Co.   109
   decentralization policies   110
   Rouge   109, 110
Fort Sumter   79
Fourteenth Amendment rights   95
Fourth Amendment protection   95
Fox News   83, 103, 122
   anchors   120
   pundits   120
framing   74
   racial   99, 105
freedom   56, 58, 66, 97, 99, 121
   Black   95
   flows   121
   human   121
   impeded   99
   movement, new   94
Freedom Rides   56, 93
Freedom School   61, 62
   local   64
freedom struggle   91
   new African-American   91
   new Black   94
Freedom Summer   55, 56, 57, 58, 59, 60, 61, 103

SUBJECT INDEX 163

student volunteer   55
Freedom Vote   54, 62
Friends of SNCC   47, 60, 62
    and SDS on campus   48
    chapters   55, 56, 58
frontier   9, 13, 26, 59, 104
    homicide   26
    wresting   11
frontlines   25, 58
Fruitvale Station   91
fundraising   54, 56, 60

game   72
    blame   117
    zero-sum   107
gaps   95
    socioeconomic   86
gender   38, 49, 92, 93, 114, 115
    constraints   116
    dimensions   6
    dynamics   114
    expressions   9
    options   130
    triadic relationships   115
General Motors   109, 112
generations   39, 93, 117, 119, 121
    younger   71
Georgia   23, 49, 53, 54, 78
ghosts   5, 68, 69, 75, 80, 94
    evil   68
    haunting   80
    racial   75
Ghosts of Mississippi   70, 72, 74
GI Bill   50
Giffords Law Center   103
globalization   33, 87
    corporate   113
    development   107
GM   112, 113
God   17, 50, 124
government   57, 96, 125
    black majority   78
    bureaucracy   42
    federal   57, 83, 95, 109, 120
    health programs   83
    position   30
Great White Father   10, 23
Greensboro sit-in   47

grievances   10
    long-standing   97
groups   79, 93
    defined   3
    dominant   39
    high-status   39
    interracial   64
    privileged   88
    racial   85, 115
    right-wing paramilitary   30
growth   33
    economic   33
    exponential   28
    massive   23
Guantanamo   28
Guatemala   24
guilt   14, 50, 52, 71, 88, 91
Gulf War   16, 30, 60, 102
    first   15
gun   13, 91, 103, 104, 105
    culture   6, 99, 100, 104, 105
    manufacturers   104
    ownership   104
    proliferate   105
    suicides   105

Haiti   41
harassment   55, 56
    constant   55
    everyday   90
    legal   28
    sexual   120
Harvard   54, 57
    student   56
hate   12, 34, 57, 83, 125
    crimes   31
    groups   31
    rhetorical   37
    vicious   77
hauntings   68, 75
    legal   69, 73
health   87
    care   40, 85
    mental   118
    reform   83
hegemonic
    global   16
    ordering   69, 92

hegemonic (*cont.*)
    reformulated   70
    reordering   75
heritage   76, 126, 131
    mixed   129
heroes   17, 19, 24, 101
hierarchy   93, 123, 124
    racial   48, 81, 88
Highland Folk School   94
Highway of Death   15
Hispanic characters   115
historians   2, 38, 59, 65, 116
historical context   48, 69, 71, 76, 82
    understanding   66, 100
history   1–2, 5, 26, 68, 70, 72, 75, 79, 80, 82, 85, 89, 104, 105–106, 108
    activity   129
    long   3, 4, 14, 23, 25, 29, 31, 104, 105, 107, 114
    measurable   123
    national   76
    racial   89
    southern   75, 77
Homeland Security   29
Honduras   24
Hoodies   92
horrors   15, 20, 100, 106
hostility   40, 42, 118
House Un-American Activities Committee   110
housing   85
    de jure segregation   27
    debacle   86
    market   91
    overpriced   62
    segregation   4
Houston   67
humanity   14, 61, 78
    basic   87
    shared   30
    surplus   97
human race   66, 113
    joining the   67
    values   34
    wreckage   114
human rights   18, 65, 66
    fundamental   96
humans   50, 119, 120, 123

humiliations   34, 37, 115
Huntingdon College   51
hyper-criminalization   92

identities   51, 60, 63, 92, 122, 124, 127, 129, 130
    commercialized   130
    counter-hegemonic   92
    economic   124
    group   86
    historically-constructed racial   38
    political party   130
    racial   86, 123, 124, 128, 129
    sexual   124
    social   128
    white political   11
    white racialized   88
identity politics   6, 82
    contested white   2
    hierarchy   123, 130
    inscribed white   42
    persistent white   31
    politics candidate   33
    weaponized whiteness and white   4, 105
ideological   32, 59, 75, 99, 100
    assistance   104
    beliefs   82
    border   9
    cloak   34
    crisis   59
    discourse   76
    expressions   4
    function   81
    media construction   74
    operation   81
    orientations   32, 86
    patterns   28
    position   88
    projections   82
    rationales   9
    tendencies   85, 88
    tropes   13, 82, 83, 84, 86
    veil   22
ideologies   12, 62, 87, 88, 102
    colorblind   96
    racial   22
    racialized   102
ignorance   35, 70, 122
    armed   37

SUBJECT INDEX   165

illegitimacy   126
illusions   5, 87, 102
   hyper patriotic   20
images   29, 43, 102
   degraded popular   31
   jingoistic   101
   negative   31
   televised   15
   visual   15
imagination   43, 47
   popular   101
   public   81
immigrants   25, 31, 36, 42, 88, 102, 130, 131
   benevolence toward   102
   communities   131
   dark-skinned   41
   high tech   130
   legal   130
   new   12
   non-white   3, 25
   status   131
immigration   6, 24, 82, 83, 99, 100, 102, 130, 131
   attorneys   25
   crisis of   102
   patterns, restrictive   31
   policy   3
   so-called illegal   41
impediments   49, 82, 89, 96
   structural   85
imperialism   19, 31
   agendas   77
   Anglo-Saxonizing   12
   soft   100
   strenuous   100
   ventures   101
incarceration   18, 28, 56, 94
incidents   14, 16, 17, 19, 22, 25, 28, 71, 91
   dramatic   61
   fabricated   30
   shooting   55
Indian   12, 13, 14, 20, 99, 126
   activist   16, 43
   Affairs   42
   hunting expeditions   11
   nations   10, 23
   race   11
   territories   10, 11

Indian Removal Act   4, 10, 23
Indian Wars   4, 13, 43, 99, 102
Indigenous   22, 126
   peoples   10, 23
Indigenous People's Day   121
industries   107, 108, 111
inequalities   33, 34, 76, 86, 100, 104
   economic   34
   income   34, 94
   inequities   29, 70, 86, 94
   racial   66, 86, 94
   structural   67, 74
inferior races   12, 14
injury   117, 120
   first   117
   hidden   37
   real   115
injustices   53, 68, 69, 86, 88, 104, 105
   white supremacist   72
innocence   10, 29, 67, 97
   whiteness of   10
institutionalization   27, 30, 71, 105, 113
institutions   63, 86, 128
   arrangements   82
   constraints   85
   financial   34
   private   3
insurgencies   27
   inspired   110
   insurrection   10
   insurrectionary interlude   107, 111
interpreter   52, 63
   critical   34
interracial   51
intersectional   49, 82, 92, 107
   gun-control movement, new   104
   injuries   6, 118
interventions   120
   early   55
   imperial   14, 19, 24
intimidation   67, 71, 101, 111
invasion   16, 19
   alien   84
Iraq   4, 9, 13, 16, 17, 18, 19, 20
   allies   18
   children   17
   civilians   19
   military raids   19

Iraq (*cont.*)
   numbering 19
   retreating 15
   torturers 15, 17
   war veterans 18
   War 16
Ireland 12
irony 9
   historical 24
Islam 31, 41, 88
Istanbul 116
Ivy League 57

Jackson, Andrew 10
   Indian Removal Act 23
   Jacksonian white terror 11
   Slave-owning 23
   Trump's hero 24
Jewish identity 52
Jewish women 66
   non-fictional 50
Jim Crow segregation 99
jobs 33, 35, 41, 51, 107, 108, 113, 115, 116, 117, 118, 126, 130
   losses 111, 115, 117
   low-paying non-union 116
   system 132
   unskilled 110
Johnson Administration 30
journalistic coverage 70
jury 27, 73, 91
   all-white 71, 72, 73
   federal 97
   grand 18
justice 28, 29, 30, 43, 56–57, 66, 69, 71, 80, 91, 95, 99, 105, 124
   equal 96
   report 94
   restorative 94
   retrospective 69
   seeking 30
   social 50

Kabul 116
Kandahar 15, 116
Kennedy assassination 54
kids 17, 57
   little 17

shoot 17
killers 71, 72
   blood-thirsty 18
killing 13, 14, 18, 29, 55, 60, 91, 126
   drone 30
   indiscriminate 16
   massive 18
   rationalized 17
   revenge 19
   sniper 20
Ku Klux Klan (KKK) 25, 27, 38, 71
   post-Civil War 77
   terrorism 120
Kuwait 15

labor 22, 30, 40, 102, 108, 131
   control 108
   costs 109
   leasing convict 120
   movement 89
   organizer 105
   resistance 108
Lahore 116
land 10, 11, 12, 29, 40, 112, 126
   native 20, 41
   policies 79
language 14, 36, 73, 122
   coded 32
Laos 14, 15
Latinos 39, 41, 95
   immigrants 41
law 1, 28, 29, 42, 68, 72, 81, 99, 104, 120
   and order 27, 83
   coded 90
   enforcement 26, 27
   gun control 105
   lax gun 105
   natural 31
   new gun-control 103
   permissive gun 104
   repressive voter ID 39
   stand-your-ground 91, 92, 104
   violated international 15
   violating campaign finance 42
leaders 21, 59, 92
leadership 54, 93
   black 59, 64
   finding indigenous 59

SUBJECT INDEX 167

group-centered 92–93
left-wing 110
male centered 93
monopolized 62
trade union 112
League of Revolutionary Black
    Workers 111–112
legacy 1–2, 26, 28, 66, 69, 80, 86, 106
    historical 33
    tortured 68
legal
    format 76
    oblivion 73
    proceedings 73
legislation 42, 49, 84, 105, 120
    initiatives 86
    manipulated 36
    new 103, 104
legitimacy 24, 49, 84
lens 117, 119, 122
    racial 48
lethal
    attacks 79
    police action 95
    white terror manifests 30
liberalism 59, 60, 61, 87
    post-racial 86
    multicultural 82
    policy analysts 86
liberation 92, 95, 97, 105, 121
    black 20, 66, 95, 97
    movements 95
liberty 22, 40, 124
    empire of 10
limitations 54
    explosive 115
link 50, 64
    missing 50
logic 79, 82, 107, 118
loss 38, 39, 84, 87
    dramatic 115
    presumed 104
Louisiana 78
Louisiana Purchase 10
Lowndes County Alabama 63, 85
lynching 2, 26, 27, 100, 121
    deployed 26
    party 27

Macedonian 35
machinery 119
    faulty 117
Mack Stamping Plant 111
Madison 56
    campus 56
    Friends of SNCC 56, 61
    group 56
    students 560
Make America Great Again (MAGA) 39, 40
management 110, 115, 117
management prerogatives 110
manufacturers 109
manufacturing jobs 38
    heartland 114
    lost 114
    started hemorrhaging 108
march 11, 60, 62, 93, 103
    peaceful 60
    provocative 22
    so-called 11
    winter 23
marginalizing 3, 94
Marjory Stoneman Douglas High School 103
markers 78, 79
    invisible 62
    promoted 78
    racial 12
market 34
    dual labor 100
    expanding world 23
    fundamentalism 34
    rules 32
Marxist analysis 89
masculine
    expression 117
    form 100
    militarism 100
    rites-of-passage 53
massacres 13, 14, 15, 20, 103
mass incarceration 121
    contrived 120
mass movement 71
materialism 118
media 15, 52, 58, 92, 104, 120, 122, 131, 132
    constructions 70, 74, 75, 84
    corporate 1, 16, 20, 103
    coverage 14

media (cont.)
   critics   34
   environment   35
   liberal   1
   mainstream   121
   mass   61, 67
   personality   35
   representations   84, 100
   right-wing   37
memorials   67, 76, 77, 79
memories   36, 70, 74
   collective   35
Memphis   77
mercy   23, 34
Meridian   50
metaphor   17, 48, 121
Methodist   50
   chaplain   72
   Minister   50
   school, all-white   51
Mexican Americans   27
Mexicans   24, 26, 30, 32, 99, 131
   degenerate   12
   territories   11
Mexican War   11, 12
Mexico   9, 11, 12, 112, 116
   feared absorbing   12
Michigan   57, 109
Michigan Law School case   87
middle class   54, 93
   suburban life   50
   upper   39
Middle East   30, 116
Midwest, rural   113
migrants   25
   abused   25
militancy   107, 111
   black   111
militant   31, 61
   grassroots credentials   61
   propaganda   20
militarists   42
militarization   29
   police   101
military   14, 16, 17, 18, 19, 33, 38, 40, 99, 104
   court   14
   engagements   10, 15
   interventions   31
   office   17

   operations   18, 23
   power   23, 101
   repression   27
   terror   17
   tradition   26
   violence   26
Million Hoodies   91
   Movement   91, 94
minorities   33, 67
   defined   49
   new oppressed   83
Mississippi   10, 23, 55, 56, 57, 58, 59, 68, 70, 71, 72, 73, 74, 75, 103
   blacks   55, 73
   court cases   75
   court   69
   Freedom Democratic Party (MFDP)   59, 60, 61
   history   74
   justice   56
   Law School   71
   life, dominated   70
   NAACP   5
   Negro   56
   racist past   73, 74
Mississippi Burning   75
Mississippi State Sovereignty Commission   71
Missouri   95, 105
mistreatment   86, 124
   alleged   120
mobilizations   4, 37, 41, 43, 53, 91, 92, 103, 110
money   32, 43, 115
   big   36
   dark   36
   funneling   30
Montgomery   51, 53, 121
   march   60
monuments   5, 76, 77, 78, 79, 80
moral
   abyss   25
   action   50, 52
   compulsion   50
   grandeur   102
   impulse   50
motivation   61
   critical   52
   key   39

SUBJECT INDEX   169

movement   5, 43, 61, 62, 70, 71, 79, 91, 92, 93, 94, 95, 96, 103, 104
   black   49, 66, 121
   centers   47
   challenges   78
   contestations   3
   environment   50
   global   111
   LGBTQ   122
   metoo   120
   new   94
MSNBC   120
multiculturalism   82, 86
   table   43
multiracial   106
   alliances   43, 103
murder   13, 14, 27, 28, 29, 30, 68, 69, 70, 71, 72, 73, 90, 91, 92
   assaults   11
   blacks   27
   cases   69
   motivated   69
   programming   19
   vigilante   91
   white racist   75
Muskogee   23
   nation in Tennessee   10
Muslims   31, 36
My Lai   14, 15
myths   10, 12, 26, 27, 40, 85, 99, 102
   liberal   61
   national   97

NAACP   71, 93
napalm   15, 126
narcissism   35
   pathological   34
   rants, daily   32
Nashville   47, 51
Natchez   61
nation   55, 58, 67, 72, 74, 75, 76, 77, 80, 100, 102, 105, 124, 125–126, 128
   postracial   74
   white dominated   88
National Action Network   93
National Domestic Workers Alliance   92
National Football League   101, 125
national identity   6, 11, 65, 99, 100, 101, 102
nationalism   25, 124
   narrow   92
   racial   4, 100
National Liberation Front   14
National Police Accountability Project   29
national/racial chauvinism   40
National Student Association   51, 54
Native Americans   10, 11, 22, 23, 24, 26, 83, 122
   condemned   99
   push   10
   resisting   10
   terrorizing   23
Native self-determination and sovereignty   42
Navajo code talkers   42
Navy seal sniper   17
Nazi expression   17
neglect   117
   benign   32
Negro   57, 78, 129
   of Mississippi   59
   leadership   55
   picket line   59
   water fountains   79
neoliberal   42, 79, 82
   discursive practice   85
   economics   33
Neoliberal Fascism   31, 32, 36
neoliberalism   33, 34, 86, 96
networks   47, 91
   pacifist   51
   social gospel   50
   terrorist   27
Never Again movement   104
New Orleans   53, 76, 78, 79, 105
   African Americans   79
New Politics   32, 90
newspapers   56
   disinformation   101
   media's coverage   70
   opinion-forming   74
New York City   29, 42, 55, 58, 95, 115, 132
New York Times   25, 74, 121, 132
   Magazine   113
Next American Revolution, The   113
Niger   30
nineteenth century   4, 11, 38, 99
   abolitionists   132
   early   26

North Carolina   47, 78
   Agricultural   47
   Governor   77
   lobbying   77
northern   48, 50, 51, 54, 55, 59, 61
   campuses   47, 60
   city   48
   college campuses   59
   front   48
   Jewish women   50
   mobilizing   55
   recruiting   55
   Student Movement   47, 57
   student   51
   white liberal   62
NRA (National Rifle Association)   103

Oakland   91
Obama, Barack   5, 37, 81, 83, 84, 86, 87, 93, 117, 132
   Administration   24, 30, 83, 87, 95, 113
   birth certificate   84
   delirium effect   87
   health care reforms   83
   Obamacare   83
   Obamaville   84
   policies and failures   86
   presidency   81, 84, 87
   response   86
   universalist prescriptions   86
occupation   18, 19
   white collar   117
Occupy Wall Street   94
officers   14, 90
   BART   91
   commanding   13, 17
   on-duty police   90
officials   14, 94
   elected   128
   federal   58
   policies   31
   political   5
   public   112
Ohio   56
   Student Association   91
oil   16
   modern day snake   130
   prices   40

   reserves, massive   40
oligarchic tendencies   36
"Only a Pawn in Their Game"   72
operation   2, 15, 28, 42, 112, 113
   militarized   78
opioid addiction   116
oppression   48, 80, 81, 85, 98
   forms   71
   historical   3
   institutional   85
   regimes   104
   role   53
   social hierarchies   75
   systemic   90
   world   56
organizations   60, 65, 71, 91, 92, 93, 111
   focus   92, 93
   male dominated   93
   new   91
   new millennial generation   93
   political   54
   religious   51
   student   58
   witnessed private   77
othering   53, 84
   rationale   123
outrage   56
   moral   56
   organized   72
   sparked   95
outrageous
   murders   90
   racist claims   30
owners   101, 116
   black gun   105
   coded white gun   105
   slave   120

Packard   109
   auto plant in Detroit   113
paranoid whiteness   5, 82, 83, 84, 85
   explicit   84
   projections   83
parents   24, 25, 30
   immigrant   24
Parkland   103, 106
   students   103
passport   115–116

SUBJECT INDEX 171

patriarchy 95, 120
patriotic 13, 101, 124
   gaze 18
   program 125
peace 29, 78, 97, 99, 124
Pennsylvania 114
   eastern 54
   western 53
Pentagon 15, 16, 18, 20, 101
   hegemonists 40
   insistence 20
peoples
   LGBTQ 36
   native 3, 10, 13, 23
   vulnerable 36
perceptions 2, 115
   misguided 81
perspective 19, 39, 40, 48, 65, 79, 86, 88, 89, 94, 105, 107, 113, 121, 126
   authentic Iraqi 19
   blinkered racial 101
   grunt level 19
   penetrating 113
   political 60
   student's 61
   truncated historical 1
Peshawar 116
Pew Research Center 29, 39
Philippines 4, 9, 13, 14, 17
philosophy 82
   coherent 123
Pittsburgh 48, 53, 60, 62, 64
   area 52, 60
   suburban 52
plants 108, 109, 110, 111, 112, 116, 117
   closures 111, 112
   dislocation 112
   location 109
   shuttered Dodge Main 112
pledges 124–125
   allegiance 124–125
   first 125
plunder 22
   imperial 11
Poletown 112
police 27, 28, 29, 30, 64, 79, 90, 91, 92, 95, 101, 104, 121, 125, 131
   Accountability Project 28

   authorities 30
   brutality 27, 28, 91, 94
   departments 94
   dogs 95
   harassment 101
   impunity 29
   killings 90, 91, 93
   misconduct 95
   officer 29
   perceptions 29
   surveillance 28
   tolerance 27
   unit 27, 28
   violence 28, 29, 90
policies 3, 4, 9, 10, 12, 16, 24, 32, 33, 40, 41, 42, 96, 102, 111
   benevolent 10
   command 14–15
   criminal justice 27
   employment 109
   neoliberal 36, 79, 111
   permissive 104
   political 96
   preferential 85
   public 4, 83, 128, 132
   racial apartheid 84
   reactionary 109
   social 85
   stop-and-frisk 30, 95
   trade 41
   zero-tolerance 24
policing 26, 27, 38, 90, 94
   aggressive militarized 28
   domestic 26
   in Detroit and Chicago 27
   punitive 27
   repressive 4
political agenda 33, 37, 79
   calculus 92
   climate 73
   changing external context 60, 64
   demagoguery 131
   development 107
   disfranchisement 54
   disputes 122
   domestic 40
   imperatives 9
   landscape 81

political agenda (*cont.*)
    mechanisms   36
    norms   37
    orientations   52
    parties   42, 128
    program   80
    project   88
    unfinished projects   70
    rule   4, 77
    socialization   57
    structure   59
    struggles   89
    task   43
    victories   96
    work   87
political establishment   28
    national   64
Political Solidarity   88–89
politicians   37, 83
    sympathetic local   76
politics   28, 35, 40, 56, 83, 84, 102, 114, 128, 132
    conservative backlash   37
    domestic   33
    exclusionary   59
    informed right-wing   84
    local   131
    moral   47
    progressive   2
    racial   108
    radical   92
    southern   85
    state's   25
    transformative   94
polls   14
    exit   39
populations   36, 101
    civilian   16
    enslaved   22
    immigrant   26, 131
    indigenous   9, 22, 23
    mixed blood   12
post-civil rights   75
    era   75, 81
post-racial America   5, 81, 83, 85, 87, 89, 96, 127
    spurious   96
post-racialism   5, 81, 82, 87
    ideological trope of   86, 87

poverty   3, 87, 92
    jobless   116
    levels   114
    war on   27
power   10, 15, 43, 65, 68, 76, 80, 83, 85, 87, 93, 94, 98, 100, 104
    corporate   33
    perceived   93
    political   83
    racialized   100
    seekers   83
    white male   120
precision bombing   15
prejudice   63, 70
    extreme   28
presidency   1, 10, 23, 30, 32, 35, 37, 86, 121
president   24, 54, 83, 94, 128
    black   83, 87
    elected   24
    George H.W. Bush   15
    Jackson   23
    Kennedy   54, 72, 93
    Obama   24, 30, 92, 93
    Reagan   33
    Trump   33, 42, 43, 101, 125
Presidential elections   35, 39, 78, 81
prison   20, 38, 68, 69, 91
    secret   19
prisoners   13
privatization   33, 79, 96
    promoted   111
privileges   38, 40, 48, 49, 50, 57, 84, 85, 86, 87, 88, 89, 104, 105, 106
    invisible   52
    maintaining   85
    national identity   38
    paternalist   55
    position   105
    racialized   66
profitability   3, 108
    high   36
progress   9, 11, 14, 87, 119
    racial   74, 85, 87
projects   55, 56, 57, 60, 74, 84, 100, 120
    governmental   33
    imperial   16
    political and economic   42
    word   120

SUBJECT INDEX 173

Project South   61, 62
prosecutions   15, 19, 69, 93
protests   15, 47, 60, 64, 77, 91, 93, 94, 101, 125
   activities   94
   black   29
   first civil rights   47
   local   90
proto-fascist   40
public goods   34
public spaces   68, 76, 77
   official   26
Pulitzer   114
pundits   1, 37, 81
   right-wing media   83
punitive policies   26, 28, 95, 96
   measures   28
   present   4
   sentencing   90

Queens College   51, 55, 58
queer movements   92, 93, 96
questions
   fascism   49
   final   20
   fundamental   59
   legitimate   128
   open   25

race   9, 12, 49, 69, 72, 74, 78, 81, 82, 86, 87, 114, 123, 124, 127
   de-emphasized   86
   matters   43
   neutral social programs   38
   privilege   38, 48
   relations   54
   standing   14
   traitors   47, 63, 88
   wars   9, 22
   white   126, 128, 132
Race and America's Long War   4
race-based hierarchies   38
   universalism   85
racial
   animosities   31, 118
   animus   3
   arguments   87
   backlash   37, 83, 84, 85
   categories   2, 3, 49

choice   128
constraints   107
despotism   102
dimensions   115
disparities   120–121
divisions   6, 114
enclaves   101
epithet   13
frame   99
gifts   12
inequalities   26, 38, 76, 85, 86, 105, 110
injuries   37
landscape   4
language choices   129
murders   29
racial/ethnic backgrounds   107
racial formations   72
racial hauntings   69, 70
   persistent   75
racial injustices   5, 9, 28, 54, 68, 74, 75, 90, 91, 94, 96, 97, 100, 101
   alleged   85
   complicit in   102
racialization   65, 102
   Asians   14
   fetishism   12
   investments   38
   nostalgia   40
   order   62
   others   4
   practices   69
   preferences   89
   purity   122
   reparations   83
   resentments   6, 22, 37, 39, 83, 89, 114, 116, 118
   stigma   116
   structures   76
   subtext   52
   verbal assaults, explicit   41
   weasel words   122
racial justice   27, 50, 51, 58, 62, 65, 66, 69, 80, 88, 102
   seeking fundamental   96
   activists   2, 26, 40, 69, 76, 104, 106
   movement   76
racial oppression   47, 48, 49, 51, 58, 91, 97
racial order   53, 74

SUBJECT INDEX

racial privilege 102
    contested white 81
racial profiling 28, 97
racial projects 82
    neo-liberal 85
racism 12, 13, 16, 17, 31, 37–38, 53, 67, 73, 74, 81, 82, 85, 86, 87
    anti-black 59, 61
    anti-Native 42
    combat 65
    dismantle 95
    explicit 100
    institutional 69, 95
    institutionalized 5, 90, 104
    so-called reverse 85
    white 65, 75, 88
racist 1, 31, 41, 59, 77, 81, 91, 105, 111, 115, 118, 127, 128
    authorities 51
    character 89
    demagoguery 101
    hostility 64
    ideology 41
    imagery 100
    mentality 17
    muck 2
    nationalism 40
    overt 32
    past, long 89
    police brutality 94
    practices 85, 86
    presumptions 27
    rantings 18
    relics 74
    rhetoric 37
    tendencies 25
    terms 17
    victimization 90
    violence 25, 27
    vocabulary 32
    wars 11
radicalization
    developing 66
    increasing 55, 61
radicals 63, 86, 88
    young 63
rape 13, 19, 20, 24, 25, 32
    occupying army committing 20

reconciliation 70
    racial 69, 102
refuge 5, 20, 79, 98
    seeking 24, 41
refugees 41
    desperate 24
    starved 23
    tie 41
regime 3, 12, 13, 24
    brutal 23
    capitalist 107
    deadly 99
    economic 26
    harsh 22
    national 42
    past 76
    unstable racial 114
rejection 42, 71
    implicit 92
relationship 2, 65, 68, 76, 112
religion 123, 124, 127–128, 131
religious affiliations 84
    fundamentalists 36
relocations 108, 109
    forced 23
removal 76, 77, 78, 79, 123
renderings 114
    racialized 99
repercussions 28, 107
    irreparable 117
    unintended 116
representations 33, 38, 82, 114
    basic 31
    discursive 86
repression 26, 55, 71, 111
    apparatus 90
    extreme 43
    regimes 26
    response 24
republic 22, 124
    early 22, 99
    slave 12, 22
Republican 24, 33, 35
    agenda 42
    establishment beholden 36
    governor 37
    Party 1, 31, 42
    presidential candidates 84

SUBJECT INDEX

presidential primaries   83
primaries   35
reactionary   42
Reconstruction   78
transformation   1
Trump   36
resistance   10, 33, 42, 43, 70, 88, 96, 108, 114, 119, 132
   continual   97
   limited   26
   massive white   71
   matters   95
resources   43, 76
   cognitive and moral   114
   extraction   42
   governmental   36
restrictions   51
   deregulating   33
   voting   39
revelations   73, 119
rights
   democratic   96
   granted citizenship   99
   modern civil   3
   natural   22
   voting   91
   white civil   65
right wing   37
   backlash   82
   incensed American   81
   populism   116
   posture   5
   Republican base   41
   state legislators   83
   white populism, resentful   83
risk   107, 121, 123, 131
roots   3, 79, 82, 90, 120
   historic   32
   historical   53
Rouge plant   109
   massive Ford   109
   workforce   109
Rust Belt   38, 117
   voters   39

sabotage   109
San Francisco   58
Sand Creek   13
Sanderistas   42
Sandy Hook   105
savage wars   4, 9, 10, 11, 13, 14, 15, 16, 17, 18, 19, 20–21
savages   9, 13, 17, 76, 102
   merciless Indian   10
   raghead   18
   work   102
scapegoating   36
schools   57, 67, 121, 125
   charter   79
   elementary   103
   high   38, 53, 103, 117
   middle   103
   public   36–37, 79, 125
   vacation Bible   51
Scientology   127
SCLC (Southern Christian Leadership Conference)   60, 61, 93
   organizer   93
   viewed   61
SCOPE (Summer Community Organizing and Political Education)   60, 76, 103
   volunteers   61, 62
   workers   61
SDS (Students for a Democratic Society)   47, 48, 60
   leader   67
Second Amendment   22, 104
Second Reconstruction   72
security   22, 41, 100
   national   31
segregation   26, 27, 57, 58, 71, 72, 78, 105, 122
   confronting   47
   practices   57
   racial   49
   restaurant   59
   residential   27, 120
Selma   60, 61
   march   79
Seminole   10, 23
Senate
   Intelligence Committee   35
   Judiciary Committee   38
separations   24
   forced   25
sexism   73, 85
sharecropper   59, 120

slaughter   15, 77
   high-tech   15
slavery   3, 12, 22, 26, 78, 80, 119, 120, 121, 122, 123, 126
   apologist   12
   defended   78
   ended   99
   labor camps   23
   patrols   26
Smith   37, 81, 85, 89
   graduate   61
SNCC (Student Nonviolent Coordinating Committee)   47, 48, 49, 50, 51, 55, 56, 58, 59, 60, 61, 62, 64, 66, 93
   activism   51
   activists   50, 56, 59, 93
   chapters   55, 56, 58
   Executive Director   57
   fieldworker   59
   Freedom Summer   60
   leaders   55, 56, 58
   memo   57
   project   51
   work   51, 61
social change   54, 60, 63, 119
   necessary   66
social
   constructs   129
   engagements   129
   isolation   118
   media   35, 37, 91, 92, 103
   media options   130
   movements   66, 82, 92, 95, 103
   order   48, 81
   practices   105
   relations   65, 75
   scientists   86, 116, 123
   stigma   123
   structural recomposition   85
   structure   61
   world   127
society   34, 48, 50, 65, 66, 67, 87, 89, 97, 104, 105
   civil   81
   color-blind   74
   democratic   43, 47
   inclusive   106
   oppressive   105

post-racial   82
sick   62
socio-cultural constructs   85
   domain   34
   process   81
socio-economic domain   34
socio-psychological domain   34, 37
   situation   63
soldiers   10, 14, 17, 18
   black Union   77
   myriad foot   70
solidarity   43, 89, 98
   active   88
   inclusive   98
   inter-union   109
   multi-racial   89, 114
   political   89
Somalia   30
souls   12, 43, 61
Souls of Black Folk   48
South   26, 27, 47, 48, 50, 51, 53, 54, 55, 57, 60, 67, 68, 76, 77
   going   48, 66
   segregated   76
South Africa   40
South Carolina   12, 47, 121
   State House   77
Southeast Asia   13, 14, 15
Southern border   24, 25
   white communities   59
   white politicians   64, 78
   white SNCC activist   59
   white students   50
Southern Human Relations Project Director   51
Southern justice   5, 54, 56
Southern movement centers   94
Southern Poverty Law Center (SPLC)   69, 76, 77, 78
   report   77
Southern Regional Council   51
Southern Student Organizing Committee (SSOC)   47
South Vietnam   14
sovereignty   42
spaces   36, 48, 92, 108, 113
   contested   74
   fixed   108

intersectional 92
liminal 66
opened 33
political 37
privileged 3
spectacle 35, 37, 43, 53
  militarized 101
  public 26
  theatrical 26
  visual 53
speech 73
  free 22, 59
standards
  basic 87
  living 6, 31
Standing Rock 43
state 22, 26, 27, 28, 71, 72, 73, 77, 78, 96, 101, 102, 103, 104, 105
  authorities 27, 43
  black 84
  carceral 94, 96
  cast 73
  control 26
  laws 78
  legislature 77
  modern nation 124
  police 60
  powers 33, 54
  practices 82
  racial 90
  regulatory 42
  sanctioned attacks 36
  southern 26, 27
  violence 22, 27, 30
  white terrorist 71
statues 77, 78, 79, 80, 125
  removing 128
status 3, 43, 104, 115
  global 40
  political 39
status quo 131
  leap 125
  racial 27
stereotypes 102
  racial 29
stories 9, 29, 49, 76, 91, 103, 122, 128, 129, 130
  coherent 89
  dangerous 32

national 91
national racial 70
news 17
palatable 2
strategy 88, 95
  effective discursive 85
  key discursive 87
structural racism 3, 68, 75, 76, 85, 87, 105
  confronting 114
  racism manifests 3
student activists 47, 54, 55, 60, 61, 64
  activism 58, 59
  black 55
  cohorts 5
  southern white 51
student leader 58
  black 51
students 47, 49, 55–58, 60, 61, 64, 65–66, 103
  alienated 65
  elementary school 103
  female 51
  northern middle class 54
  northern seminary 63
  recruit 55
  representative 64
  sit-ins 71
  survivors 103
  undergraduate 48
  white northern 57, 60
  white secular 59
  white Southern 51
  white suburban-raised 50
  young 106
  younger 103
Student Voice 51
student volunteers 50, 57
subordination 38
  permanent 12
  racial 26
Sugar Bowl 53
suicide 104, 105
  bombs 19
  rates 104
Sunni residents 16
superiority 3, 118
  racial 82
superpower 16
  dominant global economic 39

supremacy   16, 123, 126, 132
  armed   105
  white male   119, 122
Supreme Court   23, 71, 83
surveillance   92
  perpetual   26
Swarthmore   51
Sweat   6, 114–118
Sydney Morning Herald   17
symbols   23, 76, 77, 130
  white supremacist/white nationalist   125
Syria   40
  sniper   17
system   62, 67, 80, 89, 91, 94, 115, 118, 119, 120, 131, 132
  abusive   76
  court   94
  criminal justice   28, 87, 90, 94, 95, 97
  cultural   37
  electoral   128
  nationwide   120
  racialized   99
  seniority   110
  sociopolitical   2
  value   2
  white male power   122

tactics   14, 30, 96
  ill-planned   111
  new   93
  search and destroy   14
"Take 'Em Down NOLA"   76, 79
Taft-Hartley   109
taxes   33
  abatements   112
  poll   84
Tea Party   83
Tehran   116
television   15, 34, 35, 53
  and social media   35
  conventions   84
  coverage   53
  program   34
  reality   34
Tennessee   10, 23, 94
tensions   6, 114
  increased   72
  racial   115, 122

terrain   22
  contested interpretive   49
terrorism   41
  networks   27
  racial   29
  radical Islamic   42
terrors   1, 4, 7, 11, 14, 16, 27, 43, 71, 90
  conventional   20
  racial   76
  reign of   27
  war on   9, 16
  weapons   15
Texas   11, 51
  favored annexing   12
  theaters   15
  foreign   42
thinking   122, 123, 126, 127, 132
  white way of   119, 123
threats   28, 29, 35, 63, 105, 112
  constant   97
  existential   123
  global   40
  imagined   104
  obvious   84
  perceived status   39
  racialized   38
Tonkin, Gulf of   30, 60
  war resolution   60
torture   13, 17, 18, 23, 28
  constant   23
torturing   19, 100
Tougaloo College in Mississippi   71, 72, 94
Toyota   112
trade   33
  slave   123
Trail of Tears   23, 24
traitors to their race   13, 128
trajectory   107, 123
  historical   10
  long   38, 108
transcend   18, 67, 92, 105
  race   6
transformations   42, 69, 94, 99, 108, 122
  class injuries   114
  necessary   113
  personal   57
  power structures   94
  quiet   58

SUBJECT INDEX 179

relational identity 60
role 92
social 3, 92
social movement, necessary 97
structural 86
transgender 93
transition 51, 60, 64, 88
trials 5, 29, 68, 69, 70, 72, 73, 74, 75, 76
troops 15
 mandated federal 10
tropes 6, 17, 100, 102
 ahistorical 1
 common 86
 right-wing racist 40
Trump, Donald 3, 4, 24, 25, 30, 31, 32, 35, 36, 37, 38, 39, 40, 41, 43, 116, 119, 121, 128, 131
 Administration 4, 18, 24, 102
 agenda 4, 40
 airports protesting 43
 America 36
 appeal 38, 117
 Cabinet 42
 campaign promises 39
 denunciations of unfair trade 39
 electoral appeals 38
 electoral victory 39
 faux populism 39
 Islamophobia 41
 organization 35, 42
 perspective on foreign affairs 40
 politics and policies 42
 presidency 41, 42
 representation 35
 rhetoric of demonization and bigotry 31
 situates 4
 support 39
 terrors of 4, 32, 33, 35, 36, 37, 39, 41, 43
 Trumpism 1, 32–33, 36, 42, 43
 tweets 32, 41, 42, 127
 voters 39
 wall 26
Trump Tower 35
Trump White House 94
truths 2, 36, 78, 119
 moment of 126
 partial 2
twentieth century 26, 27, 100, 107, 108
 late 27

Twilight Zone 84

UAW (United Auto Workers) 109, 110, 111, 112
 members 111
 unrepresentative 111
UC Berkeley 57
unemployment 31, 110
unions 12, 96, 111, 112
 local 111
 movement 109
 struggles 107
 unionization 109
 weakened 113
United States 1, 3–5, 9, 10, 11, 13, 15, 22, 23, 24, 39, 40, 49, 84, 100, 125, 126, 131
 continental 9
University of Pittsburgh 48, 53, 60, 64
unpatriotic 101
Unveiling Whiteness 4, 47
uprisings, domestic 100
Urbana 58

vehicle 22, 26
 organizational 59
 political 59
Venezuela 40–41
 immigrant constituencies 40
veterans 13
 black 70
victimization 17, 19
victims 6, 27, 68, 69, 73, 85, 101, 114, 121
 assassinated 30
 dead 75
 defenseless 29
 doomed 12
 innocent 30
Vietnam 4, 9, 14, 15, 16, 17, 28, 65
 Viet Cong 17
Vietnam War 15, 20, 65, 67
 escalating 60
vigilantes 26, 92, 104
 actions 4
 activity 26
violence 13, 19, 23, 24, 28, 30, 31, 35, 41, 55, 71, 74, 100, 101, 123
 acts 27
 atrocious 9
 brawl 116

violence (cont.)
    brutal   67
    confrontation   116
    death   19
    gun   103, 104, 105
    intimidation   70
    massive   41
    mindless   54
    mob   26
    private   26
    racial   26, 27, 76
    redemptive   104
    removal   23
    sectarian   19
    separation   25
    settler colonialism   122
    system of   23–24
    uprooting   23
    vigilante   22, 26
    white supremacist   100
    white   121
vision   19, 66, 126
    blinkered   20
    limited   19
    moral   80
    political   50
volunteers   54, 58, 60, 66, 71
    conscious summer   61
    full-time   65
    trained   13
    white female student   57
voters   37, 39
    black   55
    identification cards   84
    registration   61, 71
    suppression   1
votes   39, 77, 78, 117
    black   73
    popular   39
Voting Rights Act   84

wage   112
    lower   111
    lowering   33
walkouts   103
war   4, 9, 10, 11–20, 22, 33, 65, 111, 123, 132
    atrocities   20
    capitalism   9, 22

    civil   23, 114, 120
    civilizational   42
    crimes   18
    domestic   20
    genocidal   10
    long Indian   14
    measures   26
    post-World   49
    racial   21
    sectarian   19
    spiritual   43
    terror   16
    unending foreign   40
    waging ideological   109
    zones   34
warfare   100
    civilized   13
Washington   40, 43, 47, 54, 62, 93
    corruption   39
    DC   103
Washington Post   74, 125
Washita   13
water-boarding   13
Watusi   52
Wave   71, 77, 93, 107, 111, 120
    destructive   36
wealth   22, 33, 35
    distribution, upward   42
    elites   36, 126
    wealthy   11, 101
weaponized whiteness   1, 4, 5, 6, 36, 39, 90, 91, 93, 95, 96, 97, 104, 105, 114
weapons   17, 20, 104
    anti-personnel   15
    clean   15
    depleted uranium   16
    nuclear   120
    political   78
welfare state   42
    expanding   96
    food   50
Western culture   123
    frontiers   4
    scholarship   31
white
    abolitionists   12
    activists   103
    affirmative action   49

SUBJECT INDEX

affirmative action programs 50
aggression 31
alliances, explored 103
allies 90
America 52, 67
Americans 11, 20, 39, 85
anti-racism 66, 88
appendage 64
autoworkers 110
auto-workers, young 111
blind spot 16, 81, 82, 89
cadre 65
Christian nation 84
citizenry 97
citizens 2, 11, 106
Citizens Councils 71
civilization 11, 128
civil rights activists 59
colorblindness 85
community 59, 65, 84, 97, 105
consciousness 89
cop 91
culture 83, 128
enslavers 23
Europeans 22
European settlers 9
fears 88
Ferguson police 28
folks 95, 127
gun ownership 104
hegemony 11, 68, 76, 88
privileged 88
identity 105, 113, 124, 129
identity cult 1
identity politics 1–7, 26, 27, 32–33, 37, 38, 43, 69, 76, 80, 90, 98–102, 105, 107, 114
immigrants 131
industrialist 78
intellectuals 87
knight 74
leadership 111
males 85
militias 104
mobs 26, 63
national identity 102
nationalism 31, 43, 88, 100, 122, 124, 125, 131
nationalism and supremacy 40

nationalist country 125
nationalist distemper 22
nationalist mythology 39
nationalist nature 125
nationalists 42, 125
northerners 55, 56, 57, 61
opponents 75
participants 5
paternalism 55, 62
people's interest 50
person 64, 126
politics 39
populations 4, 105
possession 10
power 84
privileged 60
power structure 51, 70, 76, 81
privilege 5, 42, 47, 66, 70, 81, 82, 89, 127
problem 43
racial frame 5
racial identity 38
racial politics 81
racial resentments 31, 81, 83, 87, 118
racists 74
rage 118
reactionaries 86
republic 24
resentment 83
resentful voters 41
settlers 11
sheets 27
silence 105
skin 119
socio-political hegemony, maintaining 38
solidarity 5, 101, 105
Southerners 50–51, 59
Southerners resisting 53
suburbs 53, 131
superiority 128
supporters 40, 60, 64
vigilantes 26, 27, 28
volunteers 55, 56, 57, 61
vote 1, 73
youth 52, 67, 90
White House 22, 24, 93
White League Obelisk 78, 79
White Mountain 13

whiteness 3, 5, 10, 23, 48, 49, 64, 65, 81, 82, 88, 102, 123, 124, 127
    aggrieved 38, 41
    colorblind 82, 85
    constructions of 3, 67, 80
    critiques of 1, 82
    decenter 88
    deconstructing 67
    innocence of 18
    post-racial 82, 86
    privileged 56
    privileges of 55, 87
    psychological wages of 89
    radical anti-racist 82
    social construction of 63, 105, 106
    terror 4, 9, 10, 11, 13, 15, 17, 18, 19, 20, 21
    terror unleashed 9
    terror campaign 10
    terrorism 2
    terrorists 29, 68
    tormentors 53
    transplants 11
    unveiling of 48, 49
    veil of 52, 62, 67
whites 2, 3, 27, 29, 39, 62, 85, 96, 98, 101, 122, 124, 126, 128, 129
    aggrieved 22
    angry 22
    anti-racist 4, 5, 88
    northern 48, 57
    privileged 55
    role of 1, 62
    self-conscious 103
    short-term benefit 88
    well-meaning 5
    working class 83
    young 52
    young cosmopolitan 87
white students 5, 47, 48, 49, 50, 51, 54, 55, 56, 59, 62, 63, 67
    activism 48
    activists 4, 47, 49, 50, 51, 53, 54, 55, 57, 59, 61, 62–67
    involvement 50, 55
    male 51
    volunteers 55, 57, 63
white supremacist 3, 69, 122
    Democrats 78
    extreme 77
    hate groups 38
    ideology 78
    landscape 77
    monuments 76
    oppression 90
    positions 1, 77
    residual 81
    roots 25
    status quo 79
    tropes 38
    Trump Administration 22
    vigilantes 29
    way 123
    xenophobia 41
    young 77
white supremacy 1–6, 26, 27, 69, 70, 73–75, 78, 80, 118, 119, 120, 123, 124, 125, 131–132
    act of 125, 128
    articulated 81
    constitutional 99
    ideology of 124, 132
    persistence of 33, 70, 75, 110
    reconstituted 1
    reformed 62
    rules of 27, 28
    wounded 88
    project 120
    system 120, 121, 122, 131
white woman 1, 51, 110
    first 51
    middle-aged 115
white workers 31, 37, 38, 39, 42, 98, 110
    non-unionized 39
white working class 37, 38, 39, 98, 114, 115, 117
white world 54, 63, 132
    civilized 63
WikiLeaks 18–19
Wisconsin 39, 56, 57, 61
women 13, 14, 23, 36, 39, 42, 51, 90, 93, 96, 114
    dynamic 54
    white middle class 51
women characters 115
women's movement 96
    revitalized 43
Woolworth 47
worker militancy 108
workers 6, 31, 107, 108, 109, 110, 111, 112, 117

SUBJECT INDEX 183

    intimidate   33
    low wage   130
    militancy   108
    public sector   39
    unemployed   117
workforce   109, 112
    divided   113
working class   31, 39, 40, 114
    multi-racial   113
    unemployed   117
working class families   37
working class solidarity   115
working-class stagnation   39
World War   15, 26, 70, 108, 109
Wounded Knee   13
writers   16, 82
    legendary Mississippi-bred   68

xenophobia   31, 38, 102
xenophobic   32, 40
xenophobic rhetoric   102
xenophobic tropes   41

Yale   55, 57
Yemen   30
yeomen farmers   10
youth   87, 93
    innocent   101
    local black Mississippi   55
    white middle class   52

zones, free-fire   15, 16

CPSIA information can be obtained
at www.ICGtesting.com
Printed in the USA
JSHW011715071020
8588JS00003B/87